FOUR HUNDRED AND FORTY STEPS TO THE SEA

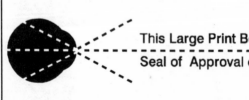

This Large Print Book carries the
Seal of Approval of N.A.V.H.

FOUR HUNDRED AND FORTY STEPS TO THE SEA

SARA ALEXANDER

THORNDIKE PRESS
A part of Gale, a Cengage Company

Farmington Hills, Mich • San Francisco • New York • Waterville, Maine
Meriden, Conn • Mason, Ohio • Chicago

Copyright © 2018 by Sara Alexander.
Thorndike Press, a part of Gale, a Cengage Company.

ALL RIGHTS RESERVED
This is a work of fiction. Names, characters, places, and incidents either are products of the author's imagination or are used fictitiously. Any resemblance to actual persons, living or dead, events, or locales is entirely coincidental.
Thorndike Press® Large Print Clean Reads.
The text of this Large Print edition is unabridged.
Other aspects of the book may vary from the original edition.
Set in 16 pt. Plantin.

**LIBRARY OF CONGRESS CIP DATA ON FILE.
CATALOGUING IN PUBLICATION FOR THIS BOOK
IS AVAILABLE FROM THE LIBRARY OF CONGRESS**

ISBN-13: 978-1-4328-5485-0 (hardcover)

Published in 2019 by arrangement with Kensington Books, an imprint of Kensington Publishing Corp.

Printed in the United States of America
1 2 3 4 5 6 7 23 22 21 20 19

To Stefan, for planting the seed

■ ■ ■ ■

POSITANO
AMALFI COAST
ITALY
2005

■ ■ ■ ■

I ought to be glad I can afford home help. The lady in question takes to my dishes with an Eastern European verve that never fails to convince me that, to her, cooking is punishment. What those blessed vegetables, reared by both our own hands, might have done to her is beyond me. Her impatience is tangible, even from here on the upper *terrazzo* beyond the kitchen. I can smell it in the bitter aroma of parsley crushed with too heavy a hand and the acidic odor of almost-singed garlic hitting the back of my throat. I've lost count of how many times I have pleaded with her to not massacre the pasta, that to feed a Neapolitan woman wet mush will find her in the dock for manslaughter. Bad food kills. It's loneliness on a plate; dishes made without love are venom. I will not hear otherwise. She's arguing with the pot now, the water is boiling too fast. It's

9

overflowed. At the three-minute mark as usual.

Not that my neighbors don't jump at the chance to come and take tea of an afternoon — every day in fact, since I decided to terminate my treatment. They sit beside me, each one believing they are my true confidante, the sole keeper of my darkest secrets. They think I don't notice the way they take in the high ceilings above my terraces or the green mist that wafts across them as they survey the riches bestowed to me, Santina Guida, no more than a peasant from the hills. They think I don't see them wonder how a street urchin ended her life in this palace. I see them picture their lives in this place after I've gone; I see it in the way their eyes linger over my lower garden *terrazzo,* in the masked longing as they drink in the view of the coast framed by the columns supporting the terraces above. The way their hands linger just a little too long upon the waxed furniture. There are those with complicated families, more worthy than I of this vast home, those who have struggled their entire lives just to place bread upon the table, the ones who have been there for me as I trawled through the endless paperwork after the major died. Each and every one of them is worthy of this home —

perhaps this is a truth. But whose truth? They think I'm tired because I'm dying. But I am tired of doing what is right, just, expected — so very tired of that.

She and I eat the wallpaper paste disguised as linguine *con* zucchini. She didn't drain the zucchini with salt, then wring out the excess water beforehand and thinks I don't notice. On the contrary, I simply choose not to point it out — for the hundredth time. Even old women get sick of their own voices.

After coffee — I use the term with trepidation, I know few people partial to boiled water with the memory of flavor — she clears up and helps me get dressed. I'm wearing the dress the major had made for me. It still fits. The pleasure of this simple thing has not evaporated. A little vanity is not wasted on the dying. I can see my skin is powder white. I still don't recognize the whisper of a person in the mirror. I know that if I live only another few days or weeks or months, this afternoon will be the most important hours of my final days.

My solicitor Antonino is waiting for me. He'll try to convince me to abandon my decision. He'll blame the treatment, or lack of it, on my apparent sudden change of heart. He won't know it is a decision I have not had the strength to make for years, a decision eating away at my heart since it all began.

"You're quite sure, Signora Guida?" Antonino asks, looking at me with condescending compassion over the rim of his glasses.

I flash him a winning smile. His eyes, even more patronizing, crinkle as if sunk into parchment.

"Antonino, I thank you from the bottom of my heart for showing such an interest in my affairs." My sarcasm is so well disguised he will mistake it for genuine politeness; men like him always do. "But I assure you that I have not taken this decision lightly."

He nods. He doesn't believe me, that much is clear. I care little for his opinion, but I need to make sure that what he says he's writing down is my request, not his. He turns the page around to me and hands me a heavy fountain pen — I can see where his greedy fees are spent. I sign below my name, trying to ignore the wash of memories swirling through my mind like a droplet of black ink in water. He passes the document to my Eastern European nurse, who, as my witness, lays down her own scrawl. It is done.

We walk home slowly. I refuse a taxi. I'd like to stifle the presentiment that this is my last climb of those four hundred and forty steps back up to the villa from the shore. We stop beneath the Virgin Mary statue placed inside a carved-out arch into the rock, a little way past the string of boutiques off Via Cristoforo Colombo. Both the votive candle's flame and I dance the precarious flicker between light and dark. Svetlana grips my arm a little tighter. She can feel my legs ever more unsteady. I nod when I've found my last reserves of strength.

Time was I sprinted these stone steps two at a time, like all respectable Positanese. I have no memory of breaking a sweat even, not like these camera-laden Americans who come to commit my town to overexposed memory. Now I am old indeed, with memories charging back to my fishing village, a huddle of homes sparse along the shingle. The fishermen keeping us all afloat until the brutal winters would leave us cut off from neighboring towns. That world almost feels imagined now: the laundry house churning through washing with the water gushing down the streets to the sea, the mill in the center of town cranking the flour. The sea was the brutal legend of invaders, the undulating history of all those rampant Greek creatures who haunt the tiny islands off our coast. Capri was the ancient seat of cantankerous Roman emperors, not lined with expensive retreats and starlets. Yes, I really am very old now.

We reach the villa and I rest upon the large wicker chairs beneath the bloom of my beloved succulents. Here on my lower terrace, I can view all my terra-cotta urns in each corner with the fuchsia spray of geraniums above the trailing flora cascading down almost to the hand-painted tiles. I can admire the canopy of vines the major and I tended with such care. I can entertain the folly of imagining crushing those grapes for one last *vendemmia*.

But the page urges me to conclude the business at hand. I sit at the major's desk in the library, surrounded by his beloved books, those unexpected swirling paths to other worlds, where he bade me follow. The memories of him poring over them each evening float to mind, windswept leaves on the cusp of winter. The hours he spent with me, leading me through these histories of great thinkers, explorers, artists, unfurling my mind like a succulent's petals at sunset, basking in the nourishing glow of discovery, is the most precious gift he gave.

This will be the last note I write; all the others are already sealed.

By the time you read this, I will be

gone. I don't write this to cast a morose or sentimental light upon my life. It is a fact like any other. You may feel sadness. You may not. You are entitled to feel whatsoever your heart dictates. Then again, I know you won't need me to remind you of that.

Your new situation will come as a shock to you. I owe an explanation, at the very least — but a woman from the Amalfitani hills could never say it in one sentence alone, however hard she may try. We're volcanic people first and foremost. Prepared for catastrophe at any moment, with a well of fervor ready to explode and annihilate those in its wake. Of this I am deeply proud, and I hope, someday, you will be too. I, sadly, am not a scribe, but I will tell the truth. And the person I need to know that truth, more than anyone, is you.

Your
Santina

15

■ ■ ■ ■

1949

■ ■ ■ ■

CHAPTER 1

Some days etch your soul. They leave scrawled scars of marrow-altering memory. Those days where you are tossed like a babe at sea, sensing the power and pull of that daunting watery mass threatening to obliterate. And despite the danger and the choking terror, you manage to wrench yourself toward the troubled sky and steal what little air you need to survive. Tuesday, November 15, of 1949 was to be a good day. Winter had been kind to us so far. The snows hadn't left us marooned. We had weathered the Germans and the Allies. We'd felt hunger and skimmed squalor by the meager amount my mother, brother, and I could gain from our truffle hunting up here in the damp crevices of the Amalfi coast's mountains.

Those mountain forests were my home. My mother was a goat; she leaped from stone to stone, fearless, focused, and precise.

I never once saw her slip, neither lose balance nor plant any seed of fear into my brother nor I. We followed her lead, limber and lithe, racing against one another to see who might discover the most. My brother and I were cradled by the scent of damp moss since I can remember. That deep green underfoot carpeted our adventures. We took the view of our dramatic coastline for granted. From up here on our hills, we could see the lower mountains sharpen up and out of the cove of Positano with its viridian water. The tiny Sirenuse islands floated just beyond, haunted by those heartless sirens luring ancient Greek adventurers to their watery deaths. Farther in the distance lay Capri, a tiny mound rising up from the water, like the scale of an underwater dragon.

Sometimes we would pass an intrepid party of travelers walking our narrow Path of the Gods, stopping to admire the view as the mountain range snaked into the hazy distance toward the Bay of Naples. Sometimes we might come across them sat upon the occasional grass clearing, a light picnic laid before them. The salty smell of prosciutto and fresh bread made our mouths water. Mother would mutter through gritted teeth to not stare like stray dogs.

We dodged the sharp crags that jutted through the living forest floor, competing to see who could be the fastest. Mother would let us stop and drink the icy mountain water as it cascaded down toward the coast. While we knelt, numbing our hands and washing our faces, she taught us which mushrooms would kill us — I can't shake the feeling that it was her peculiar way of imparting self-defense. Perhaps one day a venomous fungus would save me from a predator after all? Up in the Amalfi mountains, the danger lurking in the dark was tangible to us hill folk. Its name was Hunger.

My father drank most of what we earned. I helped Ma with her laundry runs, watching her knuckles callus against the stone washer troughs in town. After the washing was done and delivered, we would climb over a thousand steps back up from the fishing town of Positano to Nocelle, weaving our cobbled journey through Amalfitani woods toward the small fraction nestled in the hilly periphery, and from there begin our scramble to our tiny house. Arriving home we'd either find my brother huddled in a corner by a dying fire with my father nowhere to be seen, or the latter tight with drink. I knew I would be damned for thinking it, but I hated that man. I hated the scars he left my mother with. The heavy hand my brother and I were dealt for the smallest trifle, but most of all the way my courageous mother, who spoke her mind to all the gossips by the well, who was first to put any man in his place who so much as dared look at her, was reduced to a quiver when my father was in one of his thunders. I ought to have brewed a fatal *fungo* broth for him and be done with it. Too late now.

That Tuesday — *Martedi* — the sky was full of rancor, like the planet Mars it's named after. The wind whipped from the sea and blew in a thick fog. Within minutes my mother was a gray silhouette. She slowed her pace a little, ahead of me. My shoes scuffed the damp boulders, dew seeping in through the tiny holes on the worn sole. Several times I lost my footing. Mother called back to us, "Santina! Marco! Stay where you are! It's not safe today — we'll turn back." We stopped, my little brother, Marco, a few paces behind me. I heard her footsteps approach, tip-tapping with familiar confidence. Then there was a ricochet of small rocks. A cry. Marco and I froze to the sound of more rocks tumbling just beyond where I could see. We called out. I heard my mother call back to us.

The silence that followed drained the

lood from my face. My heart pounded. I called again. Marco started to cry. I couldn't hear my mother answer beyond his wails. I screamed at him to stop, but it just made him worse. I had little strength to stifle my panic. My brother took a step toward me. He slipped and fell, hitting his elbow hard on the sharp edge of a rock. His blood oozed crimson onto the moss. I yanked him up and wrapped my headscarf around his elbow. "We'll go home now," I began, trying to swallow my hot tears of terror. "I'll come back for Mamma when the sun is out, *si?*" He nodded back at me, both of us choosing to believe my promise, fat tears rolling down his little cheeks.

We never saw our mother again.

Father's mourning consisted more of fretting about what to do with the incumbent children he had to feed than grieving the loss of the fine woman who had fallen to her death. One day he declared that I was to go and live down by the shore in Positano with Signora Cavaldi, the widow now running her late husband's produce store. In return for lodging and food, I was to assist her. I felt torn; delirious with the prospect of escape from the misery of life on the mountainside with this man for a father, and terror at what life would now entail for Marco. The next day, an uncl[e] from Nocelle climbed up to speak with my father. Marco would be needed to tend to his farm. The deal was sealed. We were dispatched to new parents. I try to forget the expression on Marco's face as he was led away from me. He walked downhill, his reluctant hand in my uncle's, ripping a piece out of me with each step. I patched over the gaping hole and the fresh wound of my mother's death, with brittle bravado. My father would not see me cry. I wished that would have been the last time I ever saw him too.

Signora Cavaldi's shop was a cavern carved into the stubborn rock that enveloped the cove of Positano. She held a prime position between the mill and the laundry, minimizing competition. I now wonder whether that had more to do with her careful management of the town's politics and politicians or her not so secret connection with the men who protected the trade and tradesmen. I wouldn't like to guess whom she paid nor how much, or indeed how much others paid her, but my instinct tells me her tentacles stretched far and wide. I arrived wearing the only dress I owned, a smock of doleful gray, which matched my mood. She gave me the once-over and pieced together an opinion as deft as she would calculate someone's shopping bill. The woman was a wizard with numbers, that took me no time to figure out, but she loathed children.

"You're twelve now, Santina, *si*?"

"*Si*, Signora," I answered, trying to stop my left leg from shaking. It was an embarrassing habit since I had succumbed to polio as a younger child, and my withered calf always revealed too much about what I was feeling at any given time.

"You're here to work, yes? I'll give you two days to learn what we do, and I expect to never repeat myself, *capisci*?"

"*Si*, I understand, Signora."

She set me to work immediately, sorting the produce, laying out chestnuts in baskets, polishing the scales that grew dirty again with the weighing of earth-dusted mushrooms. I cleaned the vats of oil, swept and scrubbed the floor. As the sun dipped, she called out for me to light the stove in the kitchen of the apartment upstairs and brew a broth for dinner. At first it struck me as a little out of my remit — I had been told that I would be served food in return for working, and I will admit the idea of having regular meals was exhilarating. However, my own cooking skills were not well honed

— Mother and I permitted ourselves a full meal maybe once a week, and meat was scarce. I stood, hesitant, before the stove, in a strange kitchen not knowing where anything might be kept. I was loath to search amongst her things. I went downstairs. She scolded me for lacking initiative: "Look around you, mountain girl! We have a shop, the best grocers in the town. I have a clean kitchen, which you will keep pristine, and I want, thanks be to God, for very little. Don't let me see you down here until dinner is served." And with that she turned back toward the broccoli rabe, placing them in neat lines inside wooden crates ready for the following day.

I fought with several pans, finely chopped as many of the vegetables I could find that would not be good for selling the following day, dropped in a fist of barley, lentils, and parsley, and, eventually, there was a broth that would fill our stomachs. A little thin perhaps, and lacking in salt, as Signora Cavaldi was so quick to point out, but it was hot and reminded me that I was not on the mountains any longer.

I slept in a thin cot placed in the short hallway between Signora's room and her son, Paolino's, room. It was drafty but nothing like the limp damp of our stone mountain hut. I didn't hear my father's drunken snores — that was a degree toward comfort. Nor could I hear the soft breath of my mother, or feel Marco's fidgety feet scrambling against mine through his dreams. Silent tears trickled down my face. I felt the droplets inside my ears. I let the wetness dry there, hoping my prayers and love would reach Marco up in Nocelle, a thin line of golden thread. After a time I must have given in to sleep because the next thing I remember is Cavaldi blowing down her nose at me with strips of sun fighting into the hallway from her room.

The days merged into one, each as laborious as the one before. I was sent on deliveries, some as heavy as would warrant a porter and his donkey, but Cavaldi would not hear of it; if I had been sent down for her to look after, then it was my duty to earn my keep. I built quite a reputation amongst the porters in town, who ferried supplies up and down the steep alleys around the village. They called me Kid, alluding to my climbing skills as well as my age. It made me think of my mother. I was growing, at long last, and I noticed my muscles becoming more defined and strong. Sometimes the young boys would laugh at me for doing men's jobs. The local women were not so kind. The Positanese knew mountain people when they saw them. We had the outside about us, the air of the wild, a fearlessness which I'm sure was disconcerting. We lived closer to death than they.

When I turned sixteen, Paolino, who till then had paid me as much attention and courtesy as one might their own shadow, began speaking to me. It started in the spring, as we placed the first harvest of citrus in the crates. I liked to arrange them in an attractive pile, but Cavaldi always admonished me for trying to make art not money. I had a large *cedro* in each hand, what Americans always mistook for grapefruit. He called out to me, "Watch how you hold those fruits, eh, Santina? You make a boy have bad thoughts!" I looked at him, appalled, more for the fact that he had spoken directly to me than the inappropriate remark. I couldn't find an answer. I longed for my mother right then, to whisper a fiery return, but none came. I was mute. I had been silenced for the past four years. The sudden realization stung. I considered lobbing the fruits at him but channeled a pretense of calm. My cheeks reddened, which I know he mistook for paltry modesty, or worse, encouragement, then I fled back into the shop.

I don't know whether it was my nightly prayers, the incessant daydreams of life elsewhere, the relentless beckoning of my sea and its daily promise of potential escape, or the simple hand of fate, but three years later, on the afternoon of Friday, May 25th — *venerdi,* named after Venus, harbinger of love and tranquillity — two gentlemen entered my life and altered its course.

Mr. Benn and Mr. George were art dealers from London. They wore linen shirts in pastel shades, hid their eyes behind sunglasses, and spoke without moving their mouths very much. Mr. Benn was the smaller of the two and always held his head at a marginal incline as if he were trying to hear a song passing on the breeze or decipher messages from the shape-shifting clouds above. Mr. George was very tall and looked like he would do well to eat more pasta. His movements were slow and deliberate; his voice full of air. They admired the dancing shimmer of our emerald sea, the yellow of the mimosa tree outside Cavaldi's store, and knew that *cedro* fruits were for making exquisite *mostarda,* a thick jelly sliced thin to accompany cheese. I was easily impressed in those days.

During their stay in Positano, they made daily trips to the store, and I was happy to serve them because they always stopped to stitch together a frayed conversation in their limited Italian. They tried to tell me a little about life in London, while touching every cherry before judging which ought to be included in their half-kilo's worth. Their words spun another world before me, crisp, colorful pictures of a life I craved. I listened as Mr. Benn offered a steady commentary on what Mr. George was well advised to buy. It was a wondrous thing for me to witness lives that could afford a month's stay in a tiny Italian town. All sorts of fantasies seared my overused imagination when I served them, underscored with a restlessness that pounded louder for each day I remained within Cavaldi's prison-like walls.

Every morning, they would stop by and ask what they ought to cook with the fresh zucchini, whether the flowers were better in risotto or fried? How long I'd char an eggplant for and which olive oil would be best for *sofritto* — finely cut celery, onion, and carrot — and which would be best for drizzling over finely chopped radicchio? I began to look forward to their visits, a beacon of beauty amidst the relentless purgatory of life with Cavaldi. The obvious pleasure they took in enjoying our food made me feel proud. Their enthusiasm about our tomatoes made me wonder whether us locals appreciated the miracle of our bounty, as well as what on earth London art dealers must eat throughout the year to make our simple groceries so compelling?

As we approached the end of June, I had shared most of the recipes I knew, and sometimes, part for folly, part for necessity — as my repertoire was running thin — I'd invent ideas on the spot, improvising appropriate vegetable pairings, hoping they might work in real life too. I remember them arriving at the store, and I prepared myself for a tour of the day's deliveries. I'd been hatching a few ideas for light summery lunches that I had an inkling they'd enjoy when they asked me something unrelated to anything we'd spoken about before: Would I consider working for them in London in return for papers to America?

I will never forget that day. The way the sun bleached their white faces and lit up their pale yellow collars — they often wore the same shade. Their smiling faces are etched in my mind. Behind them, the ever increasing surge of tourism strolled past the shop. I remember watching the crowd smudge into a sun-kissed blur, the feel of the cold dark shop behind me, and that compelling stone path out of this town, away from this miserable life and the battle-axe for whom I would never be any more than a mountain-girl lackey. They must have known I would have said yes before they'd even finished the invitation. Perhaps I ought to have asked more questions, known what would have been truly expected of me, but the craving for freedom, for air, was too powerful. I think if I'd been even bolder I might have thrown off my apron there and then and walked with them straight onto their ship from the Bay of Naples with nothing but my smock. As it turned out, that was not so far from the truth. On July 1, 1956, I became part of the Neapolitan throng shuffling along the streets of London, in search of gold.

CHAPTER 2

It took six weeks of the purgatorial British drizzle before I surrendered to my first bout of homesickness. At first, the terrifying otherness was the exhilaration of a splash of spring water on a hot day; the sounds of murmured clipped vowels, the way people's hands stayed by their sides when they spoke. The way the young girls seemed to be talking out the sides of their mouths, whirring a string of incomprehensible sentences, each word looping onto the next, whirring out of what sounded like chewing gum–filled mouths. I wanted to be them. I wanted my hair pinned, curled, and set. I wanted to walk down the street with my arm linked in my best friend's, surefooted, heels that knew they belonged and where they were headed. But after just over a month of this giddy daydream, the stream of possible lives blurring before me, offering heady futures just beyond my reach, reality hit. I had no one.

Mr. Benn and Mr. George had lost the laid-back sunshine swagger of their holiday. Back in North West London they had become different people. Or rather, they had settled back into the lives they had paused. The gentlemen owned a large Georgian terraced home set a little way back from the main Heath Street that led into Hampstead. The bohemian suburb attracted a vibrant palette of artists, many of which came to call at our house, each more peculiar than the previous. Mr. Benn and Mr. George ran an art gallery on one of the back streets behind Piccadilly. I navigated my way there on my first day off. I stood upon the wooden slats of the tube carriage of the Bakerloo line, turning in a pitiful performance of confidence. Truth was, I could barely read the map in time to work out which stop was mine, so thick was the tiny carriage of others' cigarette smoke. It reminded me of my father.

When I did arrive, I was too embarrassed to step inside. I remained on the pavement, ignoring the rain. I stared at the painting in the window. Giant swirls of yellow with flecks of turquoise stuck to the canvas in stubborn blobs. Angry spurts of red protested across the central spiral. I couldn't tear my eyes away. Nothing before me could, in my opinion, be judged as art, yet the image was intimidating in the compelling way it hooked my gaze. The artist and frame had had a fight, and I couldn't decide who had won.

I left the stalemate and found a tiny booth in the sweaty New Piccadilly Café, sandwiched between the Piccadilly theater and a number of salubrious shop fronts. It was hard to decipher the goods on offer, but I had a hunch it had a lot to do with the young women huddled nearby. It took me a couple of minutes to realize that I had understood every word of what the proprietor said to the waitress. Before I congratulated myself on my progress in English, it dawned on me that the dialect I had tuned into was Neapolitan.

"Signori— you from the old country, *si*?"

I looked up at the man, unsure of what my answer ought to be. "Positano."

"I know a Napoletana when I see one!"

He scooted around the counter, leaving the blaze of short-order cooks whipping up omelettes behind him.

"You're not long here, am I right, Signorina?"

I had an inkling to suggest that I'd never met a Neapolitan man who ever thought he wasn't right about anything, but thought

35

better of it.

"You working? *Lavori?*"

"Yes," I began, realizing how much I'd cherished my anonymity up till this interrogation, how the incessant Positanese prying was very much part of my past, not present, "for two gentlemen. In Hampstead."

His eyebrows raised and his head tilted.

"Hey, Carla!" he yelled over to the waitress zipping between tables with egg-smeared plates balanced just the right side of equilibrium, "this signorina is up with the Hampstead crowd! Not one gentleman! Two! Not bad for a fishing village girl, no?"

I was back on my narrow streets, gossip climbing cobbles. I took a breath to speak without knowing what I wanted to say. He quashed my indecision before I could. "Listen, if it doesn't work out with the lords up there, you call me, *si*? Wait — two men you say? Together in one house? Brothers?"

I shook my head. His eyebrows furrowed. I wasn't convinced that he didn't mutter something to the Virgin Mary and the saints.

"I always have work for a *paesan.*" I didn't want to be a *paesan.* I wanted to be a Londoner. "This Soho," he continued, twiddling his fingers in the air like someone sprinkling *parmigiano,* "this patch belongs to us *italiani.* Out there we're immigrants.

But in Soho we help each other — *capisci?*"

I nodded, but I didn't. Or didn't want to.

I tried to let go of the vague sense that his approach was more of an offensive than a welcome. Wisdom and scrawled number on limp paper imparted, he turned and walked across the café waving singsong arms at an English couple who were sat at another Formica booth, dipping their rectangular strips of toast into soft-boiled eggs. I took a final sip and left, all remnants of homesickness hanging in the sweaty tea-smudged air of that café.

My attic room is etched in memory. It was clean and simple. My routine was described to me in great detail and it didn't take me long to adjust to the gentlemen's habits, which, it would seem, never altered independent of the day. To her credit, Signora Cavaldi's terse grip had stood me in fine stead for London life.

I hadn't meant to, nor planned to, but on my sixth visit to the police station the first cracks appeared. Small, but prominent, fissures. I was the tenth in line to have my Certificate of Registration stamped. I held it in my hand, trying not to let my nerves crease it too much. At the top was my number: 096818. And below the words: ALIENS ORDER 1956. Every other visit, I

37

had felt like it would only be a matter of time until I would no longer be alien; I would belong, click into the puzzle, be that final missing piece. But that day, as the drizzle left a damp trail on my hair like half-dried tears, I felt the sting of being the outsider. It was the first time I'd noticed the sideways glances of the people going about their regular days. Or perhaps they had always looked at us like that. I was used to being alone, I told myself. Life here was a world better than the one I'd left behind. I almost convinced myself.

Autumn and winter trundled by, and I couldn't shake the feeling that Mr. Benn and Mr. George were not impressed by my work. There was nothing major I could pinpoint about the shift in our day-to-day lives. A wave of frustration drew in, a little snatched remark here, an almost imperceptible roll of the eye; the toast being over-done, underdone, too early, not early enough. Minutiae of small failures tripped into an impressive collection, the way insignificant disappointments ferment into resentment between lovers till they can no longer bear to be together but cannot define exactly what pressure has pushed them apart. All three of us knew that I would not be working there much longer.

One morning in early May, the bell rang of a Saturday afternoon, a surprising sun casting boastful rays across the black-and-white tiles of the wide hallway, as if it too had joined in to celebrate my imminent termination of employment. I knew it would be my final weekend here, and I would, against my better judgment, give the owner of New Piccadilly Café a call after all. I turned the latch and opened the door.

Upon the step stood a man and a woman. She had a mane of strawberry blonde locks cascading in defiant curls past her shoulders. They bounced over the deep purple of her full-length woollen cardigan. Her long red chiffon slip beneath danced on the spring breeze by her bare feet, slipped into simple Roman sandals. His beard was a thing to behold, waves of thick blond tuft with streaks of red. A wide-brimmed leather hat perched on his head at an angle. His heavy leather boots stamped a few times upon the mat, scraping off imaginary snow or the memory of yet another wet day. At once, they reminded me of the painting in the window. Only this splash of color and verve came with its very own halo surround, courtesy of the bitter white sun.

I noticed I was staring just before they did and stepped aside to let them in. The woman flashed me a wide smile, flicked the hair off her face and removed her shoes, before floating into the front room where Mr. Benn had insisted I light a fire. She wrapped her arms around him, and I pretended not to notice when she kissed him on the lips and sat on his knee. So did the gentleman who accompanied her. He, rather, shook Mr. George's hand, who then nodded for me to open the wine.

I filled four glasses with prosecco and handed them out. Mr. Benn and Mr. George carried on talking. The man and the woman thanked me. I returned to the tray and lifted the small bowl of nuts Mr. Benn had asked me to prepare. As I placed them upon the low table before the fire, the woman reached out her hand. "Santina, aren't you?"

I nodded, wanting to avoid conversation.

"Henry," she began, turning to the man who had accompanied her, "this is Santina, darling. Oh she's a pip. You're like a Mediterranean stroll in the sun — you know you've found a beauty, don't you, boys?"

Mr. Benn and Mr. George smiled, one lip each.

"Santina, it's a pleasure," she continued, while I squirmed. "We've heard a great deal about you. How exquisite to have a slice of

Positano right here in North West London. Henry darling, it fills me with a great deal of hope. It's like a ray of sun through the fog."

"That'll be the morning sun actually doing what it's compelled to do," he answered, "quite naturally."

The woman rolled her eyes and jumped up from Mr. Benn's lap.

"Quite right — I'm not thinking straight at all — thank God for that! Who'd live a life through logic's narrow lens, for crying out loud?"

"I'll drink to that!" cried Mr. George and the four of them stood and clinked.

"Go easy with the wine, Adeline," Henry, who I had assumed was her husband, replied. Though in this house, when guests appeared, it wasn't always clear who belonged to whom. The boundaries I had become accustomed to back home were the suffused haze after a spring shower.

The woman's hand slipped down to her abdomen, "Good heavens, I almost forgot! Yes, we've got some marvelous news, haven't we?"

"Indeed," Henry replied, catching my eye as he did so.

"I shall be creating more than paintings this year, gentlemen!" she cried, flinging her arms up at such a speed that she almost lost half her glass's contents onto the Persian rug underfoot. "I am now producing humans also!"

It was hard to follow the conversation with accuracy, especially since I hadn't been allowed into or out of it. I could understand that the willowy figure before me was pregnant. As she stood up, it became so obvious that I wondered how I hadn't noticed before.

"Congratulations, Mr. and Mrs. Crabtree!" cried Mr. George.

"That'll be all, Santina," Mr. Benn said, with an unnecessary hand wave, adding to all the other spoken and unspoken gestures tracing my paper cut scars.

I shut the door behind me and went upstairs to pack.

The next morning Mr. Benn and Mr. George called me to the back parlor. I found Mr. Benn by his grand piano looking out toward the glass doors that led to their garden. He was puffing on a thin cigar. The smoke reached me in sorrowful swirls.

"Santina, my dear. It will come as somewhat of a surprise, to me more than anyone, that we can no longer offer you employment."

I gave a mute nod, unsure whether to express regret or surprise. Neither surfaced as it happened.

"However, there are others in our circle who are more than willing to welcome you into their home and have you offer the tireless support you have given us, up till now."

I glanced over at Mr. George, but he was looking off toward an invisible horizon behind me.

"Mr. and Mrs. Crabtree are keen for you to start with them right away. The major, for that is how you must address him from now on, has assured me that he will, like us, arrange your papers for America after your first year."

He left a pause here, which I knew he expected me to fill with grateful acceptance. I was happy that we were parting company with relative grace. Or, if not grace, at the very least that smooth veneer of some such which I had intuited was an impeccable British habit. That evening they walked me down the hill toward the heart of Hampstead village to my new home.

Adeline and the major's house snuck into a slice of land between larger old brick homes at the convergence of two narrow lanes. Its layout was more warren than house, with low-ceilinged rooms leading onto one another in a maze of unexpected connections. Tudor beams hung crooked with age. Persian rugs overlapped one another in most of the rooms. A huge hearth stood in the main living room flanked by two sofas of different shades of velveteen violet. There were masks upon the wall, Indian gods and goddesses forever mid-chase, flaunting their half-clothed bodies, or leering at the spectator. I'm ashamed to admit that I avoided looking at the one which hung by my bedroom door, so full were its wooden carved eyes of malice. Its pupils were painted red and black and hair hung in sad curls almost touching the wooden floorboards below.

At the far end of the house, squeezed in along one length of the courtyard garden, was Adeline's studio. Small glass panes lined the upper section along the entirety of one side, letting in shafts of light from over the garden wall, which backed onto Christchurch hill. The roof was formed of skylights, bathing the anarchic space in a wash of light. Several easels flanked the space, with unfinished canvases upon them, bright with moments of intense inspiration or drying paint. The floor was speckled with memories of Adeline's expressive explosions. Even in her condition, she would hide way for days at a time refusing food and rest. It frustrated the major a great deal, but I suspected that her artistic endeavors overtook both their lives with a ferocity neither could tame or understand, both succumbing to its seduction with varying degrees of resistance.

Adeline acquiesced to her imagination with abandon. I caught her once, as I headed to the major in his study with a laden tray, through the gap between the open door and the frame. She was barefoot, which was not surprising: her feet reacted to any covering as an affront to their liberty. Her white smock hung, creased about her, the growing roundness of abdomen catching the light as she swayed, a plump moon. Her fingers were splattered and quick, letting the brush lead them in muscular strokes. But it was her face that captured my attention. Her eyes were bright, the auburn flecks crisscrossing, the blue even more visible in this light; shards of intense concentration. Her head was cocked to the side. If I didn't know better, I would have said she was listening to something, music perhaps, a voice even. I was spying an intimate conversation. My eyes drifted to the canvas. I would have recognized that spiral anywhere. This was the artist whose

45

work had captured my attention all those months ago in Mr. Benn's gallery. It was beautiful. Bristles of guilt iced up my arm. I headed on to the study.

The major's hideaway smelled like the rest of the house, a compost of dusty books, sandalwood incense, and fresh flowers. He tamed the roses in their garden with intricate care and took cuttings most mornings when they were in full scent. A huge grandfather clock edged us toward the future in somber swings. His desk faced the large sash window, each framed pane offering a concise version of his beloved garden. Books lined the walls on heavy, carved mahogany shelves. Stacks mushroomed in each corner, a literary metropolis. Upon the tired green leather top was a correspondence organizer which never seemed to empty, and beside this, his pot of ink, into which he dipped between sentences as his pen scratched along his fine paper. I had gleaned that his time in the army had come to an enforced end and his hours spent in his room related to investment work of some sort. Adeline had rambled through their brief history, but she skirted details and my English didn't equip me to understand all I needed to. She also painted her own background with broad brushstrokes, a snipe at the end of sentences about her estranged family whose aristocratic wealth and abundance stood in stark contrast to the contempt they held for the artistic life she had chosen, even if the major was able to almost keep her in the manner they expected.

I stood for a moment before the clatter of the tray made him turn to me.

"Sorry, Major — I do not disturb you? Here's your four o'clock tea as you asked."

"Ah, yes, *grazie,* Santina."

He whipped straight back to his writing. The smoky steam swirled up from the narrow silver spout.

"Lapsang souchong, yes? You remembered?" he asked without taking his eyes off his letter.

"Yes," I answered, wondering how he could drink something that smelled like a bonfire.

"That'll be all."

I left and closed the heavy squat door behind me.

The remaining months of Adeline's pregnancy ripened throughout the summer. As the days lengthened, so did her energy. Several times I'd walk past the studio door finishing up my chores of the evening only to notice the lights still on and the soft

47

smudge of a brush dipping into paint and caressing the canvas. I'd listen to the quickening strokes, wondering whether this infinite burst of energy was healthy. The next morning — I think she can't have slept more than a handful of hours — she declared that we were to visit the ladies' pond in the heath. I almost dropped her egg as she did so. Then I caught the major's eyebrow rise up and lower, over the tip of the newspaper.

"Henry, don't be tiresome. Now is the time to listen to my body. I'm listening. You'd do well to do the same. It needs water. A great deal of it. This morning."

The major let out a sigh. The corner of his paper flickered on the last whispered trace of it. I placed a silver rack of fresh toast at the center of their breakfast table and, as usual, pretended not to hear very much at all.

"Adeline — you're the size of a modest whale. What on earth do you hope to achieve by thrashing around in freezing waters in this condition?"

I scooped another spoon of marmalade into a small ramekin and set it beside the toast, spreading the sounds of their conversation into a distant periphery.

As I reached the door, I heard my name

and spun back toward them.

"That's settled then, yes, Santina?"

"Pardon, Major?"

"What I just said."

He hated to repeat himself. I hated asking him to.

"I'm sorry, I didn't hear."

Another sigh. Deeper this time. He flopped his napkin beside his plate.

"After breakfast you're to accompany my bride to the pond. If she will not be convinced to avoid the icy bathing, then so be it. If you are there, you may offer assistance should she need it."

I skipped through most of the key words as he spoke, but the thought of me standing at the water's edge in charge of a heavily pregnant artist, who, to my mind, had never done a thing that anyone had ever insisted of her, sent cold trickles of fear down my neck.

I nodded, of course.

Adeline charged through the forest with long strides, ducking under lower-hanging branches, swinging her long limbs over stony patches. Her leather satchel lifted with each step, her towel draped over one shoulder, percussing her steps with a nonchalant swing. Meanwhile, I rambled behind her, walking eight steps to her three, tripping over unexpected stones, holes, muddy patches. I hated the feeling of being a stranger amongst this lush green. It reminded me of trekking light-footed amongst the mountainous wilderness of home. That was another life now. A twang of sorrow tugged. I ripped my attention away from the memories, feeling the prick of their thorns but tearing away, just as Adeline did with every bramble catch of her towel. The paths inched in again and led to a wooden gate. Adeline creaked it open and we followed the stony ridge. I could make out a jetty just beyond several oaks. As we turned, the glassy water opened up before us, shafts of morning light streaking through the branches of the trees that surrounded it. The bottle green water lay still, save for tiny ripples left from itinerant dragonflies. The reflections of the surrounding leaves dappled the surface with forest greens, ochre, sienna, and emerald, all crafted with exquisite perfection as in the hands of a skilled oil painter. I noticed I couldn't move.

"Yes, Santina — it is simply breathtaking. My very happy place. Come on!"

And with that, she reached down to the bottom of her shift and with one lithe movement lifted it clear off her body. She placed her hands on her naked hips. I wished my eyes weren't settling on her breasts, paper-thin porcelain streaked with threads of blue, ready to nourish. In the last few days, I had noticed her pregnant belly drop toward her pelvis. I knew her time was soon. Spidery-thin pink lines streaked out from her belly button.

"Have you ever seen a naked pregnant woman, Santina?"

I shook my head, feeling the heat of embarrassment color my cheeks.

"Isn't it wonderful and ghastly?"

I wished some words would come to my rescue rather than this mute stupidity.

"That's why I must simply come here today. If I feel any heavier, I may never walk again. It is a horrid feeling. And amazing of course. Henry felt it kick last night. The little monster churned across my entire belly. I saw an elbow, I think."

She spun toward the water, reached the end of the jetty, stepped off, and disappeared. I'd like to think I didn't hold my breath. I looked around for other bathers but none were to be found. I counted the seconds till she resurfaced, my chest tightening. Then her head rose with a spray of water. I sat down upon the jetty and watched her head bob over and under the green ripples, pretending that it didn't look like the perfect thing I should like to be doing at this very moment.

A week later the baby came; small, pink, and loud. Perhaps I was the only one who noticed Adeline not sleeping for those first three days. No one else seemed to pay any mind to her manic delight. The major was transfixed with the babe. The midwife was cool and brusque. Adeline was a woman possessed with a frantic happiness. It made me feel uneasy. I watched her hold the tiny baby to her bare breast, sometimes not noticing when her nipple fell out of the babe's mouth, or the wails as she flailed to reattach. I heard the cries through the night. I wasn't convinced they were those of a mother adjusting to her new reality.

On the fourth day we awoke to an almighty crash. I ran to my window. Down in the garden I saw that the major's beloved greenhouse's roof had collapsed. Jagged panes were strewn around a body.

It was Adeline's.

CHAPTER 3

I watched the major follow the ambulance crew out of the house. He shot me a fleeting glance as he left. I mustered a nod that I hoped would reassure him Elizabeth was in good hands. New End Hospital emergency department was only a few streets away, and that was some comfort. The door closed behind him. I held the screeching baby closer to my chest. I'd never felt quite so alone.

Elizabeth wailed into my ear as I carried her down the darkened hallway toward the nursery. I found several glass bottles in a neat line upon the wooden dresser, left by the midwife earlier. I cared little for that woman, but now her disinfected approach to infants was the one thing that would carry me through the night with the child.

I laid Elizabeth into her cot. She protested, jerking her limbs with deepening cries, leaving intermittent gaps between wails where her breath filled those tiny lungs before the next blast for survival. I filled a glass bottle with the contents of one of the prepared cans, picked her up, and looked at her tiny red face, contorted with anguish. I sat upon the nursing chair by the window and cradled her. She clamped her lips around the bottle's teat, and her cries gave way to the brittle silence of the house.

I tried to focus on the peace that washed over her tiny face, the dewy hair covering her cheeks that reminded me of the ripe peaches of my Amalfitani summers. For a moment, the terror of the past hour faded. She gave in to a milky sleep. I sat there for some time, feeling the flutter of her heart gallop against my belly. I didn't notice I was crying at first. Then I saw the itinerant droplets blot the muslin cloth, covering her with little damp circles. I stood up and placed the bundle back into her cot. She stirred as she left the warmth of my arms but slipped back into her quiet as my hand smoothed away from under her. I watched her chest rise and fall, fitful and erratic. I'm not sure how long I stood there, making sure she was breathing, even if I knew my gaze alone would never ensure her survival. The brief escape from the image of Adeline's crumpled face floating back into my mind was short lived.

The minutes after her fall were already a blur. A flurry of panic, glass, blood. When we first reached her, I was sure she was already dead. As the major touched her though, she let out a groan, her eyes rolling in her head. I couldn't have hoped to sail through the shock as he did. I followed his every instruction, holding Adeline's hand and doing my best to keep her conscious while he called for help.

Now, in the disquiet, my mind churns, longing for yesterday. Wishing there would have been some way to prevent this. Berating myself for not having the courage to alert the major or midwife to Adeline's erratic behavior. It was not my place. Now everything felt unsure. I was stood on floating ice, watching small pieces break off around me.

I pulled the nursing chair close to the cot. Stripes of moonlight cut through the square panes. Shadows crept through the house as it creaked into the night. Every woody sound pierced my fretful sleep. Each time Elizabeth took in several snatched breaths in a row, I awoke. I wrapped her tiny fingers in mine. That night I dreamed of my mother. The newborn and I both woke up crying.

The next few weeks snaked on between shards of silence. The major left promptly every morning after breakfast to visit Adeline, returned for a light lunch, retired to his study, then bedroom soon after.

One morning he sat at the breakfast table longer than usual. I cleared his plate. When I closed the door behind me, I heard him cry for the first time. I stood with my back against the old wood, listening for longer than I needed to. I waited, not knowing why. He did not call me, of course. I cleaned the deep ceramic sink more than I needed. I took a moment to polish the window ledge above it and take in the garden, the roofless greenhouse and its bare skeletal rusting frame. Below, the major's beloved tomatoes hung plump with fruit, oblivious to the tragedy that had crashed around them. I returned to the dining room to clear the rest of the dishes.

"Santina?" His voice was thin.

"Yes, Major?"

He looked me in the eye. I don't think he'd done so since that night.

"I'm very grateful for your help at this time."

"You're welcome."

"This is a temporary arrangement, of course. You understand. Adeline will be returning home in a few nights."

"Yes, Major."

"I will require your extra assistance during the transition. I will, of course, reimburse you fairly."

My brow furrowed before I could stop it.

"I need more help from you," he clarified, "more than your usual jobs."

"Yes," I replied, "of course."

"Thank you."

He took a deeper breath. I felt like he wanted to say something more.

"That is all for now."

I returned to the kitchen. He disappeared back into his solitary world.

Adeline returned a translucent shell. Her eyes were misty gray pools. I pretended not to notice the way her feet searched the floor, unsteady, someone trying to balance upon a moving ship. Her skin hung from her cheekbones like a fading memory. The major wrapped his arm around her and led her to the guest bedroom, which he had overseen the nurses set up for hours before she came home until it resembled a hospital room. A metal trolley stood by the window, lined with paper and a small drugstore of medicinal vials and bottles. Crisp linen towels towered upon the dresser.

A regular stream of doctors passed through the house for the next week. It was impossible to not overhear their conversations with the major because each ended in the same heated manner, with the latter crying out for the medical men to leave. That instant. The strain spread over the major's face like a drought. One morning, the more patient of the doctors sat beside him at the breakfast table.

"Henry, you must listen to our advice. Adeline will not improve. Not for a very long time. If at all. This is not an episode of hysteria. She is experiencing the trauma of postpartum psychosis. You can't just brush this off. The way you're behaving, it's like Adeline's broken her leg and you're hoping a sticking plaster will do the trick."

The major took a long breath.

"What you're doing is cruel," the doctor added.

"What I'm doing is commonly known as a basic respect for humanity! This is the woman I love! You will not experiment on her, do you hear me?" the major yelled. "How can I possibly expect any of you to understand that? We have been through this again and again —"

"And each blessed time I pray to God you'll heed my advice. You have a peculiar respect and contempt for my professional opinion."

The major wiped his mouth and flung his napkin onto the table.

"Henry," the doctor began in a familiar tone, which made me think this was more than a professional relationship, "if you insist on caring for her yourself, then at the very least take her somewhere she can find peace. Somewhere with a temperate climate. Sea air, perhaps? Somewhere she can live housebound but with some semblance of tranquillity — which, in my learned opinion, would be with us in an institution in Epsom, especially equipped for women suffering from bad nerves. You are not able to deal with this alone. You and I know this more than anyone else."

"James, I've listened to what you have to say. My wife will not be committed. She is sick, yes, but she need not be incarcerated. She's my wife, for heaven's sake!"

The major rose to his feet, slamming the table as he did so.

The doctor rose to meet him. "We both want what's best. I will do everything I can to support you, Henry, but it will not be easy."

The major nodded. His gaze bored into his hands.

"I'll give you a few days to think — then you'll tell me what you've decided."

I opened the door for the doctor. "That's quite alright, I'll see myself out, thank you."

I heard the door close as I scraped the last few crumbs off the tablecloth. Adeline cried out. The major reached the stairs before I.

"I'll go, Santina, you finish here."

The next few nights bent into a fragile routine. The major rose with Adeline, calmed her out of her night terrors, soothed the screams that tore me out of my own restless sleep, while I cradled her mewling baby, watching her mold into my arms as I fed her, then lulling her to sleep with swaying. Each feed bought me time to gaze at that tiny face, noticing the minuscule changes to the small pink mounds of her cheeks, an extra tuft of downy hair along her hairline, a second or two more of keeping her shiny slate eyes open. This temporary peace softened the house, till the next bout of unsettled cries of either mother or daughter reverberated, all the louder for the deafening quiet that encased us. Sometimes

Elizabeth would rip Adeline out of her rest and make her shake with panic. Other nights Adeline wouldn't sleep at all, but insisted on wandering the halls or walking up and down the stairs in continuous motion.

The final night before the doctor returned to hear of Henry's decision we found Adeline scrawling all over the walls. The pencil raced across the plaster, scrambling outpourings. The next day, as I tried my best to wash all the markings off I reread her stream of panic. She wrote about loving Elizabeth, of wanting to love her, of not being mad. The writing was jagged, void of punctuation. Reading her words in the cold light of day was more terrifying than watching the major try to tear her away from it in the dead of night, as she screeched at him to not set one finger upon her body or she would kill him. When the doctor arrived, the major was still asleep. I led him to the front room to wait.

"How was the night, Santina?" the doctor asked, catching me a little off guard.

"I'm not sure," I lied, trying not to think about the red circles around Adeline's eyes, or the withering panic the major tried to bury from me as he wrestled her back to bed.

"How is Elizabeth?"

"Hungry mostly," I replied. My mind spun down the hall to the warmth of the kitchen where she slept in her rattan basket. I could sense she would wake soon to be fed. I would sit by the fire and the world would slip away, replaced by Elizabeth's rhythmical suckling and an imperceptible smile I thought I could read in the peaceful slant of her closed eyes; the rise and fall of her swallows like wordless thanks.

The doctor smiled. I nodded and left the room. After a while the major came down. I placed a tray of tea between them and poured, wishing the uncertainty of the household would swirl up into thin air like the Earl Grey steam.

"And that's your final decision then, Henry?"

"I don't change my mind, James, you know me better than that."

"I'm afraid I do."

"Thank you, Santina — that will be all."

I left the men, feeling like my life in London was once again an uncharted course, headed for the rocks.

That afternoon, while Adeline was sleeping, the major called me into his study. Something about the usual considered chaos felt jagged today. A few more books were left half opened, reams of abandoned words searching for their lost reader. Time had frayed since that night, forever an unfinished paragraph.

"Santina, I must tell you something."

My stomach tightened.

"I have decided my family must move away."

Memories of the New Piccadilly Café flickered before me, darker and sweatier than I remembered it. I nodded, furious about the tears clamping my throat.

"I would dearly like you to come with us," he said, straightening.

Some hope after all, perhaps.

"It is a big move. A different country, in fact."

My body refused to offer any reaction. I stood mute, looking as stupid as I felt.

"Italy. I intend to return to the one town that has left the deepest impression on me since I first set foot there."

I held the expectant silence.

"Positano."

He read my face quicker than I could recover my expression.

"Yes, it is most likely a ridiculous shock to you, and I would understand entirely if it was the very place you would have no interest in returning to."

Any town on the globe but my own. He was rolling back the carpet to his city, hooking me back into the place I longed to leave like no other. My heart curled into a tight fist.

"I am under no illusion that the very reason you came to this city was as a gateway to America. Now, while I'm in no position to influence you, I must express that your help has been invaluable the last month. I should like to extend your time with us by one year, and, whatever the situation at that point, I will, of course, honor my promise to arrange your papers for America. As planned. I don't need an answer today, of course. Tomorrow will be fine."

He turned back to his desk. I nodded and left.

The click of the lock felt like I was shutting much more than a door behind me.

I tied a scarf around my head and left the house. My legs began marching downhill along Willow Road. I stormed past The White Bear, giving a perfunctory nod to the locals resting upon the wooden benches outside. I didn't take the time to enjoy the Edwardian terraces this time, nor the cluster of powdery-colored homes, or the line stretching a little way down Flask Walk from the public baths where the poor families from the cottages on Streatley Place would take their weekly cleanse. Thoughts ricocheted in my mind, colliding for attention and answers. How on earth could I return home? It would be like an unfinished adventure, fleeing the dream that had brought me this far. I had become the third strand in the plait of this family's drama. Perhaps it was the broken nights, the constant strain of having to cope with Adeline's reliving of terrors only she could see, but I felt a sudden wave of claustrophobia followed by a great weight of tiredness, the like I hadn't felt since my mother died.

I crossed East Heath Road and found Adeline's muddy path toward the ponds. The mixed pond was in view now, intrepid swimmers gliding through the glassy green, sending ripples across the surface. I was that net of duckweed, feeling the involuntary undulations rock me this way and that. The trees grew thicker and the trail wound in deeper into the trees, narrowing through elder and yew. The trodden leafy paths were still cooked with summer, only the yellowing tinge to the tips of occasional leaves hinted at the relentless promise of autumn. What was the sense in defying the inevitable change? Would starting a new London life alone be surrendering to the diverted path or resisting it? Was this the freedom I'd been charmed by? An unknown world, unencumbered by family dramas, newborns' demands? Now might be the very crossroads I needed to find the courage to start again.

I bent down under a low-lying branch and sank onto a fallen trunk. For a moment my mind drew a misty silence. I heard the birds celebrate high up in the trees above me. Straws of light shafted onto my feet. I let the damp, sunny air cocoon my restless mind. Could I admit to myself that I had fallen in love with someone else's child? That in the month-long care of this helpless human I had been consumed by the desire that she survive? That the first time her eyes focused on mine I was filled with the thrill of being the first human she had connected with? That the helplessness I felt in the face of Adeline's catastrophic decline was plowed into making sure this motherless child was cared for? That I loved her on behalf of the major, who I could see found it all too painful to express his feelings toward the tiny babe? Selfish perhaps, this decadent desire to save.

I was no one's savior.

I was the help.

A month or two of going beyond my remit of service would not make me part of their family. And yet, if I could keep my head down for another year, then true freedom would be mine. Giving a little more of myself to this tiny child would be a small sacrifice for what I would receive in return. I could survive one more year of gazing into those tiny eyes, each day opening wider, each day seeing the world smudge toward focus. Would I deny myself that unquestioning delight as when our eyes locked for the first time? For the mere second or two while it lasted, she saw me. Not Santina Guida, the help. Not someone's abandoned daughter. The flicker of infinity that sparkled there moved me. A bright silence ignited that fleeting, but unflinching gaze; a promise of renewal — where one dream dies, another, by necessity, is born.

What was a year in Positano compared to a lifetime in the New World?

CHAPTER 4

On October 2, 1957, I accompanied the Crabtrees upon the *Blue Star Line* ship on a return to the Bay of Naples. I was a month shy of my twentieth birthday. The crystalline turquoise of my coast was not the salve I longed for after the relentless sea voyage. The water drew me back to the place I'd fought to escape for so much of my life, I was a hapless swimmer defeated by the undertow. The major and I had shared pitiful, snatched sleep between us. Adeline received tranquilizing medication throughout the crossing from southern France, administered with precision by the major, which, to our relief, appeared to have more effect than in London. It kept her frenetic outbursts at bay and dipped her into the waking sleep to which she had become accustomed. At least in this state the major was able to keep her relaxed, or some appearance of such. He even managed to bring her out onto deck a couple of times for fresh air, though it wasn't long before the amount of people unsettled her, and the major was quick to retire back into their cabin before the situation grew out of hand.

My job was to stay with Elizabeth at all times. It would be an understatement to say I was nervous at the prospect. I had no experience of looking after a small child, let alone at sea, where the unpredictability of travel felt all the more dangerous. I tried to reassure myself that there were always doctors on board, and, most likely, experienced mothers who might help should I need it. I worked myself into such a silent state of panic that when Elizabeth was relaxed and slept the best she had since birth it came as a great wave of relief. She adored the fresh air on deck, the hundreds of strange faces. Her tiny head twisted this way and that, trying to gather the details of everything around her, the different smells, sounds, and the musical soup of languages.

Some people passed me and flashed sympathetic smiles, thinking I was her mother perhaps. I'd be lying if I didn't admit to feeling a prickle of pride as they did so. And though she was not my own, each time I lifted her close to me, and described in detail all the things around us, the girl became ever more a part of me, in spite of the sting of defeat that curdled in my stomach as we approached land.

The *Blue Star Line* ship eased into the wide bay. Shipping offices crowded the port. From the deck on this bright day I could see far into the bustling city, a mystical warren that was still a foreign land to me, and to the right, rising ancient and proud, the purple silhouette of Vesuvius. The wind caught the new tufts of Elizabeth's strawberry blonde hair; her eyes blinked away the tears left by the sea breeze. My eyes glistened too as I pretended I didn't feel like I was sinking back into my old life, retreating toward a familiar town at once unknown. Positano with an unpredictable Adeline would not be the town I left. Working for a family that might terminate my contract sooner than planned, like Mr. Benn and Mr. George had, would leave me more vulnerable than when I first fled. I wiped away my tears and with it smudged my roiling thoughts into silence.

The major helped Adeline down the gangway, a patient arm hooked around hers, following her tentative lead. If she began to tense, he would stop, take her hand in his and kiss it gently, murmuring something in her ear that always seemed to soothe. I thought about all those nights I heard him with her. Once, I had been feeding Elizabeth in the nursery, and could hear him read poetry to Adeline until she relinquished to sleep. Those nights it seemed that his care was having great effect, for a day or two afterwards she would show small flickers of her old self, but then night would fall and the wakings and railings would flare up again. The doctors had repeated their insistent requests to place Adeline in an institution, to reinstate shock therapy, to treat her psychotic episode with the internment it required. He would hear none of it. One doctor had even suggested that the major put up Elizabeth for adoption in the circumstances. That night I had seen the extent of the major's temper. I hoped I never would again.

All the images of the past fitful months floated into my periphery with each step along the sun-dipped gangway. After we shuffled through customs with the throng, we were at long last welcomed by our taxi. The major insisted I sit in the front seat with Elizabeth so that he could stay beside Adeline at the back. I saw her turn to him. A whisper of a smile skimmed her lips. His hand squeezed hers a little tighter.

Our road snaked through the cacophony

of the port, the sea of visitors embarking on their voyages. We were at a convergence of conflicting shoals swimming toward new lives, some fleeing, others, like me, returning. How many of them felt like their homeland was a strange new world? Little by little the crowds gave way to the hills I hadn't admitted I'd missed. We climbed toward the southern tip, curving in and out of the landscape till Sorrento opened up below us, clusters of pink, pale yellow, and spring blue homes rising from the gray stony cliffs, the Tyrrhenian turquoise limpid in the fattening midday sun.

Onward we drove, a sleepy Elizabeth lulled into dreams by the engine, as we began the climb toward the narrowing coastal road. The vineyards plump with purple fruit crawled up and down the hillsides beside us, the lemon trees stretched out their branches to the sun, each fruit bursts of yellow in the golden light. Another sharp turn and the coast opened up to us, defiant rocks to our left rising from deep in the cerulean water beneath us. The view of my mountains unfolded like a concertina picture book with each new bend, till the entire range was in view, each further grand cliff edge painted lighter shades of gray in the blanching sun and beside it a mineral green sea. Here we were circling its edge, tiny people in a metal box, carving through, inconsequential, at its mercy. My home hadn't missed me.

The driver took a final bend. The cluster of Positano revealed itself. The houses were more colorful than I had remembered, clutching the cliff face like a scatter of shells left by the *lingua di mare* as we called it, the tongue of the sea, which sometimes even reached the *stradone,* our main street, especially during the winter storms. My mind raced up my hills, perhaps my brother was somewhere amongst them still? Perhaps returning offered me more than the failure of my new life? Perhaps recoiling into this past was a chance to find some peace within it?

The car pulled to a standstill at the foot of the Via Giovanni Marconi. The ascent to our new home would be on foot, up the staggered steps and narrow walkways. Several porters poised at the start of the stairs, two of them with donkeys saddled with empty baskets ready to carry our luggage. When Adeline saw the animals, she reached out her hand, but the major slipped his in hers before she could touch any of them. We climbed, silenced by our weariness and anticipation. The major's steps were assured. It felt like he had been living here some time already.

The alley narrowed, and a tired Elizabeth began a hungry rouse. We passed on behind several large villas, bougainvillea trailing down toward the cobbles, a smattering of twisted paper garlands of purple and fuchsia meeting the sandy stone below, snaking garlands of succulents twisting along the boundary garden walls toward the light, gnarled wisteria branches creeping along the backs of houses. The dusty air was toasted from the warmth of the day, stony and infused with the whisper of drying pine. The alley dipped now and passed under an archway, curved round toward more steps and then a second relentless incline. Our footsteps ricocheted against those thick back walls of the neighboring villas flanking the cobbles. At last, we reached the final dozen steps, uneven with age and passage. At the top loomed the cathedral doors of the Crabtrees' new home. The major wrapped an arm around Adeline as her eyes widened to the sea view spreading out beneath us, blotting into the hazy horizon beyond Capri. Even Elizabeth quieted her hungry wails for a brief moment. We stood still, we four weary travelers, the sounds of the donkeys carrying our loads approaching with steady clops along the stony incline behind us.

The major rang the bell. We waited. One of the two enormous doors opened.

"*Buon giorno,* Signore," said a woman, stepping back to welcome us.

"*Grazie,*" he replied, hooking his arm into Adeline's and ushering her inside without hurry. A long terrace stretched out before us. At the far end there was a stone well, by the looks of it an original feature of the house. At no stage of the preparations had the major described the majesty of the home he had chosen, and I certainly had no intention of prying. Now I found myself within the wall of the baroque merchant villa that I had admired from the shore as I daydreamed of my life beyond Positano. When I had escaped the beady eyes of Signora Cavaldi just long enough to take a moment along the screaming shore of fishermen, hard at work sorting their catch, dying their nets, the air heavy with pine bark as they dipped their loads into the vats to color them, this was the pink house I had looked up at. I filled in the gaps of its fairy-tale history, played out unlikely endings of its inhabitants now lost to our shipwrecked history as a kingdom, when Amalfi was bright with mercantile riches.

I felt my leg shake a little. I walked toward the well, noticing the huge terra-cotta urns in each corner of the terrace. I pointed up to the heavy wooden-beamed ceiling above, but Elizabeth was intent on being fed. I think we all were.

"Santina, please take Elizabeth into one of the rooms. I will deal with the porters."

I nodded as I did so, catching the sight of Adeline resting in one of the lounge chairs facing the sea. The columns on either side of the lookout framed the deepening blue of the sea like a painting. The water was serene and from that view it felt as if you could trace your fingers along it just beyond the stone balustrade.

The cool dark of the rooms inside silenced Elizabeth for a moment. I looked around and saw a divan in one corner where I could lay her down while I prepared a bottle. She stretched her small body, creased with travel. I wondered if she could see the magnificent rococo painted decoration above her, great swirls of red, yellow, and blue upon the wooden beams. Bottle in hand, I raised her onto my lap and she suckled with eagerness. It was stony quiet, but for the soft swallows of the child.

A large wooden dining table was at one end of the room, surrounded by six high-backed green velvet upholstered chairs. A heavy mahogany dresser was beside it. The wooden shutters were closed against the heat and we sat in the wide shaft of light from the terrace. It felt like the home had been empty for some time. It smelled like a forgotten place, a locked-up palace whose tiles had not been stepped across till now. I imagined the woman who had let us in must have been paid to prepare it for our arrival, yet the sensation of a place awakening without hurry was palpable. No sooner had I thought about her than her face appeared around the doorway.

"*Salve,* I'm Rosalia," she said, offering a hand, which I struggled to shake.

"*Piacere* — Santina," I replied.

"Yes! I thought I recognized you — aren't you the Cavaldi girl?"

Her question made me bristle. I was no more the Cavaldi girl than she was my mother.

"I worked there for a while, yes," I replied.

"You work with the English now?"

"Yes."

"What's wrong with the lady?"

"She's just had a baby."

The young woman waited for me to elaborate, her little black eyes twinkling with anticipation. We both realized I wouldn't.

"Well, Santina," she began, breaking my silence, "if you need anything, please just ask — I live just down the way, Via Stefano Andres, number 8."

"Thank you, Rosalia."

She flashed me a wide grin. I mirrored her, intrigued by her clumsy curiosity in spite of myself.

Elizabeth had drifted into a brief afternoon nap, which afforded me time to unpack the little we had brought with us. The major led me up the wide stone steps that wove through the core of the house to the two upper floors. When we reached the top, he showed me to Adeline's room.

"I will take care of the initial arrangements over the next week or so. There will be daily deliveries which I've coordinated in such a manner as I deem most beneficial to all of us."

He read my furrowed brow.

"And I assure you that your education, besides the matters at hand, is high on my list of priorities. I have little care to look at your creased confusion any more than you must do feeling it."

I creased a little more.

"You will learn English. Properly. Starting tomorrow. I want you to understand every-

78

thing I have to say. You understand?"

That I did. I would have sighed out loud with relief, but I was too proud.

"Today you will get basic provisions. Cook a light dinner and organize your room on the floor below, and Elizabeth's beside you, as you see fit. I will sleep in this room here" — he pointed across the hallway to a darkened room on the other side of the stairwell — "so I can be sure to be near Adeline. That is all for now."

I left without asking any more questions, though I could have sat upon that bed and gazed up at the deep red squares painted on the wood above, palatial trompe l'oeil within each panel, a fanfare of bold golds, maroons, and deep blues. Adeline would be sleeping in a cathedral.

When Elizabeth awoke, I changed her, fed her a little before we left the house, stuffed the huge key in the pocket of my skirt, and pretended I wasn't nervous at the prospect of my first excursion with a baby in tow. It was five o'clock now, the shops beginning to open their doors to customers after siesta. Each tap of my shoe percussed the jagged memories fighting for attention. It wasn't nostalgia, the town that opened up underfoot as I wound down the steps toward the center felt like one I had known in the final fitful moments of a bad dream.

The streets appeared the same but there had been a subtle shift. The colors were different. A little more care was taken over the window boxes. Some homes had been painted pastel shades. The town was rousing from a slumber. Of course it was still the fishing village I had always known, but there seemed to be more people now, a more resolute swagger to the Positanese.

A voice drew me round. "Well, well — if it isn't the mountain girl! I see you didn't waste any time over in the city by the looks of things." Signora Cavaldi raised an eyebrow at the strawberry blonde bundle in my arms and traced me with a glare I hadn't missed.

"*Buon giorno,* Signora. This is the little girl I look after."

"Yes, I can see that. You've come back after all. Dreams a little too big for a mountain kid after all?"

I smiled so I didn't say anything rude.

"You should see what Paolino has done to our modest shop." She swept her arm through the air to the unrecognizable store behind her. I had left it a darkened cave of fresh produce; now it was framed by flowering window boxes of vermillion geraniums, beautiful wicker baskets laden with lemons and fat peaches. Tall terracotta urns stood with pots of fresh herbs growing inside them. The plain wooden door had been replaced with glass, held open by slabs of granite, beckoning you into the display of fresh legs of prosciutto and glass bowls filled with white clouds of fresh mozzarella. Behind the counter, upon the slanted wooden shelves, the last of the day's fresh loaves beckoned, all the ingredients for a light dinner. I stepped inside.

"We've become quite the talk of the town," she resumed, her chest puffing out. "Something all the new foreigners are seduced by of course — so many of them coming now. All a little strange if I do say so, but money's money, whatever your hair color, no?"

I wasn't sure what answer to offer.

"You'll be wanting something for dinner, no? I'll call Paolino." She walked back to the skinny stairwell I had dreaded climbing each night, and yelled.

She turned, heaving with heavy steps up to her burgeoning empire. I stood still, watching till she'd disappeared around the corner.

I breathed in the salty prosciutto, realizing that it had been hours since I ate. My mind took a bite of the fresh figs in the basket upon the counter, and I imagined the smooth mozzarella softening upon a hunk of the fresh bread. The sound of steps drew me out of my imaginings. Someone stood before me, the air of familiarity but with a face I couldn't place. Only when he spoke did I realize the awkward Paolino I had fled had been replaced by a relaxed young man, proud purveyor of the beautiful creation around him.

"Bet you don't recognize it, Santina?"

I smiled without thinking, wondering how to reconcile that gawky, rude teenager with the man who had chosen baskets for fruit, or laid out these terra-cotta bowls of charred eggplant floating in luscious green olive oil beside tall jars of green olives scenting the shop with an herby air I could almost resist.

"It's beautiful, Paolino!"

"I know. I can hardly believe it myself. These new people coming now, Santina. They like these things. We sell double what we used to. Artist types. They look strange. Act strange. But they spend on the good things, you know?"

"I suppose, yes."

"But enough about me — you look . . ."

I braced myself for one of his cutting remarks, hating myself for being lured in, in the first place. Now I'd be constrained to buy. It was only polite.

". . . English!"

I laughed at that. Out of relief if nothing else.

"And who is this?"

"Elizabeth — I look after her."

"Really? You hold her like she's your own — I thought you'd found some British prince already."

I smiled, feeling a twitch of disappointment prick the corner of my lips. I tried to ignore the surfacing memories; my last conversation with Mr. Benn, the confusion of Adeline's fall, the whisper of failure. All these things Elizabeth made me forget.

"I'd like to buy some things for dinner," I said, focusing on the task at hand.

"I didn't think you'd come just to visit me!"

His face cracked into a wide grin. I had remembered his eyes a hard brown, glassy with pompous adolescence; now they were warm, full of humor. I watched him wrap the bread in wax paper with deft hands, and fill a crate with other provisions I saw fit; a crisp head of bright romaine, a handful of red tomatoes clinging to their vine, several scoops of olives and charred eggplant, and an *etto* or two of prosciutto, pancetta, and

83

coppa, wrapped between thin layers of paper. My stomach rumbled in anticipation.

"Don't worry, Santina — I'll send this to your house with Gennaro, you remember him, no?"

I'd tried to forget that toothless porter — he'd never been kind about mountain folk.

"Where are you living now?"

"Villa San Vito," I replied, watching his eyebrows rise in astonishment.

"No prince, you say?"

"I know the major and his wife will be wanting to dine early — is Gennaro free now?"

"I'll send him right away."

I set the small table on the terrace just outside the stone-walled kitchen and tried to keep Elizabeth occupied, bouncing her on my hip, hoping her cot was due to arrive with the first of the furniture shipment from London the following day. The heavy bell at the front door clanged. I jumped. I reached the door and heaved it open. Paolino stood before me. I looked down at the crate. It was loaded with several things I hadn't ordered.

"A welcome home, Santina."

I didn't want it to feel that way. This year was my detour, nothing more.

"Few things on the house."

I smiled, baffled by his kindness, then noticing his racing eyes dart past me gathering information.

"*Grazie,* Paolino — I'd better be getting on."

"Yes. No rest for the wicked."

I sighed a faint laugh; the travel day was beginning to wear me down.

"Or donkeys," he added.

The major's voice rattled down from the stairwell. I reached for the crate, but Paolino shook his head. "Don't be a crazy, English girl. Let me." Before I could close the door, he strode across the terrace. My heart raced.

"It's fine, Paolino, really, I can manage," I insisted, breaking into a skipped walk to keep up with him.

"I'm no barbarian," he replied, pushing on toward the farthest end of the terrace, where the garden began. The major met us. Paolino stopped.

"You are?" the major asked, looking down his nose at Paolino, his eyes flashing an icy blue.

"Delivery from the grocery," I said, interrupting.

"Very well. Do hand me the crate. *Per piacere.*"

I watched Paolino take in the major's fiery

red hair, the spray of freckles upon his cheeks, and wither a little under his sharp stare. I realized the major no longer made me feel I was being interrogated. He reached for the box and walked to the far end of the terrace, where double doors led to the kitchen. "He may go," he called back to us as he disappeared inside.

"No prince, no," Paolino muttered, shuffling back toward the door, "they all like that in London?"

I felt a familiar irritation rise and heaved the door open. Paolino turned before he began his descent down the first dozen steps toward the alley, flashing me a knowing smile. Then his footsteps tip-tapped down into the dusk along the rose glow of the sunset cobbles.

CHAPTER 5

I awoke the next morning with a start. Adeline was screaming. I heard the major's heavy footsteps above, thudding staccato feet across my ceiling. I wrapped myself in my dressing gown and ran upstairs.

The stench hit me before I turned the corner at the top of the stairs. An acrid smell snubbed the air. I knocked on Adeline's door before opening.

"Santina, I would welcome some assistance, yes!" the major called from within.

The tiles were splattered with vomit. Adeline was crunched into a ball at the corner of her bed. She rocked. The major's pajama sleeves were rolled up past his elbows. He was on his hands and knees using towels to clean up the mess.

"Please, Major, let me, you see to Adeline."

It was the proper thing to do, but my stomach twisted at the sight of it all. He left to wash his hands in the attached bathroom. I swabbed the pools. No sooner than I did, Elizabeth cried out. The major stepped back inside the bedroom.

"All the women in my life have the devil in them this morning — that will be all, Santina, go to the child."

I left, no doubt with too much eagerness.

The major always referred to Elizabeth as The Child. With each day that passed, that small bundle of life was becoming more a part of me. Each time he flicked this title at her, it was as if he pressed a fresh bruise of mine. I could count the times I had seen him hold her. He looked without seeing. A perfunctory glance now and then, someone cross-checking an inventory. It wasn't hard to understand why, but it smarted nonetheless. This child broke his wife. The devotion he bored into Adeline consumed all his passion. How could there be anything left for this needy babe? That was what I was there for. He paid me to love her for him. And I did.

Elizabeth's lament was soon lost to milky nourishment. We sat in the corner of my room, on the chair I had prepared for night feeds. I always opened the shutters for her first morning feed, letting the light stream in through the tall glass double doors. The

October sun was reluctant to acquiesce to autumn. How different from my first October in London, where the damp air already furled the decaying tips of bronzed leaves. Here, grapes swelled to picking, the mountain air was sweet with chestnuts. I watched the shadows of a passing cloud dance across the tiles. This morning's sun was proud, radiating with the pretense of summer, mocking the promise of autumn. Perhaps Adeline's recovery would stay a hope lost to the past too?

When Elizabeth had finished, I sat her up on my lap, noticing how her back strengthened each day. I could lose myself in this small human. She absorbed my restlessness, distracted me from the gnawing sadness for having been dragged back to Positano, away from the life I'd planned. It was impossible for me to sink into those thoughts while I rubbed my palm in circles around her middle till she let out several belches and looked pleased with herself. The pull of this girl was both a balm and unsettling; this time the following year, I would have to leave her. Allowing myself to become attached would cause me nothing but more unnecessary heartache. I laid her down in her cot to stretch out for a little so I could return to the major.

The door was open. I stepped in.

I found him curled around his wife. His hand locked into hers. Her hair was matted with nightmares and sweat. Their breath rose and fell together. I stood, trespassing. My eye caught sight of the dirty towels. I decided to finish the job at hand regardless of the imposition. I heaved the pungent pile and caught a bitter whiff.

"Santina?" I heard him call.

I turned, feeling even more the intruder.

"Thank you."

I always hesitated after he thanked me. It would be rude to say that he was welcome because that would insinuate we were equals, which of course we weren't. It was rude to say nothing too, of course. Awkwardness puffed through me like a snake of smoke despite, or maybe because of, my best efforts to smother it.

"I'll take breakfast at my usual time, then we will begin your first lesson," said the major.

I swallowed a stammer. "Will you not rest, sir?"

"I will take breakfast at the usual hour. You will not shirk your commitments."

I turned and left. If I had been nervous about my first lesson before, now I was on the precipice of panic.

He ate on the terrace just beyond the kitchen; two eggs, cooked for three and a half minutes once the water reached a rolling boil, two slices of toast, light brown on one side, one spoon of marmalade, two cups of tea from a pot. I added a fig on a small saucer as well. It needed to be eaten that morning; it would be jam by the afternoon otherwise. He peeled the papery purple skin, sliced it into four wedges, chewed each piece several times and wiped his mouth clean afterward. I cleared the table and wished Elizabeth would call out for me, but the warm breeze seemed to lull her into a nap in the Moses basket upon the kitchen table. I liked her close to me. It helped me intuit every nuance and, with enough concentration, nip hysteria before fear of famine took hold and that round face of hers creased into the kind of fury you'd expect from a spurned woman intent on everyone knowing so.

"Let us begin," he said.

I placed the last of the dishes into the ceramic sink.

"You may finish your house duties afterward," he announced.

I think he expected me to do something other than stand mute in the doorway.

"Good heavens, Santina, am I really all

that terrifying?"

It was one of those lingering questions that pierce the air, leaving a small, unanswered tear.

"Sit here."

He gestured at the chair beside him where Adeline had managed to eat a light supper yesterday evening. That had filled us both with a tentative hope — nothing that this morning wouldn't have dashed, no doubt. He was a fixer. I suspected that what he couldn't immediately fix with Adeline, nor Elizabeth for that matter, he'd make up for with me, and my tentative English.

I sat down, trying to unclasp my hands and failing.

"You speak fairly well," he began.

My lips rose into an unsure smile.

"Enough to understand instructions, yes. But if I allowed you to sail to America as promised, without a true grasp of English, I would be failing on my word. That is to say, what is English to you, Santina?"

"What is it, sir?"

"That's what I asked."

"A language. To talk."

He took a deep breath now, and as he let it out again, his gaze drifted toward the sea. It was a deeper blue than yesterday at this time, but still clear enough to see the watercolor patches of algae swirling toward Capri. His eyes snapped back to me. I noticed the tiny licks of darker blue that cut across the aqua, framed by thick blond-copper eyelashes.

"It is not only to talk, Santina. We do that already. I will educate you in a cohesive manner. I will not ask how to buy cheese and bread. Any donkey can do that. I will teach you English — in all its startling, crisp beauty."

He had lost me several sentences ago.

I watched him open a small book, marked by a slim leather bookmark that looked well loved. He straightened. " 'Oh ye! Who have your eye-balls vexed and tired, Feast them upon the wideness of the Sea.' "

He stopped and looked at me.

"Keats, a poet, wrote that, in 1817."

"Is that all of it?"

"You want to know the rest?"

I nodded. I hadn't understood everything, but I liked the way his voice changed when he recited it. He twisted the book to face me.

"There." He pointed toward the bottom of the page.

I looked at the jumble of letters on the page. I couldn't bear to raise my eyes to meet his.

"You see? You carry on where I left off —"

I swallowed.

"Don't worry about mistakes, Santina, there's no one here to laugh at you."

My ears became attuned to the minutiae of sounds around me, a twitch of a leaf as a grasshopper skimmed its surface, the breeze lifting the sprinkle of crumbs he hadn't allowed me to sweep away yet. I realized he was calling my name.

"Santina," he said, his voice softer now — it was his Adeline voice, the one he used when her speech began to corkscrew toward ramblings — "you can't read, can you?"

I felt furious that he had cornered me like this. What need had I for poetry? How on earth was that going to help me survive America? Here I was, dragged back to the tiny town that had smothered my childhood, following a man and his sick wife, caring for his daughter night and day, a responsibility I had never sought, and his repayment was a promise and a poem!

He wasn't afraid of the bristling silence. He let it hang, unhurried, like a dank February morning in London where the clouds merge into one purgatorial white canopy.

His hand smoothed his beard.

"Would you like me to help you, Santina?"

A sigh escaped before I could stop it, then a solitary tear, which I hated myself for. I brushed it off my cheek, but we both knew it had been there.

"Please say you'll consider my offer?" he asked.

I hadn't invited these blurred lines; he was my employer, not a teacher. I didn't want to be helped. I wanted to work, survive a year here in exchange for my escape from this town; this place that had never taught me to read, or think about poetry, or hope to live off course from the mountain girl. I was prepared to commit to this time with his daughter and do the job as best I could, but my eyes were set on a horizon far from here. Now I sat, within one of my town's palaces, feeling more imprisoned than when I first left. His face relaxed into something close to a smile.

"I think I can offer you more than just money, Santina." His voice lowered to a syrupy murmur, his expression softened. "In return for everything you are doing for my family and me."

I lifted my eyes. His offer came from a genuine place. He was no more trying to imprison me than I was. I took a breath to answer, but a metallic clatter cut through

95

my pause, followed by a bucket cascading down from the terrace above, crashing into the lemon trees below, tumbling down the brush toward the wall at the end of the garden. We ran upstairs. Adeline ~~was~~ stood before the balustrade that ran the length of her terrace. She was closer to it than made me feel safe. I stopped by the doorway. The major walked through the bedroom toward the terrace, his feet soundless, as if he were wading through water.

I watched him coax her back inside. When she returned to bed, he crushed a pill into a spoon. He leaned in to give it to her. She spat in his face.

"I'll hold her and you give it to her, Santina."

I took the spoon. She jerked in his grip.

"Now, Santina!"

I placed it in her mouth. He closed her lips around it. After a few seconds, he released his grip. She crawled to the top of her bed, grabbed the sheet, and cocooned herself inside.

Her breathing began to even. The crease of bed linen eased down onto the mattress.

"I will take lunch at the usual time, Santina. That will be all for now."

I left. My footsteps echoed down the stone stairwell.

96

It was clear then, that the more unpredictable Adeline became, the more rigid his own routine would be. My lessons would be inescapable after all.

After breakfast the next day, the major strode into the kitchen and laid a notebook and a wooden box inlaid with geometric patterns of mother-of-pearl upon the kitchen table. His height made the kitchen feel all the smaller. Unlike me, his head reached a foot or so from the ceiling, which arched over us, like a cellar. The walls were painted a brushed pink and behind the marble counter that stretched the length of one wall there were a dozen lines of decorated tiles of geometric designs in yellow, emerald, and turquoise, hopeful swirls of pomp. A wider squat arch graced the space where the hearth stood. A wooden table, dipping in the center with age, stretched halfway across the room.

"I have decided, Santina, that I was quite in the wrong yesterday."

I looked at him.

"I will be grateful if you'd forget my clumsy start, yes?"

It was my turn to let a question evaporate, answerless.

"Today," he resumed, "I am going to teach

97

you how to cook one of the dishes I brought home with me to England after my years in India."

"Cook?"

His face brightened. I knew he had spent several years in India working for the British Army, Adeline had told me that much. She'd intimated that his role was shrouded in secrecy, but I'd never paid it too much mind because Adeline had a wonderful way of painting stories with a brush of mystery, whatever the subject. For the first time, I allowed myself to miss her. The eccentric little talks she might indulge me in after breakfast before she began her day in the studio. The way she'd shown off her Heath in Hampstead to me, her paintings, bright with freedom and questions and passion. Now I understood. He needed the lessons more than I. It was impossible to shirk the sense that they were as much about the major having another to converse with as opening my mind up to the poetry he loved best.

"Cook, yes, Santina, and afterward you will write the recipe into this little book here." He picked it up and gave it an optimistic waggle. The cover was black leather, and the center of the front panel featured a tiny painted rose.

We spent the next hour trawling through

the details of the dish. First, he asked me to dice an onion. He stood beside me while directing me on how to soften it in a pan with olive oil. It was something I did almost every day, but that didn't stop him inspecting my timing. As the pieces began to sweat, he placed the box next to the stove and opened it. Inside were five jars filled with different-colored powders: a palette of deep browns, golden yellows, and fiery reds.

"This box goes with me whenever I travel. I knew we wouldn't be able to source these spices here, so I arranged for them to be sent to me in London before we came."

He lifted one of the jars, unscrewed its lid, and handed it to me: "Smell."

I dipped my nose close toward the opening, trying not to worry about the onions that were starting to caramelize. A pungent flowery scent powdered up into the back of my cheeks. I couldn't place it.

"This is ground coriander, Santina. Next growing season, I shall be planting it in my garden and you will help me."

He handed me each of the jars in turn: aromatic cumin with its sweet and smoky herbal scent that brought church incense to mind, the barky smell of golden turmeric, and the provocative punch of ground chili — my eyes watered in an instant. The final jar contained a fine deep brown powder. This was the most complex smell of all of them. There was smoke, fire, citrus, and a muddy tang to it. My eyebrows creased.

"This is curry powder. Ground in the hills of Jaipur, Santina, by an elderly lady I came to know well. I watched her large wooden pestle and mortar create this pot of wonder. She taught me everything I know about how to use it too."

His eyes twinkled with the pleasurable memory. I wondered how long it had been since he had been able to talk to someone about this. I knew him as a solitary man, but it was clear that the loneliness stirred by the incessant care of Adeline needed remedy. These five little jars contained just that. He held each of them as if it was a precious jewel, presenting me in turn with reverence and a bottled excitement I'd never noticed before.

Next he gave me specific measurements for each of them. As I sprinkled a spoonful of turmeric, coriander, and curry powder over the translucent onions the small stone kitchen filled with a potent earthy steam. Next, we stirred in two fistfuls of rice until each grain was coated with the sticky yellow mixture. The major poured in almost half a liter of water, put the lid on, simmered it

100

for ten minutes, then took it off the heat, but left the lid on to let the steam finish the job. Meanwhile, he instructed me to boil six eggs, this time for four and a half minutes. I rinsed them under cold water, peeled them, and cut them into wedges, as directed. Finally, we brought a little milk in a frying pan to a gentle simmer and placed two bay leaves inside. He opened up a paper package with two fillets of fish and slipped them in the warm milk.

"This ought to be haddock of course, Santina, but I'm using what I could find yesterday afternoon at the fishmongers, which was very little, I might add, because I made the mistake of waiting till the afternoon to get it. Foolish."

He removed the fish pan from the heat and let it continue to poach while he instructed me to lift the lid on the rice. It was fluffy and golden; the fragrant ribbons of steam that lifted up from it made my mouth water. I watched him stir in the egg wedges, then flake the fish and fold it into the rice. He lifted the pan and put it on top of an iron potholder in the center of the table. He handed me a fork and gestured for me to taste. The caramel of the onion gave way to a woody perfume, a musky taste balanced by the creamy yolk and the tender aromatic fish flesh. My eyes gave away my delight.

"First poetry lesson complete."

My head tilted.

"Now I help you write it. Title: Kedgeree."

The rest of the morning he sat next to me, a fastidious but patient teacher, as I wrote the list of the ingredients. My scrawl was tentative and messy. He wouldn't let me leave the table until I had finished. In between hesitations, whirring doubts ricocheted about my mind as I tried to understand how any of this would serve me in my new life.

"Tomorrow, we will write the method. That is all for now. I will take lunch at midday. You may take an hour to take a stroll with Elizabeth perhaps? I will rest awhile."

He turned and left, leaving the scent of another world suffusing the air.

CHAPTER 6

The following May, the major and Adeline's belongings at last found their appropriate places in the villa. New packages arrived throughout the frigid winter and temperamental spring, then were sorted with care. By midsummer, the major's library, up a few steps behind the kitchen, was complete, his sanctuary at the opposite side of the house from the large dining room. Oil-painted landscapes graced the walls. After my final chores of the evening, I'd linger over the depictions of the humid mountainous coffee plantations above the Malabar coast in India, or the city of Jodhpur with its square blue houses clustering the valley, the stone alleys reminding me of an exotic version of Positano. It was clear to me that he'd always been drawn to these landscapes. The major loved the mountains as much as I. His early morning walks, before the now hordes of tourists began their jaunts, often took him high above our town, into the mossy depths of my childhood. I was relieved, however, that those grotesque carved masks from the London hallways remained in his library.

Although the major refused to entrust Elizabeth to anyone but me, we had come to an arrangement that I could leave the house for an extended time on Sunday afternoons and take her with me. Rosalia, who had strong-armed her way into my heart, huffed and puffed that this did not, in fact, constitute anything close to a day off. She wouldn't believe me, but Sundays spent at her home were just that. They forced me to relax, to forget my inconclusive search for my brother who had run away from our uncle's farm and all but disappeared in Naples not long after I left for London.

Elizabeth and I took our time climbing the narrow alleys that ran behind the neighboring villas. Her hair was a fluff of bright red waves that made the Positanese reach out and touch it out of instinct, so different was she from the dark-haired toddlers discovering gravity along the cobbles. She loved these Sundays as much as I. Rosalia's sisters and sisters-in-law took turns to hold her and coo into her bright little blue eyes, teasing me that I'd left town only to kidnap a foreigner's daughter.

One morning in late summer, we negotiated the steep steps down toward Rosalia's gate and pushed it open. A fragrant canopy of kiwi and lemon trees entwined a high bamboo frame above. The excited chirps of birds greeted us. Along the slim walkway toward the main door, five cages hung with yellow and pale blue budgerigars twittering to each other and out toward the coast.

The door flung open. "Just in time!" Rosalia said, greeting me with a kiss on each cheek, wrenching Elizabeth out of my arms and into hers. "You've been a good girl, yes? You eat all my food today, yes? No *sorbetto* if you don't eat your lunch, young lady!"

I followed her into the kitchen. A huge oak table dominated the squat room. At the far end was her wooden oven, etched into the wall where the mountain rock was varnished but still craggy. This was a room wedged into the stone. Upon the stove in a heavy iron skillet, fresh anchovies melted into warm oil, softening several crushed cloves of garlic. The smell of artichokes followed soon after from a larger pan, their lustrous purple doused with fresh parsley. A simmering stockpot of linguine raced to al dente. Rosalia's sisters busied themselves with the final fixings on the table, yelling for the men to join us. I could hear the rumble of their husbands and brothers coming down from the terrace above following the scent toward lunch. In a few minutes the small room ricocheted with too many voices and conversations colliding at once. It was my weekly dose of cacophony, the perfect antidote to the church-like silence at the villa.

Rosalia balanced Elizabeth on one hip, scooping linguine out of the pan with the other.

"Please, let me take her," I offered, reaching out my hands, which she shooed off with the back of the wooden spoon. One of her sisters swooped in and took over by the stove for the final hungry minute before the pasta was cooked.

The door swung open. In strolled Paolino, a basket in his hands laden with fresh Romanesco cauliflowers, zucchini, *cedri,* and a pile of *sfogliatelle,* small crisp pastries stuffed with a rich lemon crème. As he walked by me, their vanilla scent powdered the air.

Rosalia had decided several months ago that he and I ought to be the perfect pairing. I loved her for many things but this was not one of them.

106

"You see, Santi'," she began, bouncing Elizabeth beside me, "the man bakes too now."

This meddling in others' personal affairs was a pernicious local habit I longed to escape; it made my scheduled sailing to America, toward the latter part of this autumn, feel like part of a very distant future.

"You already love him more than I ever could," I whispered to her cackle that followed.

"What are you witches plotting over there? You mind it doesn't spoil our food now," Paolino called out from the far end of the table, where Rosalia's brothers poured him their homemade wine.

"You just wait, Paoli'," Rosalia called out to him, "you get under our spell and there'll be no helping you!"

Everyone laughed. The late September sun syruped through the windows. I took Elizabeth onto my lap and watched her eye the strands of oily linguine Rosalia lifted up with an oversized fork, swirls of garlic steam wafting across the plates. I cut her portion into small pieces. She dove in with two hands. All meals at Rosalia's ended with a salty smear of lunch across her happy face. The sisters would pinch her rosy cheeks in praise of her appetite. Paolino teased me that I wasn't feeding the child enough and perhaps we ought to raise our weekly orders from him. He caught the roll of my eyes.

"Oh come on, Santina — it's a little joke between friends."

I had no memory of friendship.

"Well, you'd better get used to it. Men around here don't just sit around and let beauty slip between their fingers like water, no? You've been around the British too long."

I returned a forced smile, thankful Rosalia's family's laughter drowned my silence.

"You've changed," he continued, mistaking my silence as an invitation for conversation. "You left a polio-struck orphan with a tatty dress and a half-hearted smile. Now you look —"

His hands waved in the air, as if they might pluck the word out from it somehow. I worried about the gesture that might follow.

"Eat your food and save us all from this drivel!" Rosalia's grandmother piped up from the opposite end of the table, her wrinkled skin creasing into even more tiny folds.

"*Salud* to that!" the men cried as the rest

of the lunch simmered through the afternoon.

After the men left to sip limoncello outside on the small concrete terrace, and Rosalia, myself, and the rest of the women had cleared the kitchen, it was time for me to return. Rosalia walked me to the gate, running a proud hand over her lemon trees overhead as she did so.

"I know a joke from the truth, Santi'."

I turned to her, feeling Elizabeth's weight pull on my back.

"Don't look at me like that," she replied off my look, "you know perfectly well what I'm on about."

"I don't."

"It's that mountain air in your lungs. Too near the sky to see what's on the ground in front of you."

Rosalia talked in riddles.

"Paolino, Santina. You think it's all sing-song. I can tell it's more than that."

"Aren't you tired of weaving stories where there aren't any?"

Her eyebrows did a little dance, and her dimples deepened.

"See you next week, Rosali'. Thank you."

"Don't ever say thank you. You're family now. You say thank you, it's like I'm just a neighbor."

She flicked a playful slap on my arm. I went on my way.

I jogged home to prepare a light late lunch for the major, Elizabeth bobbing up and down, delighted with the insane pace of her guardian. I would have liked to remember keeping a calm hand upon the plates while setting the table after I returned home. I would have liked to forget the way I dropped not one, but two plates upon the unforgiving tiles, blaming myself on rushing, knowing it had more to do with the memory of Paolino's claustrophobia-inducing grin across Rosalia's loud lunch, the way his eyes managed to connect with mine every time I looked toward his end of the table. Now my fingers quarreled with one another while my mind chased silence. The major strode through the kitchen just as I placed a few leaves of romaine into a bowl with the last of the tomatoes.

"Whatever have these plates done to you, Santina?" he asked, looking down at the heap of shards swept out of the way in haste.

"I'm so sorry." I was starting to gabble. The appearance of Adeline in the doorway plunged us both into silence.

"I smell Kedgeree," she said, flat.

I looked at the major. His eyes were alight.

"Yes. I made it this morning," I said, filling the silence, hoping that if I spoke close to normalcy it might uphold her spell of sanity. Throughout the spring and summer, we had seen a marked improvement in Adeline. On occasion she even held Elizabeth for snatched moments.

"So you did," she replied, "it got me out of bed. I fell in love with Henry after I ate the first forkful he ever gave me."

She looked at him. There was a simmer of a smile beyond her exhaustion. The spark was still there, the snap of a match as it ignites against sandpaper even if the flame fails into smoke. He took her hand and walked her out onto the terrace. They sat in silence for a moment. He cradled her fingers in his.

They shared an apple after their food, then Adeline returned upstairs. The major did not retire to the library as usual. He sat looking out toward the sea while I cleared around him. Elizabeth refused to stay in her wooden chair I'd set in the kitchen. She fretted until I released her, so I delayed my tidying till she took her nap. I walked with her down the steps that led into the garden and sat her down on the last one, beside me. She crawled a little way down the hill,

111

paused, squatted, then heaved herself up to standing. I'd seen her do this many times, but she'd never held herself upright for so long. The breeze lifted her curls. Her nose scrunched. Then one foot lifted. She wavered but didn't fall. A step. Then another. Then another. Several more determined paces followed, before she collapsed again onto the grass. I ran to her, wrapped my arms around her, and swung her around.

"You're walking, *ciccia*! You're doing it! *Brava!*"

She giggled into my ear as I squeezed her. I saw the major over her shoulder. He was laughing. I'd never seen his expression so relaxed.

That afternoon Elizabeth took the longest nap of her life. I returned to the kitchen to finish clearing up and found a large bowl of oranges and lemons upon the table.

"There you are, Santina. I've been waiting."

The major's buoyant mood caught me off guard. Adeline must be sleeping too.

"I took a short stroll to the end of the garden this morning as the sun rose," he said. "I gathered another load of oranges and lemons. Glorious."

"Are you ready for tea, sir?"

"Not just now. I thought as the women in

my life are finally sleeping, and it's a little cooler, we would prepare a British breakfast staple."

"Sorry, sir?"

"This afternoon, your English lesson is marmalade."

We never had lessons on a Sunday.

"This is not to be rushed," he began. "You may relinquish your dinner duties; Adeline and I can fix something for ourselves to-night. Once we start we have to keep a close eye on the proceedings."

I gave a feeble nod, imagining how good my bed would feel at this very moment.

"Where is your notebook, Santina?"

I lifted it out of my pocket, where I kept it.

"Excellent. Now, while the marmalade is cooking, we will write up the method. No time will be left idle. There is much to do."

I had made some jams in the past but this process was a different beast. He stood over me, marshaling the way I dropped the scrubbed ten oranges and four lemons into a large stockpot, covering them with water, and describing in more detail than was necessary how we would let it reach a boil, and then simmer for the next three hours, clamping the lid down to stop valuable vapors escaping. "A perfect poach is required, not an exacerbated boil, you understand?" Though his words were clipped and could be mistaken for a military pace, there was a boyish lilt to his speech when he and I worked in the kitchen. He was in his late thirties, but when he spoke of food or poetry, the years fell away, lifting veils through which I could spy the major as a much younger man.

While the room filled with the uplifting citrus smell, we set to work on my handwriting. It wasn't the scrawl of last autumn, but there was still hesitation. He wrote a sentence and I copied. Any mistakes were noted and required me to repeat the word in question. The afternoon should have felt interminable, but I loved the intimate focus of these moments: the sound of the dish of the day brewing behind us, the soft scratch of my pencil upon the paper. The quiet way he would speak, directing my hand with gentle instructions, wooing my pencil to do the right thing.

Finally we removed the pot from the heat and set it aside to cool.

"I shall take tea now. Please call Adeline to join me."

He left.

I stood in the empty kitchen, steamy with the fresh, hopeful scent.

I could hear Elizabeth beginning to stir but decided to leave her a while longer while I fetched her mother. I ran up two stairs at a time. Adeline's door was shut. I tapped softly, then a little louder. Still no answer. I eased the door open and peeked inside. Adeline was at the far side, crouched down. She had a pencil in her hand and was tracing intricate patterns across the length of the wall where the floor tiles met the plaster. I'd noticed the major had set a sketchbook upon the table. I didn't think he had scrawling on the antique walls in mind when he had done so.

"Madam?"

No answer. The artist was lost in her work.

I coughed. She stopped, then froze me with an icy glare. My mouth opened a little, but no sound came out. She returned to her creation.

"Madam, the major has asked you to join him for tea."

The speed of her pencil accelerated. Elizabeth's cries reached us from the kitchen two floors down. These stone walls were unforgiving; thick but live, amplifying every sound.

Adeline began to weep. I went toward her.

"Stay where you are!" she yelled without looking at me. "Stop that God-awful screeching." She whipped round to me; I could see her eyes were bloodshot, spidered with anguish. "Now!"

She rose to her feet and lunged toward me, sending me flying out of the room toward the stairwell. The major was at the table now, oblivious to the protests of his daughter.

I prepared a bottle, lifted Elizabeth, and before I returned to the dining room to feed her, I told the major about Adeline's current mood.

He gave a stiff nod. I felt like a student who had displeased her teacher.

He stood up from the table, walked through the kitchen, and placed a hand on the lower side of the cooling pot. "Forty-five minutes more and we will continue," he announced, then left. I heard the library door close behind him.

I returned to a major tetchy with impatience. "You're three minutes late."

"I'm sorry, sir."

"This is alchemy, Santina. It requires precision. I expect deeper understanding from you."

Together, we lifted the oranges out of the cooled liquid, sliced them open, and scooped out the pulp and pits into a smaller pan, reserving the peel. To the pulp we added a jug of water and set it on a medium heat for about ten minutes. I held a colander while the major lined it with cheesecloth, placing the cooked pulp into it.

While it cooled in the cloth, dripping into a bowl underneath, we sat at the table and cut the orange peel into thin strips, his eyes darting over my work to make sure each piece was the same length and width. I followed his instructions to gather the corners of the cheesecloth, squeezing the pulpy contents into a tight ball. My hands were sticky with the juice. He handed me a towel to blot them dry and then a large wooden spoon so I could stir these juices back into the original poaching liquid. He tipped in the peel and placed the lid back on top. As soon as I became aware of the comforting quiet in which we worked, it hardened into an awkward silence, like a tray of boiled sugar crisping into brittle.

"This, we leave overnight," he said.

My eyebrows raised before I could stop them.

"You had no idea about the importance of time in this process, did you?"

I couldn't tell whether he was about to castigate or educate. The lines between the two were random, dirty twists of floured dough upon a tired wooden counter. He took a breath, his eyes softened. " 'O Time! who know'st a lenient hand to lay, Softest on sorrow's wound, and slowly thence, Lulling to sad repose the weary sense, The faint pang stealest unperceived away.' "

This time I was tired enough to let my confusion float around me and hover, lost and soothed in the tone of incomprehensible words.

"William Lisle Bowles wrote that, Santina. Why do you think we started the process of marmalade?"

We returned to exhausting questions: short, sharp arrows whizzing by my ear.

"I will tell you why. Because the process is long but finite. It requires attention, stamina, and precision. And so does educating oneself in another language. I do not tire easily, and I expect you to be collaborative with your attention. When you returned from your luncheon elsewhere, you were skittish, forgetful, and a little frantic, dare I say it. In this vein, you will learn absolutely nothing. Now, I could have chosen a different dish, something we may have eaten right away, like the Kedgeree, but I didn't. Language, education, must be savored and labored. But it is a joyful thing. Smell this room, Santina" — his hand swept through the air — "smell the optimistic spray of citrus grown in this very garden beyond the terrace. How can it fail to touch you?"

His words caressed and taunted me. I could tell that he was full of something more than facts alone, but my mind prodded with uncertainty. I offered a tentative smile.

"Look outside, Santina." He placed stiff hands upon my shoulders and twisted me round toward the open wooden doors. The last hands I had upon me were my father's. The memory prickled down my spine to a sting. I felt the weight of his hands upon me, noticing the tips of his thumbs pressing into my shoulder blades. The garden rolled down a steep incline and the trees stretched out their branches in greedy gnarls toward the early autumn rays. Beyond, the sea had begun its descent into dusky purple, Capri's tip golden in the dipping sun. I wanted to move but daren't, hating myself for it.

His voice fell toward a whisper, I could feel the breath skim the top of my ear. " 'Educating the mind without educating the heart is no education at all.' "

My body softened out of trained fear to the lull of his voice.

"That is what Aristotle said, and I'm inclined to agree."

He straightened. "Tomorrow," he began, removing his hands, his voice once again crisp, "we will heat sugar in the oven upon a tray for ten minutes. Then we will reheat the preserving liquid and add the warmed sugar. When it has all dissolved in the liquid, and not before, we will turn up the heat. We will allow it to reach a rolling boil. We will remove the pan from the burner, allow to cool for thirty minutes, and finally pour into sterilized jars. Then what?"

Another prickle of a question, which required no remedy.

"Then, Santina, you, Adeline, and I may taste the glorious marmalade throughout the winter. And when the fog rolls in once again, and the tiresome visitors have abandoned the streets at last, we will sit and savor the memory of my trees once plump with bounty. Is that clear?"

Of course it wasn't. He turned on his heels and closed the door behind him.

I breathed in the aroma, the citrus deepening toward a warm caramel now. The setting sun streaked in from behind me, burnishing the tiny kitchen with russet rays. Only a month remained before I left for America. I couldn't shake the sense that the lessons that remained, like the marmalade of this afternoon, would be nothing besides bittersweet.

The midmorning sun cast hopeful arcs of light upon the curve of the cobbles as I walked Elizabeth up the hill on her new-found legs. We'd stop every now and again, for me to catch my breath if nothing else, while I held her facing out toward the sea which spread out in a turquoise sheen toward the gray cliffs. Onward we climbed, as the path narrowed. To my right, beyond a squat wall, was a jagged drop to the water below. I walked without any particular aim, the smell of citrus and caramelized sugar still clinging to my hair from the previous afternoon, floating into focus every now and then on the breeze.

The path ended by the entrance to the cemetery. The dead had the best view in town. There was a small bench just outside. We sat for a moment to rest before return-ing home. I longed to lay flowers for my mother. I envied those little tombs, perched upon the uneven hill, goat-like, defying gravity with stubborn marble. At least all these people could find rest. Their loved ones could sit by them, remember them while the wide expanse of the sea and mountains comforted them with awe and tranquillity, the landscape assuring them that their grief was all part of the natural fabric of the world, no more, no less. But I had none of these. There was a gaping hole where my mother should be and another wherever my brother roamed; love without the freedom to be expressed.

The sound of footsteps drew me round. A figure stood by the gated entrance, fiddling with a heavy chain. I rose to my feet. It must be getting close to lunchtime if the gates were already being shut. I turned to begin my descent but something about the man playing with his lethargic lock spiked a memory. I turned back to take a closer look. I didn't know this man, but there was something about the shape of his round face, the gentle slant of his almond eyes that stirred me. His hair looked like it hadn't been washed in a while, and it clung to his scalp in sweaty strands. He looked up at me for a brief glance. My heart twisted with sorrow and joy.

It was my little brother.

Chapter 7

"Marco?" I called out, my mouth so dry the word almost stuck to it.

He turned, nonchalant. *"Sì?"*

We looked at one another. I fought seeping doubt. Perhaps my memory was playing a cruel trick on me? But there was no mistaking the pointed arch of his eyebrows, just like Mother's, or the tiny mole on his left temple.

"The cemetery opens again at five o'clock," he said, as if I was just another visitor muted by grief, which of course, I was.

"It's me. Santina."

His face marbled into stillness. I noticed my breath change. I watched his expression shift through a painful spectrum, much like the sea behind me rippling with light and shade beneath the moving clouds. I ran, wrapped my one free arm around him, grasping Elizabeth in the other. After a moment, I felt his around us. I looked up at him. I wiped his cheek and kissed the tear streaks twice each, knowing that a lifetime of them could never make up for the way I abandoned him.

"I'm so, so sorry, my Marco," I stuttered through snatched breaths.

He shook his head and took my hand in his, then kissed it. That's when I noticed how very thin he was. That's when I took in his uncertain pallor, a gray day that hovers, expectant of a forgotten sun. His nails were chewed and his cuticles an aching pink with nervous strands of skin pulling away from them.

"Is it really you, Santina?" he whispered at last, looking at my face like someone determined to put the parts of a puzzle together, rearranging my features into the picture he remembered.

"It's really me."

"And this? *Tua bambina?*"

"No — I look after her. I'm living just down the hill, Marco. I'm home again!"

The words honeyed my mouth. It was the first time I had used the term.

He turned away from me, as if unsure. "I have to go now. You'll come back and see me?"

Through the neglected hair falling down

over his face, and the tension scarring his nails, I saw a glimmer of the child walking down the mountainside only weeks after we lost our mother. "Of course."

His face creased into a bleak frown.

"You must believe me, Marco — I'm here now, working for a family at Villa San Vito."

His eyes widened. The words felt an accidental betrayal. Till this moment I'd been counting the days till my departure.

"I'd have you come back with me right away, only I have this little one to feed and her mother and father are very particular about when they eat and —"

A yell from another young man farther up the steps leading toward Nocelle interrupted my excited blabbering. Marco gave him a perfunctory glance, before looking back at me. His features hardened.

"I have to go now, Santina. Come back tomorrow?"

I nodded, wondering if I could bear to watch him leave.

He turned and climbed the steps up to the man. I watched his shadow lengthen before him, zigzagging up the stones. The vise around my middle tightened. I wiped away the pictures of my father that bludgeoned my mind. Marco disappeared around the corner. I turned back toward the sea. The wind tousled gentle waves toward the shore. Do people, like water, always reach their natural level?

I made several feeble attempts to stay calm on my return to the villa. I simmered a small pan of water, infusing it with a fistful of chamomile flowers. I tried to allow the earthy steam of porcini mushrooms, wilting with garlic and parsley, ground me in the kitchen and the tasks at hand. I stirred the tagliatelle around the tall pot of boiling water, but hard as I tried, my thoughts tumbled across one another like those fierce, salty bubbles racing to evaporation. Elizabeth banged her spoon on the counter of her wooden high chair. The sound irritated the major but usually left me unruffled. Today it percussed my noisy thoughts with increasing irritation. I grabbed the spoon from her. She burst into tears. The major walked in.

"Is the child not getting her own way once again? Or is this some personal vendetta that's escaped me?"

His sarcasm smarted. Off my look, he retracted. It wasn't something I was accustomed to witnessing. The turn toward genuine concern caught me off guard. For a moment I thought I might let myself cry.

"Sorry, sir. I was impatient. It's been an unusual morning."

"Indeed," he said, running a hand over Elizabeth's head. The small act of tenderness caught both she and I by surprise. " 'The buttercups, the little children's dower, Far brighter than this gaudy melon-flower.' " He looked between the two of us, left muted by his poetic interruption.

"What on earth did Robert Browning understand about the great beauty of Italy, Elizabeth?" he asked, running a finger under her chin. "Fancy comparing a melon flower, full of the promise of delicious fruit, to the blasted buttercup!"

My heart raced. Was the major careening toward the same kind of breakdown as his wife? His behavior was peculiar, even for him. Any doubts about leaving disappeared in an instant. The sooner I left, the better. Elizabeth fell silent.

"Lunch is almost ready, sir. Am I to call Adeline?"

"But of course, Santina. You will find her in agreeable spirits this afternoon. Have you not noticed the marked changes in her? Her energy is returning little by little, a sapling of herself. Owed in a huge part to your tender care. Of the both of us."

The expression in his eyes made me feel

uncomfortable. There was an unfamiliar streak of sorrow, different from when he spoke of Adeline. I turned to leave.

"Santina?"

I looked back at the major. The sunlight streamed in behind him like a halo.

"Take this note, please."

I reached out for the small vanilla envelope, expecting him to bark out instructions for delivery, though in the past ten months I could count on one hand the number of people he'd conversed with in town. If he carried on in this manner, the gossips would have a field day concocting elaborate fictions about him and the wife imprisoned on the third floor of this merchant's palace.

I looked at the addressee. It was my name.

"It is rather unorthodox perhaps, but it struck me that writing my thoughts to you would allow you the space and privacy to consider my proposition in the most honest way you can. I'm loath to put you on the spot. Goodness knows I've had a lifetime of that from my seniors. It's excruciating. In every way."

I still hadn't learned how to mask my frown.

"Excruciating: painful, embarrassing."

A pause. Elizabeth looked from me to him and back again.

"So there we are. That is all. You're to read this tonight. Sleep on it. I would hate it to ruffle your day any more than is necessary. You've obviously been challenged enough already. That much is clear."

His thoughts were rambling again. He lifted Elizabeth out of her seat and took her outside with him. Had he fallen in love with his child at last? I could see the feeling terrified him. That's why he tripped over the words. Where was the man who used the vast spectrum of language with such confidence, throwing descriptions into the air like puffs of Adeline's vibrant paint powders?

This was a man who had been grieving for his disappearing wife. As her life force made a quiet return, he allowed Elizabeth in. Before today, he would have rather cut himself off than risk the pain of losing another woman. He'd have said something to the effect that the very existence of children reminds us of our own fleeting fragment of time. . . . That the new person entrusted to us to love must leave. . . . How this is the very nature of nurture, the truest test of love.

Such was his poetry, I had learned.

I watched him place her down and take her chubby hand in his. They walked toward the steps into the garden. Perhaps she would feel the tender attention of her father after all. The thought uncorked a deluge of silenced memories. What pain must my father have been in to inflict so much on us? The tiny flame of compassion flickered but faded at the picture of my mother's bruised face. Marco replaced that painful recollection. I left the kitchen in case the major should turn back and see my tears.

Rosalia rang the bell just after lunch. She knew better than to do so, as the major had told me several times that any visitors, business or otherwise, were to call midmorning or not at all. Trying to impart this stringent guideline to the local fishmonger, butcher, and woodsman elicited nothing short of sighed laughter, a nod at best, terse irritation at worst.

"You're incorrigible, Rosali' — be quick and go," I said, poking my head round the side of the door. "He's in a strange mood today as it is."

"What's new?"

"I'm serious."

"My sisters and I are going up to Nocelle for a *spuntino* later this afternoon. It's our youngest one's saint's day. I want you to come."

I grew suspicious.

"Oh for heaven's sake, Santina, it's just for some fresh air, why the look?"

"You're meddling, and I can't put my finger on what."

She straightened her blouse over her middle, revealing a little more cleavage. I loved how at home she felt in her skin. Perhaps I envied it a little. Her hair curled down her back, fringe lifted off her face in soft waves.

"And also," she carried on, "the new folks who moved in two houses down are looking for occasional help. They'll be doing lots of entertaining over this coming year. Two sisters. German, I think. I told them I could gather some girls. Thought you'd like some extra money before you leave?"

"And Elizabeth?"

"I can look after her."

I shook my head. "I don't know." The thought of floating the suggestion to the major made me uneasy.

"Suit yourself, Santi', I'll call for you in a couple of hours."

Before I could reply, she sauntered up the steps, toward the alley that ran the length of the back of the villa leading to her house.

Nocelle was Positano's sister; smaller, older,

remote. The one thousand steps that led us up to it were unrelenting, passing through the gorge of the valley. Deep green rose on either side of us, as the stairs wound in and around ragged rocks, undulating through the ancient pines, till we reached the outskirts of the small village. Here, the stone steps took us in between homes, bright red geranium blooms cascading from terra-cotta pots balanced on a prayer along uneven walls, palms offering regal salutes, cacti in the warm glow, their fruits ripening in the sun.

Rosalia's sister's home was modest, perched along the precipice of the cliff. She had a small terrace and two rooms. The table was laid with *sfogliatelle* and a large cake. The linen tablecloth lifted on the breeze. We took our seats upon the wooden benches and heaved a sigh of collective delight when she brought out a jug of homemade *limonata*. My legs were accustomed to walking these inclines but even I welcomed the respite. Elizabeth guzzled her drink. Rosalia lifted her up from me and sat her upon her lap; then gave her the reins to an imaginary horse so she could jiggle her into the infectious laughter of a toddler.

We toasted Rosalia's sister. Then their brother brought out a huge box. From inside he lifted an enormous record player to squeals of delight. He placed it upon the table and wound it up. Marino Marini began to tinkle his latest hit, "Piccolissima Serenata." Everybody rose to their feet. Rosalia danced with Elizabeth upon her hip. Her sister held her husband. I turned toward the feeling of a tap at my elbow.

"Shall we?" Paolino asked. I hadn't noticed him slip into the party. I could have avoided this had I done so.

"Just one dance. Then I'll leave you in peace."

Perhaps it was the atmosphere, the folks about me caring little about their troubles for a short pause. They had neither the comfort nor security of wealth, nor regular work, but were full of celebration. I longed to know what that felt like. So long had I been fixed on my next voyage that I failed to enjoy these moments passing by. I watched the family around me, my mind filled with Marco. How long would I have to knit our pasts together before I departed again?

Without thinking, I let my hand slip into Paolino's. It was square and strong, a little rough along the tips of the fingers. He held mine with more grace than I would have expected and kept a polite distance, much to my relief. I felt a sudden awareness of my calf as we spun, then admonished my vanity. No one here cared whether it was half the size of my other one. I wasn't here to impress anybody — most of all not my dance partner.

"You think they dance under the sun in America, Santina?" he whispered in my ear. I stiffened.

"I'm sorry," he said, his face relaxing into an expression close to genuine embarrassment. We swayed for a few beats. Rosalia's family filled in the quiet gaps of our own dwindling conversation.

He stopped dancing, but didn't let go of my hands.

"Can we talk somewhere?"

I noticed Mr. Marini had moved on to "Perdoname," his lament begging for forgiveness from his lover. Paolino led me out of the terrace and sat upon the wall surrounding the house. I felt for the donkey grappling the stairs as it passed by us, loaded with lemons in deep baskets hanging either side of his body, an unrelenting porter behind, jeering him on.

"Santina, I need to say these things. If I wait, I'll never forgive myself."

I looked at my hands for a moment. Where was my mother's fire to spit some wise retort at him, just enough to steer the conversation away from where I intuited it was headed?

"You won't believe me, for whatever reason. But truly, you are the most beautiful woman in this town."

I took a breath but should have known he would misunderstand it as a signal of studied feminine modesty.

"You're different," he added, "you're not like the others. You've got your sights set on a bigger, brighter future than this little fishing village. I know that. I love that."

"Paolino, please," I interrupted at last, "stop before you say something you'll be embarrassed about later."

"Nothing I want to tell you can embarrass me. I'm not scared of the truth. You shouldn't be either."

I stood up.

"But you are," he said.

I hovered, angry that he was using his words to prod uncertainty out of me. His charm was as clumsy as I would have expected it to be after all.

"I don't think you'd know what the truth was if it slapped you round the face, Paolino. You know nothing about me."

"I know you're compelling. You're not like those girls who strut around town plastered with makeup to grab the attention of the foreigners. And you've survived living with my mother — that's a small victory in itself!"

My involuntary laughter annoyed me. His smile changed his face. If I squinted, I might even catch the bud of humility there.

"Santina, I know nothing about you, it's true. And I want to know everything."

His eyes turned a deeper chestnut. I'd never noticed how thick his eyelashes were.

"I've said too much. Sorry, Santina. You must have a lot on your mind. This is my final act of selfishness."

He shrugged.

I said nothing.

He took my hand and kissed it.

My stomach tightened.

"Come on, Rosalia's tongue will be wagging!" He smiled, changing trajectory with surprising ease.

We walked back onto the terrace. The sun had begun its descent.

"I'll be heading home now, Rosalia," I said, lifting Elizabeth out of her arms.

Her eyes twinkled with a familiar mischief. At last her plan unfurled.

"And before you say what you're thinking: No."

"No, what?"

"No to whatever scheme or romantic plan you're been salivating over. Paolino likes to say things he doesn't mean. Or understand. You of all people can see that, surely?"

"I see a lot of things, but that's not one of them."

I turned before she could tease me any further, kissed her sister on both cheeks, and hiked downhill through the valley.

The house was quiet as we stepped back inside, the dusky pink plaster deepening in the final rays. Elizabeth, full of fresh air and exercise, gave in to sleep just as the stars twinkled in the midnight blue of early evening. I took my chair out onto the terrace outside my room. It was a warm evening that mocked the onset of autumn, whose creep over the valley felt a long way off even though it was almost October. The moon was full tonight, casting watery beams upon the glassy sea surrounding the tiny islands of Li Galli. There was a lot of talk in town of the Russian choreographer and the open-air theater he had built there for dance recitals. I imagined ballerinas twirling in the moonlight, their limbs long and lean, allowing every expression to ripple through them. What must that feel like?

I unfolded the major's letter.

28th September 1958
Villa San Vito
Positano

Dear Santina,

Ahead of your imminent preparations to leave our family, I felt it only proper to express our deepest gratitude. If I were to do this in person, I have no doubt that your face would crease into the embarrassment I have come to see all too often, especially during my intensive approach to teaching. I put you very much on the spot, and I know this. But I did it for good reason.

When you arrive on those new shores, there will be scores of people hoping to catch the same dreams as you. No one will care too much about who you are or want to be. You will have to prove yourself. The reserves of inner strength and determination I have observed in you over the past few months reassures me you will find your place wherever you decide to settle.

Furthermore, I have come to understand over the past difficult year what Wordsworth described as, "The Child is father of the Man." Elizabeth has taught me more than I care to admit. Her birth heralded the start of the hardest year of our lives. My darling wife is a shadow of the woman I married. Her recovery is slower than I hoped. Yet in spite of this, Elizabeth is a sunbeam. And this is all down to you.

I knew you were a special young woman the moment I met you that afternoon in London, the way your eyes lit up with an insatiable curiosity, something so similar to my own. What I couldn't have known is how you would shower my daughter with a care that only a mother can give. I can offer her a fraction of what you can, or indeed what Adeline may, one day, if ever. Only time will tell.

I have decided the best course of action is to send Elizabeth to boarding school after she turns five. To send her before then seems brutal somehow, though in all likelihood it probably would be the best thing for her. I want to keep her with us until she reaches the age where her mother's condition might start to weigh upon her in any way.

If there was any part of you that might even for a moment consider remaining here as her caregiver until she returns to Great Britain, I would do everything in my power to make it worthwhile. It goes without saying that I would offer you a reasonable raise in wages, and, I think only fair, one day off a week where I can schedule additional help.

If you have reached this part of the letter and have understood everything, I congratulate you on all the hard work you have invested in learning this new language. I hope, one day, I might be able to speak Italian as well as you do English. I gave up hope of cooking linguine with fresh clams and garlic as well as you do, long ago. Perhaps you might teach me before you leave? In Italian of course.

Whatever your decision I will honor it. The choice is entirely yours. I hope the sun has set by the time you read this. In my experience sleeping upon a decision delivers the truest answer.

Sincerely yours,
Henry Crabtree

I let the letter fall to my lap. The sky was onyx. The air was still. I could hear the faint sound of the sea beckoning to the shore. Which way was the tide pulling?

CHAPTER 8

The next morning the clouds darkened. Claps of thunder shook the house. The sea churned gray, and the whole of Positano retreated into their homes while the rain lashed the narrow alleys into scurries of water chasing over the cobbles down to the sea. The major watched, sat at the table on the terrace outside the kitchen. As the wind whipped and flashes of light blanched the leaden sky, he sat in perfect stillness; the eye of the storm.

I should have liked to imitate his poise. My thoughts raced, clanging against one another like the copper pans I hung back on the wall in a vain attempt to coerce clear thinking. There was another fury of thunder. Elizabeth ran under the table and burst into tears. I threw the tea towel I used to dry the pans over my shoulder and crouched down till my face was level with hers. Her cheeks were crimson with terror. Tears streaked the

141

sides of her face. I took her hand in mine. I tried to sit with her terror rather than brush it away. The latter approach I had found to be a pointless task, serving only to fill me with the same frustration as her own, which did nothing to expel it, and more often than not exacerbated it. I smoothed the back of her hand with my thumb and kissed her forehead. For a flicker, I considered how liberating it was to be a child and let each of these emotions ripple through without boundary. Perhaps she was crying for my benefit? She shed the tears of confusion and fear I couldn't. What would happen if, for a moment, I surrendered to the conflicting emotions swirling inside me? Would it be so very disastrous? What if I acknowledged, with unabridged simplicity, that the idea of sailing away to a place where I knew no one and nothing of the English spoken upon the American streets, abandoning my friends and Marco, filled me with palpable sadness?

I had been running all my life. My earliest memories are chasing behind my mother in search of something, food to sell, riches to dig up, laundry to deliver. We ran from my suffocating father and the dread of hunger. After my mother died, I ran away from the memory of her.

As the shutters clattered against the wind,

I wrapped Elizabeth in my arms and allowed my American daydream to ebb. I wanted to feel comforted by the realization that it was nothing but that — an ephemeral wish, another wisp of a life. Yet it smarted. It was so much easier to chase. Perhaps that way I might never get what I wanted and risk the chance of losing it?

I watched the major take another sip of his tea, thin ribbons of steam lifting up into the furious air beyond the balustrade. Elizabeth grew heavy in my arms, her breath slowed. I didn't realize I'd been rocking, soothing the both of us. She had fallen asleep. I walked through the dining room and up the stairwell to lay her down in the bed I still kept close to mine.

As I retraced my steps back to the kitchen a draft curled up behind me. I knew I'd shut all the windows at the first darkening promise of a storm. I checked the major's — they were still closed.

I knocked on Adeline's door. No answer. My stomach tightened. I hoped she was sleeping. I creaked the door open a little. The damp air blew on my face. The tall shutter door swung against the frame in the draft. Upon the roofless terrace stood Adeline. Her arms were outstretched. Rain pelted down her nightdress. Hair clung to

143

her scalp, matted to the back of it. I fought the instinct to rush to her. I knew from experience that it would jar her into defensiveness, if not aggression. I ought to call the major, but something stopped me. He seemed so peaceful down below on the kitchen terrace. This time I could handle Adeline. I stepped inside the room.

Perhaps I envied her abandon. She never did anything without entire commitment, to the detriment of herself. And yet, watching this woman, making tiny steps toward healing, standing fearless in the storm, filled me with an awkward admiration. All until I snapped back into myself and ran to gather towels so she might not catch her death. I stood in the doorway to the terrace, holding them. The water cut across the space between us; diagonal flights of tiny arrows.

"Signora Adeline!" I called out.

She turned toward me. Her face spread into a warm smile.

"Please, come inside!"

I reached out a hand. She placed hers in mine. Her fingers were strong, still callused from her work. I didn't want to pull her, but my forearm was already drenched. I began to regret my decision to take on the challenge of bringing her inside. Her grip tightened. She pulled. I took a step outside.

"Come," she beckoned.

I didn't want to fight. The sea shimmered silver as a vein of electricity splintered down from above. I didn't want to be struck by lightning either.

She took my other hand and pulled. I stood opposite her. My face was drenched. My worn soles blotted with rainwater seeping in at the edges.

"Isn't it glorious, Santina?!" she yelled over the din.

I had no answer.

"Do you remember when you came swimming with me?"

I nodded.

"You're so very good to me, Santina. You come from these mountains. It's a blessing. Such power, don't you think? Listen to the mountains roar!"

I was cold. I cared little to listen to silent mountains. The lightning and thunder were loud enough.

"That rage! Pure energy. That's all it is. That's what we all are. I love you, Santina!"

Now her blue eyes deepened. For a moment I caught a flash of that woman jumping into the pond water in London. For a second she was there, in all her fiery glory. It made my heart hope and ache.

"Signora Adeline — please let me wrap

this around you now."

"I don't need looking after, Santina. I need the water. I always have to be in water. Henry knew that. That's why he brought me here."

I tried to smile, while easing a towel around her.

"That's how you tell if someone really loves you, Santina. If they give you what they know you need, whether or not they need it too. Do you understand that, Santina?"

I wanted to. I also wanted to be inside.

"Stop pulling me, Santina!" She flung off the towel and held my face with both her hands. "Look up! I mean really look!"

She lifted my face toward the sky. I half expected a shot of lightning to strike through me. Perhaps I would crisp in her arms.

"How many colors?" she asked.

"Sorry?"

"How many colors?"

Perhaps the major would hear this outburst and rescue the both of us.

"Gray?"

"No — look closer. See the tinge of yellow? Can you see the hint of light green around the edge of that cloud just about the house? See how many grays there are,

Santina — so many. Gray isn't in between, it's not simply neither white nor black. It's not indecision, Santina. It's full of blues and greens and browns and purple. So full. We only see the surface."

And then she laughed. She wrapped her arms around me and squeezed me into her wet dress.

"There's no storm, Santina! We *are* it."

Her laughter peeled into soft tears, ebbing and flowing between the two. She softened, so much so that I could actually lead her inside. I peeled her wet clothes off and wrapped another towel around her. She had grown thinner these past few months. I noticed the protrusion of her bones, the way the skin around it hung, a mournful ivory.

As I turned for another dry towel she walked away from me. I wasn't quick enough to stop her. She stepped back out onto the wet terra-cotta tiles of the terrace, raised her arms up to the heavens, naked, stretching out her body, uncovered breasts for anyone to see. I was thankful that most Positanese would be shut away inside. I ran downstairs for the major. No sooner had we returned than he stepped out into the storm to Adeline without a moment's hesitation. I collected the wet towels.

As I turned to close the door behind me,

my eyes were drawn back to the terrace. I'd expected him to lose his temper somehow, interrupted as he was from his meditative tea. Instead, he placed both his hands around Adeline's face. He pulled her in close and placed his lips upon hers. She leaned back. Rain cascaded down her cheeks like tears. His mouth moved down her neck. I caught the tip of his tongue trace its brittle line. I closed the door, pretending I hadn't seen his hands ease down her naked back. I pressed the door closed, wishing the feeling pulsing in my chest was closer to embarrassment.

Like a Neapolitan temper, the storm was swallowed out to sea as swift as it had erupted. Thankful that the rumbles of thunder had been nothing but that, and not prescient to an earthquake, the town resurrected to business with renewed gratitude. We had survived, once again. I pretended not to have noticed how long the major stayed with Adeline before he returned to his abandoned tea and ordered a second pot. As I laid it down, he looked up and caught my gaze.

"I expect you are wondering when will be the appropriate time to discuss my letter?"

I straightened, trying my best to not allow

his unexpected question to leave me hanging for a studied answer. I decided not to give in to mute embarrassment.

"When would you like to discuss it, sir?"

"This moment. I'm sure you've arrived at a decision. We always arrive at these sorts of decisions far quicker than we'd like to admit. It takes our stubborn brains longer to articulate it. Indecision is only the marker of resistance to our first impulse." He cleared his throat. If I didn't know better, I would have sensed a sting of nerves. "No time like the present."

I noticed he hadn't done up the top two buttons of his shirt. Usually he only kept the top one undone.

"I think," I began, trying with every fiber not to allow the quiver in my voice to take over, "I think that I am happy to stay in my hometown a little longer." This wasn't the answer that had pounded my brain all night. I chose to ignore the other versions of my reply fighting to get out. The ones where I spoke of the family, of feeling flattered that they had thought my work good, of how much of a bond I felt with someone else's daughter. I chose to make him think that it was Positano only that kept me here. I don't think I'd realized it was far more than that. Or maybe I did, and that's why I said nothing to that effect. I couldn't articulate the way his lessons had changed me in this short time. I loved the way they worked a tangible magic upon my mind and way of seeing — the idea of stopping now was not an option.

"Then it is settled?"

"Yes, sir. I will remain until Elizabeth begins school."

I didn't think it appropriate to gush, or thank him. This was a business conversation. He creased his paper back up to cover his eyes.

"This afternoon we must plant some of the newer tomato plants, Santina."

I stood still.

"It's high time you and I instill some order to this garden. We are somewhat askew this year, but you can rest assured it will not happen again. If we work quickly, we will avoid a dreadful glut of zucchini. Even with your culinary prowess, I'm sure you'll struggle to handle an endless supply of the blasted things. One can't ever have enough tomatoes though. I shall be glad of some jarred sunshine come November."

He closed the conversation. There was nothing left for me to do but unpack the clothes I'd packed in my mind, and be sure to reach Marco before he closed the gates for the evening.

I wasn't sure whether it was my state of mind, or whether the tumult of a storm made the blue skies that followed all the brighter. The cemetery looked luminous that afternoon. The bright white of the tombs crisper than usual, any leafy debris washed away by the rains to reveal the delicate veins within the marble. Elizabeth and I wove in between the high tombs, sometimes stopping as she looked up at the towering angels above the richer dead, or insisting we take a moment by the tomb that marked the picturesque spot where a Muslim prince lay, his head scarf carved atop an engraved obelisk.

We followed the narrow walkway onwards, which curved back into the rock where two wide stone benches were sculpted into the indentation. Elizabeth sat down upon the hot cement, happy to perform careful reexaminations of a handful of stones and a couple of pine cones we'd found along the way. I waited for Marco, holding a warm roll I'd just baked stuffed with prosciutto and thin slices of eggplant wrapped in a tea towel. In my other hand, I'd filled a small cloth bag with oranges from the garden. I turned toward oncoming footsteps. I stood up and wrapped my arms around Marco.

"*Calma,* Santina, you make me feel like you're saying goodbye!"

I didn't let go.

"Something smells good!"

I handed him the warm tea towel. He sat and attacked the contents. I wondered when he had last eaten.

"I'm sorry I didn't come straightaway like I'd promised," I said, after I'd let him enjoy several mouthfuls in silence. He shook his head, brushing away my apology. "It will be different now. I will have every Sunday off. We can be together."

He straightened and swallowed. His eyes creased toward the sea. It was a deep turquoise this afternoon. I followed his gaze. I thought about Adeline and squinted to see how many other colors I could see within the blue.

"I would like that, Santina. Can I come to you? My house —"

He trailed off.

I filled in the gaps. "Let me speak with the major — that's what we call him, he was in the British army, India — I'm sure we can work something out. Perhaps a picnic up in our mountains?"

My question hung, unanswered. Then he gave a tiny dip of his chin, which I took as a nod. He seemed to withdraw before me.

"How are you, Marco?"

"Bene, grazie."

"You don't need to give me the polite answer."

He turned and looked into me. I still struggled to marry the scrawny child darting behind me along the rocks with this tall young man. His eyelids lowered as if to hide the images rolling through his mind.

"I live with the dead, Santina."

His words lay between us, a slab of marble.

"We all do. A little."

He smiled then.

"Do you still live with our uncle?" I probed.

"No. He threw me out after Papà didn't give him the money he had loaned him."

My heart tightened. "Where did you go?"

"Nowhere for a while, then to another farm in the hills of Amalfi. I thought about working the ships in Sorrento. Heard about some jobs there. I tried it for a while too. Things got a little . . ."

I held back from interrupting.

His face darkened. "Let's just say they're not the nicest crowd to work with."

I wrapped my arm around his back.

"Thank you for the food. You can come again."

"Sunday?"

"Amen to that."

I kissed him on each cheek and hauled Elizabeth off the seat. "We've got a lot of time to make up, Marco."

His smile looked better fed now. Whatever was preying on his mind had been put on pause for a while. The food I had prepared with such care took his full attention. My mind began to flick through ideas of what I might make for us on my day off.

"*Grazie,* Santina."

"Don't say thank you. We're family."

He stood up and gave a slight tip of his head.

"I'll meet you at the gate after Mass, yes?" I asked.

He smiled, brushed his hand over Elizabeth's head, turned, and wove back up around the corner.

Elizabeth and I took our time returning home. Her new legs grew stronger by the day, and she relished the newfound independence even if holding my hand as she did so proved to be an ever growing battle of wills. Rosalia met us halfway on her return from town.

"My brother's fixing a leak in the roof! I thought we were all going to die!"

"It was a loud one, yes," I replied, trying

to mop away the image of Adeline naked on the wet terrace.

"I've just been asked to help out on Sunday evening at the German women next to your house. You're coming too. They pay well."

"I don't know, Rosalia."

"I do. It's going to be mayhem. All the artists will be there."

"I don't need to gawk at artists, Rosalia."

"Yes you do. I'll call for you at four thirty."

She puckered a noisy kiss on each of Elizabeth's cheeks and one on mine, then left. I was glad to be in her company for another few years. I could but imagine the scale of her plans for Paolino and me once I broke the news to her that I was no longer leaving.

My steps grew light. The weight of the sudden change of plans had lifted. I'd thrown a scatter of seeds in the air and they now landed in perfect order on fertile, volcanic earth beneath me.

The breeze caressed our faces as we carried on our downward wind. Where the backs of houses allowed but for a thin alley to pass through, Elizabeth stomped her feet to feel the echo bounce off the white walls either side of her. The sun's heat intensified.

We reached our last turn before the villa. At the foot of the final set of steps I caught sight of a small figure before the villa's door. It was a man, small and hunched over. A sorrowful excuse for a sweater hung from tired shoulders. His face was gaunt, darkened with drink from the looks of it, prickled with stubble. He turned toward us. For a moment the sun shone a bitter halo around his silhouette. He took a step down and his features shifted into focus. The tourniquet around my middle tightened.

I don't know how long we stood there like alley cats before a fight.

The sounds of the streets below clammed silent. I felt no breeze.

"Santina?" the man croaked.

I didn't reply.

"They told me you lived here."

My heart raced.

I'd never been so glad to see Paolino arrive. He pounded up the steps loaded with a heavy crate of deliveries. He stopped, sweat beading at his brow with the load resting on his shoulder.

"Am I interrupting a street party or is anyone invited?" he asked with a crooked grin.

Off our silence, he lifted the crate from

his shoulder and placed it down on the wide step.

"This man bothering you, Santina?"

I nodded.

"Hey, Signo', do your begging someplace else, *si*? This lady has work to do."

The man cackled. Paolino climbed the half dozen steps between us to reach him. "Old man, go make trouble someplace else. Lots of tourists down the hill, you never know, they might take pity on a tramp like you."

As he spoke he led the man down the steps. The smell reached me before he did. Alcohol, urine, cow shit. My throat clamped tighter. When Paolino returned, I was in the exact spot he'd left me.

"You know that man, Santi'?"

I gave a stiff shake of my head.

"He didn't hurt you?"

I shook my head again.

"Well, come on then, let us in."

I opened the door, and he followed me into the kitchen, placing the crate on the table as he always did.

"Every time I come in here, it feels like you've made it a little bit more like your home. It takes time for a kitchen to become a cook's. Like a good pan, you know? So many dishes have to be cooked before the metal is truly seasoned."

We stood for a moment. The troubling silhouette planted in my mind like a boiled-in stain.

"I have to run — orders on the rise," he said, filling in for my lack of conversation. I followed him to the door.

He turned back toward me. "You alright, Santina? You look like you've just seen a ghost."

I feigned a smile, then closed the door.

I had buried all memory of my father a long time ago.

CHAPTER 9

That last Sunday the following June, I should have been at church. I should have been intoning with all the other women, fingering the tiny black beads of the rosary, falling into the familiar droned rhythm like I did each Sunday morning and Thursday afternoon. But when I reached the church of Santa Margherita, passing the *nonnas* I once served at Cavaldi's along the way, I didn't go inside. They were drawn to worship. I was carried down to the sea.

I stood upon the sharp black stones feeling the pull of the deep turquoise before me. Sheer heights of jagged jet mountain rose from the bay, dipping the beach in shade, a shadow before the glittering water. The expanse spread out before me toward the haze of the horizon, the pointed tips of Li Galli reaching out of the water, and far over to my right the allure of Capri. Our town lay open to this endless water, yet we clung to the mountains as if the houses sought refuge from centuries-old memories embedded in the rock; those Arabian invaders who sailed in, robbers, ransackers, terrifying pirates. Our sea wasn't an intimate pool, a demure bay. Ours was an ancient force of nature.

This year's June was a choral song on light, the promising prelude of a blinding summer. The water turned emerald. I looked down. My feet were wet. I lifted them out of my shoes and waded in a little way. My cotton dress reached halfway down my calves. No one could notice how withered the right one was in this dress. I looked around. Nobody. I lifted my skirt up a little more and felt the cool reach my thighs.

I thought of Adeline. If she were here, she would have swum halfway to Capri by now. I could picture her with ease, cutting through the glassy surface, passing the cliffs in long, smooth strokes, water rippling from her in liquid arrows. I listened to the rock and lap of the water against my legs, wondering if I would resist diving in then and there without a care of whether I had worn the appropriate suit, whether I had a towel? Would I ever have a taste of the abandon of an Adeline? Or would I always stay the dutiful help? The tireless carer? That's what I'd agreed to do, for these next few years after all. What sense in these swirling thoughts?

Today, the call of the open air stirred a playfulness I'd kept in the dark. My first day off without Elizabeth had made me giddy. It was an intoxicating taste of freedom and more than a little overwhelming. I looked down at the glinting light. My fingers reached in and swirled through it. I thought about the congregation replying to the priest in unison, facing toward the altar, turned away from a powerful ocean. I thought about the cool gray of the church inside, a world away from these gleaming stones, of the people echoing repetitions rather than losing themselves upon the beach like the tourists. What would it take for me to swim here, now, fully clothed and walk back, dripping behind me like a wet dog? Would it matter what anyone would say? I pictured Cavaldi's scorn. It made me laugh out loud.

Voices began to fill the beach. I saw Giacomino wheeling his lemon ice trolley along the far end of the sand. His brow was as weary as during the winter. His family lived in a one-room house not too far from where I had grown up. A couple of tourists swaggered to him and exchanged their coins for cups of freshly squeezed lemon juice with sugar and crushed ice. These beachcombers splashed the beach with synthetic color. They wore large hats, larger glasses, bold swimsuits made to be looked at; how different from the deserted bay I knew as a child. My life inside the major's villa was all encompassing — looking after a toddler and her family was a round-the-clock job — and I hadn't realized quite how much the small piece of world beyond our walls was bursting into life.

These people had chosen our bay to play. Theirs was the passionate pursuit of happiness. For the Positanese high up in our church, it was worship and protection. Because of these visitors, Giacomino's family would have enough to eat through winter from what he might hope to earn over the summer. Just beyond the beach cafés shaking up cocktails for the visiting artists, families like this scraped by on bread and sauce or scant drippings of olive oil and freshly picked oregano, to keep hunger at bay. All this time I had been aching for a life beyond these waters but the waves had carried it to me. There was no one clambering along these pebbles that I knew. Everyone who knew me as Santina the polio girl from the hills who worked for the English soldier was either inside the church I'd just left, or the larger church down in the main square, or creating feasts for their families or the tourists they worked for.

I thought about those tiny ceramic shepherds' houses placed inside the small cave I'd passed along the curve of road this morning. The models were fixed amongst the crags, taking up only the tiniest of spaces. It was a miniature version of our world; honoring the power those mountains wielded over us. Like those terra-cotta houses, we stuck steadfast to what tiny space we could carve out.

Today I let the bubbling sense of liberty tingle through me. Renewed, I was a mountain girl. I belonged higher up, amongst those rocks, in the damp green. I squinted toward the hill on the opposite side of the farther bay. I could see the major's villa from down here. What would Elizabeth be doing now? Would the major be taking his tea on the terrace? Might he spot me, a small puff of yellow dress against the dark stones? My chest tightened. I shifted my gaze back to the water. I watched the bubbles crawl up toward my feet and slink back again.

The world was coming to Positano.

When I stepped back inside the house I found Rosalia's cousin chasing Elizabeth around the ground floor. She shrieked in delight, and I suppressed the urge to run and wrap my arms around the child. Of course I was relieved Elizabeth was happy, yet felt uncomfortable with the subtle twist of envy squeezing my middle. I chastised myself for it and returned my attention to the picnic for my brother and I.

In the kitchen I'd already set aside a loaf inside a basket, a slab of cheese, and a handful of tomatoes. I added a small bottle of wine I had decanted from the large glass urn that Paolino refilled with his grandfather's own brew. I placed a mozzarella in a glass dish and tied a plate to the top, slid in some paper-thin prosciutto slices in their brown package around the side of the basket. It felt heavy. I stopped my compulsion to add any more.

"How was Mass, Santina?" the major called out to me as I reached the front door. I ignored the tight arch of his eyebrow and offered my usual reply: "The same."

His mute nod spoke volumes.

I imagined myself telling him I'd left after the first reading, that the scorch of the sun and abandoned beach was too tempting. That I would have swum in my sea then and there. That I looked up toward the terrace and imagined him watching me disappear under the water. The sound of the water lapping over my feet returned to my mind.

"And that, I suppose, is its very draw." He took a sip of the fresh lemonade I'd squeezed earlier this morning. The dappled light through the canopy rippled over his white linen trousers and shirt. I'd not seen him quite so relaxed in a while. Something about this surprising serenity softened his features. Gone was the subtle frown, the quick, incisive glare with which he attacked any task. For the first time I would have even come close to calling him handsome. His red-tinged beard still framed his face in severe outlines. He was as angular as any day, yet his demeanor had shifted. Perhaps he too went to the deserted beaches before the crowds on his early morning walks? He never spoke to me about them, but it seemed so obvious to me now that the one place he would lose himself in was the water. This place wasn't for Adeline alone. I imagined him gliding through the undulating morning sea before it swished with noisemakers.

Adeline entered through the main double doors onto the terrace. She sat beside the major without a sound, then turned to me and smiled. I was accustomed to the major's moods being entangled with Adeline's. Today was a good morning. When Elizabeth dashed by her, she even lifted her hand to reach her. Rosalia's cousin scooped Elizabeth up and, perching her upon her hip, brought her to her mother. That's when she kissed her child. It was the first time I'd seen her do so. My eyes darted to the major. His eyes were light.

"Don't waste any moment of today, Santina!" he called, returning to a book open upon the table. I opened the door and stepped out onto the alley. The sunbeam of my childhood waited for me up there in our hills.

All the shimmer of my morning lost its luster by the time one o'clock rolled around and still my brother did not show. I fell into worry. I recounted our conversation, his caged remarks about the dubious ship folk in Sorrento. I tried to remember the face of the young man I'd first seen him with. I forced myself to suffocate images of my father laying into him for my stilted reaction on seeing him for the first time in an age. I waited until almost two o'clock. I no longer had an appetite.

I could hear the sounds of the beach from up here, fearless frolics from out-of-towners.

Word had got around about tonight's party. Rosalia was beside herself with excitement. I wondered how I would be able to concentrate while worrying about my brother. I slumped down onto the bench outside the cemetery gates. I pulled out my rosary and fingered a few of the beads, trying to conjure the intoned calm of our little church creased into the cliffs, but in vain. I looked down at the beads. Crescents of light curved around their diameter. The rest ebbed into the darkness of my palm. The warm roundness of them filled my hand. In themselves they did not transmit light, but the actions that accompanied them could. Or should. Or did. I longed to make new memories of my family but couldn't help wondering whether this daydream was a meager replacement of my American one.

Villa Santa Croce was a few hundred meters along the alley that ran behind our villa, and almost a replica of the major's in layout. Its plaster was deep damask, unlike our pale pink, and its terraces were wider. It lacked the intimacy and faded allure of the major's house, but inside it was a veritable treasure trove in stark contrast to the major's collection of bizarre artifacts from faraway lands. Here, the dressers that lined the halls shimmered with fine china, goldrimmed and adorned with exquisite designs. Chandeliers hung in each of the grand rooms, glimmering with heavy cut crystal. On one floor the parlor's centerpiece was a grand piano. I could but imagine how on earth they would have transported it up here. I pictured a caravan of donkeys each hauling up a separate piece to be puzzled back together. The kitchen ran the entire far side of the house, rather than taking up a small nook of the ground floor like the major's. Here, a broad hearth overpowered one wall, with long stone counters running the length of each side of the room. The range was at its center, colorful tiles either side upon the stone island. In our villa this area had become surplus book storage for those texts that couldn't find a place in the major's study.

A small army of staff were deep in preparations. There were four regular domestics including a cook who I took great pains to stay on the right side of. She was a small, stout woman, with thick, fast fingers and a hot tongue. As I walked into the kitchen for the first time to collect some dishes, I overheard her slam one of the regular girls with a blast of Neapolitan I'd rather not repeat. Her standards were exacting and, from what I could sense, never achievable.

Rosalia sidled in beside me and whispered, "What did I tell you? Can you believe this place?"

"It's a palace," I answered, trying not to move my lips. Our heels clipped along the polished tiles to the far room where an enormous dining table was strewn with mouthwatering arrays of festive dishes. There were several seafood salads, a great pile of charred shrimp, a small mountain of steamed clams. A tempting aroma of garlic, dense olive oil, fresh mint, rosemary, basil, and laurel moistened the air above the display. Another girl entered with an enormous basket of fresh bread. Its yeasty warmth as she passed made my mouth water. I ought to have eaten more before I came. The grandfather clock chimed six. We were called to the kitchen.

"Now listen up — *asco' ma bene!*" the cook exclaimed, wiping her hands on her starched apron. "I make a lot of food perfect. You don't talk, you don't stare. You don't behave like peasants from the *montagne* — no mountain goats here, *si*? We do things properly here. The family is *Tedesch'*, from Germany. Lots of *artisti* coming here tonight. Any trouble, you talk to me. But I don't want to talk to nobody. *Capisci?!*"

169

I joined the general mumble of agreement. The bell rang. We took to our stations. I wished I had had the sense to defer the job of balancing a tray of prosecco for the guests on arrival. Then I realized, as the stream of guests flowed, that I had a vantage point. The German sisters, who lived here with their brother, received their friends in the dining room. Rosalia took great pains to describe their escape from Germany. She threw around the word Bauhaus as if she and I knew what it meant, though we were both a little embarrassed to admit that we didn't. Reading between the lines, I sensed the brother had no place to express himself back home. But here, in the hills of our town, people were glad to accept a poet and artists into our midst. This is what Rosalia explained to me with colorful expression, proud to be part of the Positanese, who held an inherent esteem for art and artists. "It's in our blood, Santi'," she sang.

I was to offer a cordial welcome. The first to take drinks were a pair of gentlemen that reminded me of Mr. Benn and Mr. George. I think they may have been German too, but I often confused them with Russians. A small herd of dancers followed. You could recognize them by their sinewy limbs, the way their backs were stretched long and straight, with the gait that suggested they might leap through the air at any given moment. Their skin looked taut, as all fat reserves had been consumed by their great muscularity. They skittered by me, glasses in hand, giggling into the next room. I believe their choreographer, Massine, followed. I know this because Rosalia made a point of elbowing me to attention. She gave a discreet commentary from the opposite side of the wide hallway, an enormous portrait of a half naked woman swaying by a waterfall behind her. Her head reached just high enough to block my unadulterated view of the naked buttocks. Massine was smaller than I had imagined but had lively eyes with the same bounce to his gait. He followed his dancing army.

A small, older, bald man followed with ochre skin and large piercing brown eyes. He took two glasses. I didn't think it proper to comment. Rosalia did — with her eyes at least. She managed to stay quiet, for that I was thankful. A rainbow of others lit up the corridor for the next half hour or so, each luminous in their attire, speech, and the space they took up with grand gestures. None exhibited any inhibition about how loud they spoke, nor how overstated their reactions to one another's stories were. I was a sparrow amongst lions.

Rosalia beamed. She adored the opulence, this great waterfall of energy. I found the noise deafening. Confusing even. When it felt like most of the guests had arrived, we took our places in the main dining area, monitoring the plates and judging when refills were needed. I caught sight of the two sisters floating amongst their guests. In contrast to their friends, they were demure, in dark purples and blacks. Their dresses were plain, their hair scraped back from their thin faces, drawing observers only to the bright intelligence of their small blue eyes. Their brother held court in the corner of the lower terrace, surrounded by a group of young men who seemed to be ordering the universe with a complex mixture of animation and thoughtful contemplation. They all wore black. What were they mourning?

When the last guest arrived, she turned heads. I would have liked to think I paid her no mind. That I too didn't stand and gawk at her flame-red mass of hair shrieking out of her head like a Medusa fury. I would have liked to take in the tattoos upon her face, weblike lines of ink, as if they were nothing more than a little makeup. But I couldn't, of course. She prowled in, full lipped, black pencil around her eyes like thick smudges of soot. Several guests lounged to her and wrapped their arms around her, calling out "Vali!" and "Ms. Myers, darling!" She purred into them. The prosecco drained dry. Spirits were passed out. Someone started at the piano. The whole room swayed into dance, or rather undulated into a collective swagger, like passengers on a ship in a storm, flicking random fragments of shapes to one another. Rosalia signaled for me to return to the kitchen. As I passed through the large room, which we used as a dining room at the major's villa, a voice called to me.

"Ah, the *signorina* with the bubbles at the door!"

I turned, doing my best performance of professional calm. The man pulled out a small notebook from his pocket with a stub of charcoal. "Don't move, *per piacere.*"

I had no plans to. I was concentrating on breathing.

Black lines swooped over the page. I could hear somewhere far off percussive laughter underscored with an improbable mix of piano notes in crescendo. Inside the darkened quiet of this room, the scrawl echoed.

"This, *per te* — for you." He reached out

the small piece of paper. I wasn't sure what to do.

"*Per piacere,* you take. It's a bird."

I took the sheet in my fingers. My eyes raised back to him.

"Bird of peace, no? You like?"

I smiled then. It escaped before I could stop it. I had visions of being fired on the spot should the cook or any of the regular staff see me here like this. "Yes, very much. Thank you."

"Oh wait!" he said, grabbing it back from me. He laid it on top of his notebook and scratched a signature. Then without turning back, he left me alone with the sheet in my hand. I folded it and slipped it into my pocket.

That's when I saw them.

The major and Adeline stood in a slant of moonlight a little farther down the corridor. He hadn't mentioned anything about coming tonight, even when I'd asked permission to do these extra hours outside their home. Adeline had not left Villa San Vito since we arrived. At first I didn't recognize him. His beard had been shaven clean away, revealing a face far younger than I had supposed. Now they stood, the major whispering into her ear while a tentative smile penciled across her lips. The moon fell over her white skin, translucent in the metallic glow. She wore a long red dress with small floral details raised in darker velvet. It hung on her; as she moved, the protrusion of her hips brushed the fabric. Her hair was held off her face by a loose strip of ribbon. Even from where I stood I could notice the intricate amethyst clusters of her long earrings. Her mournful beauty was compelling.

This is why the major brought her to my town. He knew it was growing. He knew we welcomed the misfits, the foreigners, the artists, the people who imagined. She was one of them. I left the corridor and returned to the kitchen.

Cook led an armada with a huge skillet of more shrimp, flaming in sweet wine as they turned pink. My stomach ached to try some. I was sent back to the drawing room with the loaded plate, placing the heavy ceramic dish in the center where there was space, to a collective gasp of delight. Hands dove into them with abandon. What must it feel like to relish food with such passion? There were murmurs of delight I would have liked to join in with. Rosalia tapped my elbow. "We can stay here and carry on with drinks, says Cook."

I felt his hand upon my back. I turned to see the major standing tall in his crisp blue linen shirt and pressed khaki trousers.

"How does Cook's food compare then?"

I had no answer. Rosalia's smile widened; his apparent newfound youth wasn't lost on her.

"And thank you once again, Rosalia, your cousin is doing a fine job with Elizabeth. I can see that Santina's day off has done her the world of good!" He looked down at me, his eyes dancing. How different from the man who first arrived here, holding on to his wife as if she might collapse or run away. Rosalia nodded as if she understood each word. The major looked across the table at Adeline, now engaged in conversation with a man wearing a purple shirt and shorts that left little to the imagination. The major left us to join them.

The evening oozed on, the dancing slowing as the crowd shifted toward the poets and singers in the group. A silence fuzzed over the room as people took it in turns to recite or sing. Warm applause followed. Then the brother stood up. "Paolino!" he called. "Where's Paolino?"

Rosalia turned to me, conspiratorial. "Eduard just loves Paolino's singing. Heard him one day as he delivered the groceries, forced him to sing the whole thing to him right then and there."

"I didn't know he was here."

"That's hardly surprising, you've barely looked up this evening. You can't get fired if you're a temporary, you know!"

The room ricocheted with applause. Paolino brushed behind me, his guitar strapped on him. Eduard stood up, his English fluent but heavy with a German intonation. "And so, my friends, this is the wonderful Paolino, who braves the hills for our sakes, and makes sure that we are kept fed in the most wonderful way imaginable. This is a song, which made me fall in love with him even more. It's called 'Scalinatella,' or, for those ignoramuses among us, 'Little Stairway.' A latest hit, perhaps, but as you will hear, it is scribed in the ancient passion only a Neapolitan can ever truly understand."

They cheered at that. I looked across the room. The major saw me. His eyebrow raised into a question mark. A smile crept over my lips without me intending it to.

"But enough of this German man — listen, and, like me, fall in love."

A hush fell. I didn't think it possible this crowd could curtail its self-expression for that long. I was washed up into the golden quiet with everyone else. Paolino caressed the first chord. The tune sounded familiar.

177

His woody timbre held the space. Then the lyrics reached me, at the far side of the room, like a forgotten memory. I'd never heard him express himself with such unself-conscious honesty. It bewitched the room. He reached the closing verse.

That's when he saw me.

"Little stairway," he crooned, "climb to the sky or go down to the sea."

A few guests traced his gaze in my direction. My cheeks betrayed me.

"In the next few days a steamship will leave," he sang, slowing down for dramatic effect, "within a few days my love will throw itself to the sea!"

I allowed myself to see him. For the first time I cast no judgment, I wasn't flinching from his attention, nor batting off his glib patter. He stood before a room of strangers, artists, and dancers and was bare. He let them in. In turn, they courted what it felt like to experience this unrequited passion. From their intense hush, I couldn't doubt their powers of empathy surpassed anyone I had met. His vulnerability penetrated us. Not his usual dancing lilt, his flyaway hands, the self-assured swagger with which he held himself. It was clear to me for the first time that this was a man capable of expressing his feelings with compelling simplicity. The artists were seduced. He was singing to me; another girl would be quivering with embarrassment or pleasure. Paolino imbued the complexity of life and love into one simple melodic line. I let the light and dark of his voice glow around me.

The final chord hummed into the shimmering bubble of concentration, till Eduard rose to his feet. Everyone followed. Paolino beamed. His face widened into a sunny grin, his eyes a deepening shade of chocolate. He looked beautiful. I'd never paid much attention to his posture before today. He grew before his audience. His chest widened. The obvious muscularity of his thighs did not go unnoticed by most of the women, and several of the men, in the crowd. As the cheers grew, the partygoers obstructed my view of him. I didn't see him shift to try to find me through the human shield because I sought refuge in the darkened hallway outside. Thoughts plucked my mind, one by one, like a ghost tiptoeing across strings of an unfinished chord; the resonance of doubt.

The major's house was silent as I stepped back inside. The water swayed with mercurial threads. It was the type of full moon that made our little town feel smaller and insignificant, desperate to cling on to its little indentation. We were barnacles riding the whale.

"It is particularly boastful tonight, wouldn't you say?"

The major's voice startled me. I hadn't noticed him sat in the shadows of one of the lemon trees down beyond the terrace where I stood. As I focused toward the voice, I could pick out threads of moonlight upon his hair, though he still looked like a stranger with his newly shaven face. I couldn't shake the sense of the major as a younger man. I walked toward the steps down to the garden, not wanting to call out over the balustrade.

"It looks like a harvest moon, even," he said.

"Yes."

He fell back into silence, save the soft clink of his melting ice cube as he swirled the remnants of his whisky.

"Santina, would you mind to fill this up for me?"

I walked down the steps. My feet crunched across the crisp grass. I took his glass. His fingers brushed mine. He looked up at me and smiled. I wondered how much he had drunk.

"I can read Rumi in this bright light, quite

well." I noticed a book lying facedown upon his knee.

"An astonishing man from the thirteenth century. Born in Turkey. Wrote in Sufi. Wandered the planet searching for what in the West we might use that obtuse word: God. Something you claim to know a great deal about, I should think."

His eyes smiled. I couldn't tell where his sarcasm would lead us. I hoped he hadn't been drinking since they'd returned home. "Here — read this top line."

I took a breath, trying to steady myself despite his unpredictable demeanor. " 'At night, I open the window and ask the moon to come and press its face against mine. Breathe into me.' "

How long had the major sat here, stupefied by the moon, churning Rumi's writing around in his mind? I hadn't noticed him leave the party.

"Well, Santina? What do you say to that?"

I looked at his smiling eyes.

"I say . . . Positano is the perfect place to be moonkissed."

He laughed at that. Or laughed at me. I didn't care which. I caught a titillating glimpse of something beyond his wiry self-control. Our grins faded into an almost comfortable silence. He tapped the glass.

"On second thoughts, Santina. I ought to let you get to bed. This is supposed to be your day off. I apologize."

"It's already tomorrow."

He stood up. "Then it's far too early to start drinking."

He closed his book and walked toward the steps. When he reached the balustrade, he placed the book upon the base rim of one of the columns supporting the upper terrace.

"I shall leave this here for you, Santina. I think you have a closer affinity to your Positanese moon than I. Do let me know if it presses its face against yours, won't you? The moon, I mean — not the book. Unless you're in a particularly clumsy mood. I've heard parties do that to people."

With a chuckle he disappeared into the shadows of the house. I picked up the book and let it fall open at a random page: "Let the water settle, and you will see the moon and the stars in your own being."

I reached inside my pocket for the little drawing, straightened it to place it between the pages to press the creases away. I read the signature: "Picasso." Alone in the garden, I felt I'd been gifted that very moon. Those party people from a parallel world had muddied my thinking after all.

CHAPTER 10

Dawn teased the horizon with strands of pink. The major and I bent over the zucchini patch, which was shooting out in all directions, thick tubular stems threatening to dominate everything in its wake. It was impossible to water or garden at any time other than this, or during the abating warmth of dusk. In between, the humidity of July steamed toward a ferocious August that even the locals struggled to survive. We took this time, before Elizabeth stirred and the sun rose, to tend to the vegetable garden. Paolino joked about the major's military layout. Every time he brought up deliveries he asked whether I was sure he hadn't used a ruler to measure the distance between the plants.

"The fact of the matter is, Santina, Mother Nature is not so much of an attentive listener as a law unto herself." His trowel tucked into the small tufts of weeds eking an existence near the base of the zucchini plant. "Just as it ought to be, I should imagine. But good heavens, what are we to do with all these zucchini?"

I had tried, with diplomacy, to convince the major that planting more than three to four indentations with seeds would lead to a glut, but he would hear none of it. It was the first time he had planted this garden with full force, and, still accustomed in his mind to the damp London summer, he anticipated several seeds to fail. All of them grew.

His maintenance of it edged toward obsession in the face of its unrelenting bounty. Even he had to admit, there was only so much linguine coated in the sweet grated vegetable that he could eat, even if he knew I infused the olive oil with garlic to perfection and had the patience to wring out all moisture inside the zucchini before sautéing.

"I will pickle some later, Major, and make *verdure giardiniera.* I can add some cauliflower too."

He looked at me while still bent over, attacking the pernicious intruders. He wiped a bead of sweat from his brow.

"Our Lady of the Zucchini. I'll speak to the mayor. Perhaps I can convince him to add one more saint festa to the never ending list?"

I sighed a laugh and snipped away several male flowers that would not bear fruit, placing them with care into a small basket at my feet. In my mind, I was already coating them around warmed translucent onions and garlic as the base for a risotto. The major bent down toward several of the smaller zucchini and cut them away with his knife. He reached over the top of the foliage and handed them over.

"How many's that, then? Enough to feed half the inhabitants of Li Parlati, wouldn't you say?"

He loved throwing around the name of our area. I noticed he'd begun even to roll his "r's" in an effort to prove that his promise of learning Italian had been in earnest. Our hill had been christened "dead city" not only because of the cemetery that reigned over it at its peak, but because the houses around us were the ones left abandoned during the first wave of Positanese escaping to America. I hated the term. Ours was the place where most of the larger mercantile houses stood. One by one they now filled with people who were far from dead. Here were the people celebrating life, committing the colorful burst of our town to page, canvas, and screen.

I straightened.

"Good heavens, Santina, don't tire just yet! We've got several rows of tomatoes that need pricking out."

I made my way over to them and crouched down. I loved their herbaceous smell, the way the scent deepened as I broke away the extraneous green shoots, allowing the plant's energy to feed the growing fruit alone. Would this be good practice for people? How could I cut away unwanted shoots — of thoughts, dreams — so that my energy could be directed only to the fruit I bore? What would I leave behind me? I brushed away the vanity of my own legacy. How fortunate I felt, to have these daily dawns of peaceful gardening to clear away needless thoughts like weeds.

We worked in silence as the sun climbed. Only the *scritch-scratch* of dry earth beneath the claws of the major's small garden fork and the quiet snap of stems as I removed them scraped our fading thoughts.

Over the past summer months the major had expressed a preference for conducting our lessons in this manner. From ten o'clock till no earlier than tea time, he would prefer the shade of indoors, reinstating his reign over the garden only once the sun had softened its blaze. I prepared lunch alone, spent the days with Elizabeth within the cool of our shuttered room, lulling her to afternoon rest under the shade of the lemon trees, now widening with maturity and entwining into a thick canopy beyond the vegetables. Most days I'd take the time to rest myself. I loved lying upon the reed mat underneath those flat leaves, Elizabeth's slowing breaths edging me to sleep, like lying on the floor of a rocking sailboat.

The major stretched his back. "My word, they're making quite some progress with those carnival boats this year!"

I followed his gaze down toward the water. Around a small bend from the main beach, Spiaggia Grande, there was a rocky bay where several dozen old fishing boats were moored — a hidden location ahead of tonight's celebrations — beside the tourist vessels that transported visitors to town from the larger ships from Naples and Sorrento which could not dock on our bay.

It was August 15th, *Ferragosto,* Assumption Day. The day we honored our Madonna's ascent to heaven. The day our town fizzed about with anticipation as summer began. Each year all the local fishermen and traders outdid one another's inventions as they masked their working boats as pirate

187

ships or enormous sea creatures. Everyone would watch tonight's sea ritual. It was the most magical evening of my childhood memories. Perhaps the only one. It wasn't Sunday though. I would not be joining the festa down on the beach this year.

"Your face is a child's, Santina."

My eyes darted to him.

"The idea of standing in a hot crowd fills me with cool terror," he added.

I smiled. The sun stretched its rays. We'd have to water soon or it would evaporate. I went to the faucet at the far end of the patch, turned it on, and reached the end of the hose just in time. If I placed my thumb over the water, it would squirt down onto my wrists. I tried to remember this feeling when the midday heat beat down.

"Such a promising smell, isn't it?"

"The water, Major?"

"The water, the damp earth underneath, the plants filling the moisture with a thankful, herby scent."

I must have raised an eyebrow without meaning to.

"That's why poets write about these things, Santina. Such simplicity cocoons complex biochemical manifestations — such utter perfection in all things. I mean, look at this flower" — he lifted a zucchini petal from my basket — "look at all those spider veins flowing through these papery petals." He held it up against the sun so that the light shone through, silhouetting the thin green lines. "You see, this little zucchini blossom is sending messages to the very tip: survive. It's a compulsion."

"I suppose."

"And while a flower is so very beautiful, it's a plant's parting song, one last desperate attempt to survive. It offers its seeds back to the earth whence it came."

He took off his hat and fanned his face in smooth strokes.

"Before my grandmother died, she was overtaken by a great wave of energy. I remember it well. We were in India. She'd gone into the kitchen, placed an apron on, and decided to cook alongside the staff. She instructed them on the art of the perfect roast dinner. Every detail was attended to. She didn't sit down until everything was done, despite the heat. She didn't order me out of the kitchen that day, rather insisted I too help. For a month she'd been bed-bound, but that day she was resurrected."

"She sounds wonderful."

"She was an abhorrent, terrifying woman. But that day she was beautiful. Dead, the next."

Off my look, he smiled.

"It's quite alright. No need for maudlin. I'm just saying that people, like vegetables, blossom at the end of their lives. The seeds were passed on to me, if you like. Oh dear, the heat's already cloying my brain. You are to learn to stop me when I begin talking nonsense, Santina."

I wouldn't dream of it. I liked his nonsense. I admired the way his thoughts brambled over one another. I adored the way he would step back after an observation and pick it apart, dismiss it, judge it. And I loved the way his face would crease several years younger as he did so; at once philosopher and curious child.

Elizabeth's voice echoed down the stairwell.

"And so another morning is over," he said, cleaning off the dirt from his fork and trowel with a rag from his pocket. He always returned the tools to the potting station he'd set up along the side of the house, polished. "You see to madam. I've quite the appetite this morning. I'll eat outside. With the child. Only do let us teach her how to eat like a human, not a small ape, yes?" His face was a playful grin. "There's time yet before we're cooked."

He slipped the tools into the top drawer,

slammed it shut, and went upstairs to wash and change for breakfast.

The cicadas' morning chorus deepened.

Elizabeth was settled into an early bedtime as usual, before the major and Adeline took to the terrace for dinner. I could sense the energy down in the bay. The heat had been furious, but I hadn't stopped in the kitchen all day, simmering the freshly picked zucchini and cauliflower in vinegar, then jarring them with peppercorns, laurel, thin slices of shallots, and whole peeled garlic cloves to preserve for the winter. I counted twenty jars in a row, then permitted myself to finish a small plate of *totani* with *patate* — local squid cooked with homegrown potatoes. The heat hadn't drained me today. I'd kept the shutter closed tight against its beams, and the kitchen became mine and Elizabeth's cave for the day.

Inside, I'd taken time to let the *totani* bubble with thin slices of garlic and skinned tomatoes from the garden. I'd diced the potatoes with precision, then let the mixture simmer for almost an hour. I knew that by the time the major and Adeline ate dinner the flavors of the sea and our fresh produce would have infused to a perfect balance. If I couldn't eat the dish from any of the stalls down at the bay at the festa, I would be sure to take part from up here.

I never minded dining alone. It was a welcome moment of solitude after the day, but this evening, I could hear the voices drift up to me from the beach. The performance would begin soon. I wiped my small bowl with a heel of bread, enjoyed the sweet garlicky tomatoes, then headed outside to clear the plates.

"Santina, that was absolutely delicious!" the major called out. His spirits were still buoyant.

"Whatever is happening down there, Santina? Is someone getting married?" Adeline asked, still wearing her nightdress. One of the straps hung listless over her arm.

"Darling, I just told you — it's *Ferragosto,* the whole town is erupting on account of the Madonna."

I stacked their plates, careful not to make a clatter.

"Would you like to go down with them, Santina?" Adeline asked. I stopped scooping up the crumbs on the table into the dirty plates.

"Are you sending Cinderella to the ball after all?" the major asked.

"Don't be abhorrent, Henry — look at her!"

"I can't imagine that carousing with fishermen is what Santina is after this evening."

"Do you imagine what Santina is after very often, Henry?"

I didn't want to watch this tennis match. "Shall I bring fruit now?"

"Only if you want to, Santina," Adeline said, spikes on her tongue. "Why don't you ask Henry — he'll know what you really want."

She threw her napkin on the table and glared at her husband.

"Thank you, Santina, yes."

I retreated to my kitchen. The world was in order there. I knew Rosalia looked upon me as a slave to this family, doing more than my share of duties. She told me every other day that most families had several help. I couldn't imagine being part of a team in such close quarters, day in, day out. Listening to the gossip. Defending the major. Having my loyalty criticized, teased. No, ours was an intimate unit, and it worked, unless Adeline was in the temper of this evening. Or the major for that matter.

That's when this room became my sanctuary. Rosalia and Paolino were all too ready to call it servitude, but in here, I was in charge. I was the alchemist. What I chose to cook could shift moods. Hot day: fresh fish to cool the blood. Spiteful moods: fennel, bitter chicory leaves for the liver. Too much restless energy: anything with and including fresh tomatoes, their rich juice, sweet and smart, perfect to balance hot and cold. I intuited more along the way. I dared not tell Rosalia. She would have called me a witch, splashed holy water in my face, and sent me to confession.

I placed a glass bowl of peaches on the table outside.

"Our Lady of the Nightgown has proclaimed it cruel for me to imprison you in this ivory tower. Take the evening off."

I stood, silent. He looked at his wife.

"The exact level of joy I would have expected, Adeline — do you see that?"

Adeline bit into a peach. A trickle of juice sweetened her chin.

"You may use my knife, Adeline."

He handed it to her. She didn't move. "Off you go, Santina."

"Elizabeth?" I asked.

"A sleeping child is a blissful ward. I won't repeat myself," the major replied.

I'd never run down to the bay quicker.

The beach was crushed with hot bodies. An accordion played beside a drummer thumping his tambourine. The band's singer wailed a dancing tune. Stands lined the farthest end of the beach near the most popular haunt, especially with the visitors, *Buca di Bacco*. This is where the stars were photographed and their particulars telegraphed to me via Rosalia, who could somehow remember every detail about their appearance, from the slight crease around their eye to the width of their hem. The smells made my mouth water. The salty citrus scent of fried *totani* and calamari, tempting vanilla and citrus sweetening the air by the *Bacco*'s gelateria — doing as much trade in this one night as a whole month.

Then the drums pummeled into life. A dozen men from the town lined the shore, pounding their barrels. The crowd grew quiet. Far in the distance, the flickering of lights heralded the start of the show. They floated closer till at last we could make out the fishing boats in their disguises. Torn tea-stained sheets hung high, like pirates' ragged sails; paper crows' nests were attached to make them look like old, tall ships. Farther behind, other ships had attached huge reed frames covered with bright cloth to mimic enormous sea creatures chomping through the water toward us. When their red eyes lit up, the children squealed with terrified delight. It didn't feel so long ago that I stood here with my mamma and did the same.

That's when I saw Marco, on the far end of the beach. He was sat upon a rock with a group of young men. I wove in and out of the bodies looking over one another's shoulders to get a good view. I called out to him.

He waved, then reached down a hand for me.

"Some things never change, no?" I looked at him, my face warm and grinning.

"You look beautiful tonight, Santina."

"I'm happy to see you."

In a moment I forgot all those afternoons he wouldn't show up at our picnics. I forgave the Sunday evenings I would linger outside the main church square, by Chiesa Nuova, in the hopes that he would come with me to get gelato. Elizabeth and I would walk up to the cemetery a couple of afternoons a week instead. While he was working I knew I could leave him food and my thoughts without wondering.

The men beside him shook my hand. Marco told them to keep their hands off his "little" sister. We laughed at that. Before I could carry on the conversation, the bellowing started. Deep throated cries from the boats where the local woodworkers, butchers, fishermen, and bakers pretended to be those ancient Saracen invaders. To the roar of the crowd, they pulled onto the beach, wading through the shallows toward a huge statue of the Madonna planted on the jetty. They lifted it and, returning the float with them, set about lighting the hay piles around the jetty. The flames flapped up into the black night. Everyone jeered. Then, with great aplomb, they pantomimed contrition. Their arms swayed in guilt. They cried up to the heavens. The flames were extinguished and the statue of the Madonna of Positano returned to its place. The crowd erupted then, just as the fireworks burst into the sky. I looked at Marco, his face flashing blue and red and green. His smile was a boy's.

The "actors" waded out of the water to their families, undoing the scarves tied around their heads, laughing at each other, patting one another on the back as if they'd sailed around the world. One masked figure caught my eye. He was aping around a group of young men. His hands danced in silhouette, recounting the great adventure. I watched him pull his scarf off his head and wipe his face. That's when he turned toward the rock where Marco and I sat. He waved his scarf up at me. I'd never seen Paolino look so beautiful.

He was beside me quicker than I thought anyone could crunch across those stones.

"You know this clown, Santina?" Marco asked, his face hard behind the grin.

"Doesn't everyone?" I laughed, allowing the buoyant atmosphere to lift me.

"After that master performance?" Paolino strutted. "There's film directors on the beach tonight — I'll be surprised if I don't have some offer of work come across my countertop tomorrow morning."

"I don't doubt it." I laughed.

He puffed out his chest, miming a producer puffing on a cigar. "Two *etti* of prosciutto and a part opposite Loren, yes?"

A couple more men came and patted him on the back as they walked past.

"Can I get you a drink, Santina? Gelato?" Paolino asked.

"That would be nice," I replied without thinking.

"The major letting you stray the streets most nights now, Santi'?"

I turned to Marco, confused and appalled by his snide remark.

"You want something too, Marco?" I asked.

"I'm going." He turned to the men sat with him, who peeled themselves off the rocks and flanked him. They looked taller now. Their eyes shifted across the crowd, as if they were counting the entire beach.

"We'll walk you home, Santina," Marco said.

"Oh I'll be fine — I've missed being down here."

Marco looked at Paolino. Neither blinked.

"I'll be at work tomorrow," Marco said, "if you need anything."

"Grazie."

I never thought I'd be glad to see him leave, but as I watched him sway through the crowd, I couldn't help but acknowledge a hidden wave of relief.

Paolino took my hand before I had time to retract it. We wove through the bodies, some dancing, most drinking, all of them eating and shouting. He ordered two cones and before I knew it we were sat on a bench next to Chiesa Nuova.

"I love crowds. And I hate them," he said, breaking the sugary silence.

"This is delicious," I replied, taking another lick of gelato.

His lips were coated with a vanilla gleam in the lamplight.

"So he let you out?" he asked, as always.

"It's not prison."

"Tell his wife."

I rolled my eyes.

"You look different tonight, Santi'."

"So do you."

My chest tightened. I crunched into my sugar cone. A couple of pieces fell onto my lap. He picked them off and ate them.

"You're a pig."

"Absolutely. You never met a Saracen before?"

My laughter escaped.

"You've been drinking," he teased.

"All day." I giggled. "Must be the fumes from the vinegar have gone to my head."

"Not more zucchini?"

"It may never end."

He laughed now. I'd never noticed the faint dimple on his one cheek.

He finished his cone and wiped his mouth.

"I'll take you back before you tell me to go to hell like you normally do?"

He stood up and offered his hand. I slipped mine in.

We walked in silence. Everyone who lived along these alleys was at the beach. The sounds of music and cooking swirled up along the cobbles. It spun around the moonlit silence between us. He stopped at the mouth of a tiny stairwell leading off the main ascent.

We stepped into the shadows.

I noticed my breathing. Or lack of it. His breath brushed my lips.

He leaned in. I didn't move.

My first kiss was toasted hazelnut and vanilla.

CHAPTER 11

That night, I slipped into the slice between consciousness and dreams. Thoughts tripped over one another, little dust motes spiraling in the moonlight. At last I gave up the fight to rest and stepped out onto the terrace outside my room. I sat there watching the stars fade. With each breath another warren of thoughts: Paolino's lips, the feel of his hands around me, the electricity splintering down my spine, the thrill of his touch, and the ache for him to stop.

He had walked me to our door after we left the alley. I did not kiss him there. All of a sudden it felt tawdry. I silenced the sensation of feeling conquered. I reassured myself that Paolino, contrary to my intuition, was more sensitive than I had thought. His touch was gentle. His lips danced over mine. They eased them open. There was no force. No violent edge to his passion. So why was I sat here, looking at the changing sky, unwilling to acquiesce to a skittish excitement? I ought to be floating in a delicious haze.

Instead, unanswered questions and doubts raced to the surface of my mind like water on a rolling boil. When sleep edged further still, just before the purple sky creased orange, I gave up the fight and went downstairs to the kitchen. I filled the small room with the scent of three freshly squeezed lemons and their grated zest. I lit the oven, not caring that it would add unnecessary heat — by the time the sun rose, this lemon cake would be cooled. I drew a silence around me, beating the eggs, softening the butter, toasting and crunching the hazelnuts into small pieces. I let the swirl of the batter around my whisk paint over my thoughts. I buttered and dusted a molded tin with flour, poured the mixture in, and let it cook on low. I drank my coffee on the lower terrace, watching the rose beams sketch an outline around the clouds. Every ten minutes or so, as the cake cooled, I poured a couple of spoons of the lemon juice mixed with water and sugar over the sponge, watching the sweet-sour sink into the warmth.

It was almost time to water the garden. I tipped the cake onto a dish, poured the last spoon of sugary lemon juice over the bundt and let the hopeful citrus cleanse my mind. Outside, in the perfect still of the garden, I took my time to visit each plant, the water hitting the dry ground and circling into the earth.

"I couldn't sleep either."

The major's voice gave me a fright. I almost dropped the hose.

I had been lost deeper into my thoughts than I had realized. How did I not see him sat at the far end of the garden?

"Don't look quite so alarmed, Santina. I wasn't here spying on you. I just found more pleasure in watching the dawn than twisting around my bedsheets. Also, the smell of what promises to be a rather delicious breakfast was near impossible to tear myself away from."

I lifted the hose over the brush of fennel leaves toward the tomatoes.

"I did almost invite myself to share your coffeepot though. I don't particularly drink the stuff, but when you make it I'm very tempted indeed."

He pulled himself off the deck chair, brushed his trousers down. That's when I saw he was in his pajamas. It was the first time I'd seen him out of pressed clothes. We noticed it in unison.

"I suppose Adeline is having an effect on me at last. If you see me wandering aimlessly around the garden in a nightdress, you will tell me, won't you?"

I laughed at that. His eyes smiled, catching flints of dawn through the trees.

He reached me, rolled up his sleeves, fetched a trowel from the potting drawers, and began building up the patches of earth around the fennel. I tried to concentrate on the celery, the thirsty rows of parsley and coriander. My eyes kept wandering over to his deft work. The gentle way he cocooned the fattening bulbs with earth. I watched his large hands raise the mounds up and over the base of the plants: a man wrapping a bedsheet around a sleeping lover.

His eyes met mine. For a moment neither of us spoke. The hose spilled onto my toes.

"Was the festa memorable, Santina?"

A smart of embarrassment.

Had he heard me return with Paolino? Had he slipped me under his judgmental gaze? Could he see how I had held Paolino's hand as we walked the darkened alley? Why did I need to know he hadn't compartmentalized me as another local girl whose sole aim was to find a man and procreate? I washed away the memory of Paolino's mouth with difficulty.

"It was beautiful," I replied.

"I can see that. Your expression shifted through a palette of colors in a moment."

I felt naked.

"When the arrow strikes, Santina, the fine line between pleasure and pain opens up a whole new world, does it not?"

I pretended not to understand the rhetoric. I just wanted him to keep on talking. I wanted his thoughts to eclipse mine.

"I felt the same with Adeline. Her entire family warned me not to devote myself to her. Her own *family*, Santina. Friends of mine who knew them were quite blunt about what they thought to be her mental instability. Her brothers were the worst. They didn't understand her. They abhorred the fact that she did as she pleased, that she would swim naked with them and their friends because if the boys could, why not her? That she would curse any who saw that as an invitation to use her as they pleased. Faced with a woman's unbridled mind and body, man turns defensive. So very disappointing."

I stayed silent, hoping he would elaborate before his openness clammed into practiced reserve. It worked; his confession was directed more to the tousled fennel leaves than me.

"I couldn't ignore the burning need to be with her. It was all-consuming. She was free. She stretched her wings however she chose. She cared little for what was expected of her. That is what I fell in love with. She followed her every instinct." He sighed a sad laugh. "I almost envied her that. Then I saw her art. She was life itself, in all its vibrant, muddy, terrifying glory."

He stopped short. We looked at one another. I held the space between us, his intimate description hanging in the golden pause. I'd never heard a man couch love in those terms. It was bittersweet. I thought about the Adeline at the table last night, about the Adeline scrawling along the walls. My heart ached for the love affair I couldn't be sure would ever be his again.

"And so it is true. Sleep is magical indeed. Without it, man is mad. Why do you let me prattle on like that?"

"Because it's beautiful."

The words slipped out ahead of me.

His face opened into an unhurried smile. "Beauty is sat on that kitchen table. My nose tells me so. And so does my stomach. Have a slice with me?"

My head started a rehearsed polite rejection. He would hear none of it.

We ate my cake in silence as the morning

207

sun stretched its beams down the mountains and across the azure ocean before us.

The next few days were a flurry of preparations. The major's friend Dr. Simmons, the man I'd first met in those dark postpartum days in London, sent a telegram to announce he would be taking up the major's offer of coming to stay at the villa. He would offer his professional opinion on how Adeline was coping with their new lives. We could both see a clear improvement. I suspected the invitation was more for company than medical expertise. Her spirit still trailed her like a damp shadow most of the time, but she ate well. She slept well for the most part. Sometimes she held Elizabeth on the good days, though out of instinct, I always stayed close by, pretending to be dead-heading the geraniums in the terracotta pots along the terrace, or dusting the shelves for the third time that morning. The way she touched her child remained stilted, as if she were observing herself do so from a distance, but there was no anger now. Some days she even sparkled into bright focus, but those moments were brief; a hopeful candle flame in a draft. Adeline waded through invisible water. Her steps were braced, as if in fear of something unexpected underfoot. I tried to insist upon her wearing slippers, but after receiving her wrath the first few times, the major and I let her do as she pleased. It set me on edge. To my mind, it was only a matter of time before she caught pneumonia.

The major insisted I give the entire villa a deep clean. This was no small task with a toddler intent on dismantling whatever work I did. At last the major saw that Elizabeth was hindering my valiant efforts. On the morning ahead of the doctor's arrival day, the major played with her, often wherever I was. To mark her careening through toddlerhood — she had entered an attached phase. If I was out of her sight for too long, she would swerve around the villa until she found me, wailing her lament as she did so. I didn't love having company while I sweated through the arduous tasks of changing beds, dusting, sweeping, mopping, polishing. Nor could I find a polite way to ask my employer to leave me to work alone, but even I had to admit that hearing the two of them tumble into laughter was a delicious sound.

Sometimes they slid into deep silence, which drew my attention more than the noise. It was a compelling sight, watching the major study his daughter, as she reexamined whatever object had commanded her full concentration; the caulk between the tiles, a doorknob, the shadows cast through the shutters. His face relaxed into a humble elegance, his eyes bright with curious benevolence. He was at ease allowing his child to wade in her wonder. He didn't need to qualify what she saw, label it nor explain it. Their intimate simplicity was magnetic. She crouched down and traced her little finger along the sweeping designs upon the turquoise and yellow painted tiles. The major looked up and caught me wrapped into her quiet alongside him. The light streamed a halo around his copper-blonde hair. In his smile, I caught a glimpse of the playful new father he allowed himself to become. I turned back to the drawers behind me and polished them a second time.

"Adeline and I shall return toward early evening, I should imagine, unless you hear otherwise." The major was doing a fine job of ironing away his nerves. I had tried to suggest he leave Adeline with me, but he would not be convinced. I ought to have known better than to attempt it in the first place. We both knew that it was his way of proving to his friend what a wonderful job he was doing. I wouldn't be convinced that it was the right thing for Adeline however — a long bus journey to Naples was not the best way for her to spend a day. The major insisted it was time to start acclimating her to the outside world. His stubbornness infuriated me, more so because the trip was about his abilities rather than her well-being. In his current frame of mind, there would be no hope of anyone changing his decision. They left before the late August sun began to cook the streets.

Elizabeth and I turned toward the cool silence of the villa. My mind danced through all the things I might have her do while I finished preparations for the guest. Perhaps I'd fill one of the wider tin buckets with water and let her splash about? She loved that. Then we'd make a messy lunch together, visit Marco, stop into Rosalia's house on our return. With any luck, I might be able to finish my tasks.

A knock at the door. My chest tightened.

I didn't feel ready to face Paolino just yet, even if I knew avoiding him was both childish and impossible. I ripped the scarf off my head and ran my fingers through my hair, finding my vanity surprising and disappointing. My hands smoothed my apron. I opened the door.

My father stepped in before I could stop him.

"Well, well, landed on your feet after all, haven't you, Santina?"

Every muscle contracted. Elizabeth ran up to me. I lifted her into my arms before she made her escape out of the door, forcing me to close it.

"*Bella fanciulla!* She yours?"

"Yes. No."

"We will stand here all day? By the door like two corpses?"

My mouth tasted bitter.

"I have work to do," I replied, trying to stay polite, but firm.

"No rest for the wicked as they say. Beggars, choosers. Lots of sayings that mean nothing but we repeat and repeat . . ."

His breath fumed last night's drinking.

I watched him walk to the table and pull out a chair. He sat down, uninvited. I couldn't remove him by force. That much became an obnoxious fact. I scrambled my mind for options. Numb darkness was its feeble reply.

"Come sit with your father, Santi', so much time has gone." He tapped the chair as if I'd just stepped into his home. I didn't move.

"You married yet?" he asked with a stupid smile.

"No."

"No one wants you?"

His words were the mistaken scrape of a razor, lifting the top layer of skin.

"What do you want, Papà?"

He ran his crooked fingers over the stubble on his chin. "What do any of us want?"

"Any minute now my boss is walking through that door. He will take one look at you and drag you by your shirt back onto the street," I lied, hoping my feeble fib would become a self-fulfilling prophecy. Perhaps the bus had broken down? Perhaps Adeline would have an inconsolable panic attack and they were halfway back up the hill already?

"He can try," my father answered with a sneer. "English snobs. Coming here, making their little colony. You should be ashamed of yourself, dribbling behind them like a stray dog. You think they care about you like family? Yes, you live in their palace, walk their gardens, but you're just their servant, you know that, don't you? None of this is yours."

"I don't have any money to give you. That's what you're here for, isn't it? The only one groveling in this house is you!"

213

Another knock at the door reined in my inevitable loss of control. Paolino stood with a huge box in his arms. On top of our usual deliveries lay a bunch of orange, yellow, and pink roses. He took one look at my flushed face and the gnarled man behind me, then walked straight in past me.

"*Buon giorno* — we meet again, Signore," he said, striding over to the table. He placed the box on top of it. His arms folded.

"Flowers for my girl, I see." My father chuckled, flicking a look back at me. My cheeks deepened with fury that he mistook for embarrassment. "So this is the prince, is it? Mr. Grocer Boy? How sweet."

That's when Paolino lunged at him and grabbed his dirty collar. He lifted my father up off his seat. Their struggle scuffed the tiles. Elizabeth burst into tears. She ran toward me. I lunged at the men, leaving her wailing by the open door.

"Stop!" I hollered, prizing them apart. "This is my father, Paolino!"

Paolino loosened his grip. My father shuffled from foot to foot, shaken.

"I want you to leave, Papà," I said.

My father looked up at me, a wounded pup.

"You heard the *signorina*. Get out!" Paolino yelled.

214

"Paolino — please."

I watched him walk toward the door. Paolino flanked me, waiting for my father to go.

"This how you treat the man who raised you?" he hissed, inching toward my face. "You're a stuck-up little bitch. Always were," he whispered. I watched him leave.

My eyes darted around the garden for Elizabeth. I couldn't see her. I called her. No answer. I walked into the kitchen, the dining room, I even ran up to her room. The last time I'd seen her was by the open door.

My feet pelted down the alley. I didn't hear their ricochet. I heard nothing but the heavy thud in my ears. The white panic eclipsed everything else. How far would she have got to by now? Someone would have seen her, stopped her, brought her up to me. But as I reached the bottom of the hill where it met the main road, there was nothing and no one. Where was everyone? I turned facing back uphill, panting with panic. Paolino ran down toward me.

"Santina, relax — how far could she have got to?"

I wanted to stop the fits of sobs. I had to focus. It was impossible. Between the festa, my father's visit, and now losing the child entrusted to me, my resolve broke. I felt his hands wrap around me. I pushed them away. My feet returned to their crazed search. I retraced my steps, her steps. I headed up toward the cemetery. She knew that walk well.

That's when I saw her shoes.

They poked out from a step that led up toward another area of Li Parlati. She had found a nook of shade. I ran to reach her. She looked up with a smile. Her little fingers dismantled a weed that clawed its way up for sun and air between the cobbles. I lifted her and squeezed her into me. A deep cry of relief shuddered through me. I sobbed like a second child, feeling Paolino cradle us. I wish I hadn't murmured apologies. As my senses returned, I could hear the footsteps of our neighbors. I think one or two tried to say hello. I didn't need anyone to see Paolino comfort me.

I could have cried longer. My stomach ached with a familiar grief. Memories of my mother returned and flew around me, tufts of ash from a dying fire, their glowing tips fading fast. We began a weary walk back uphill to the house. We stepped inside and shut the door. Elizabeth grew heavy in my arms. I straightened.

Paolino took my tear-streaked face in his

hands. I hated him seeing me like this. He looked into me. I ought to have been glad for him, but I couldn't shake the feeling he adored his role of savior more than he made me feel comfortable.

"Everything's okay now," he murmured, wiping the tears off my cheek with his thumb. "We found her. He's gone."

"He'll never go. She could have been hurt. Anything . . ."

He kissed my forehead, then lifted my chin up to face him. "Where's the commander?"

I wanted to believe he was trying to joke me out of my soggy mess, but I could hear the prickle of sarcasm even more than usual.

"The major and Adeline are on their way to Naples." I craned my head toward a quiet Elizabeth. Her eyes were half closed now.

"I'll unload the shopping — you lay her down, Santina."

"*Grazie,* Paolino."

By the time I reached her bed upstairs, Elizabeth was deep asleep. She didn't even stir as I laid her down. This was not the morning I had planned for her. I stepped out without a noise.

Hands raced around my waist.

"Relax!" Paolino giggled into my tension. "Who did you think it was?" He leaned into my neck and smothered it with kisses. My spine tingled.

"Don't — not here . . ." I said, my hands pushing him off me.

"Why not?" he whispered in my ear. I felt the tip of his teeth trace along the top of my shoulder. "No one's here. When else can we feel like royals? You want to slink around alleyways all our life?"

I didn't know what overwhelmed me more. His fast hands, the way they traced my thigh under my skirt, or his fast words? What life? Which part of our lives had become inextricably joined? We had kissed. Once. In the shadows of the festa. Now he was intent on playing make-believe in the major's villa. Everything about it felt wrong. His fingers teased my body. The pull I felt was as compulsive as the retreat. My confusion bristled with longing and a fearful emptiness.

I couldn't say what happened first, me pushing his hand away as it reached the heat at the top of my thigh, or the sounds of the lock opening downstairs. All I remember was racing down the stairwell and meeting the major and Adeline as they came in. My hair and clothes looked touched and ruffled. Paolino walked into a guilty spotlight behind me. The major's face was flint. Mine crimson with shame.

"*Buon giorno,* Signore!" Paolino beamed, unruffled. "I just finished unloading the groceries."

"I imagine you did," the major answered without moving.

Paolino looked to me. I hoped my eyes said nothing.

"Well," he began, tiptoeing through the awkward pause, "I'll see you later in the week. *Buona giornata.*"

He nodded at Adeline and the major, resisted looking back at me, and closed the door behind him.

No one spoke.

"Is everything alright, Signore?" I offered, wishing I'd stayed quiet.

"Clearly it's not."

Nothing about this morning was alright.

"Accident on the road to Sorrento," he began tersely, "absolute God-awful chaos on the roads. We were forced to turn back. Shambles. I'll try again in an hour or so. Adeline will remain here — unless you have more pressing duties to attend to, of course?"

I looked at him, expressionless.

"I trust you won't be entertaining *all* of Positano each time I set foot out of my house?"

He walked by me, leading Adeline by the hand. As they passed, I felt the humiliation of his condescension.

My anger wound into a tight ball. I couldn't decide whom I'd launch it at first.

CHAPTER 12

The doctor arrived looking several shades lighter than I remembered. In London I hadn't noticed his pallor, but here he was panna cotta to our caramel. The major, in his customary way of churning events to fall in line with his will, managed not only to get himself to Naples in time for the doctor's boat's arrival but return with the traveler for an early supper. I took Dr. Simmons's bag as they entered. He removed his panama hat and gave a weary wave over his face, reddened by the climb from the main road.

"Good heavens, Henry — you don't mean to tell me you walk them every day? I'm not sure that's a terribly wise thing to do."

"No. Double. Before the crowds and sun, obviously. You'll join me in the water tomorrow morning, James, whether you want to or not."

Dr. Simmons simpered a laugh. "Pleasure to see you again, Santina," he said, "what a beautiful place to call home."

I replied with a polite welcome.

The doctor stepped in onto the lower terrace that stretched out from the main doors and ran along the entire width of the house. He passed me, gawked at the overhead vines gnarling a ceiling. He ran a hand over my huge begonia plants twisting their stems up from the tall terra-cotta pots. I watched him nosey down the antique well at the center of this terrace, then look out, as everyone was compelled to do, toward the ocean. He breathed in the late afternoon glow, looking out toward the golden-tipped snaking cliffs. His face ebbed from London vanilla toward a hint of color.

"Well, Henry, you might have found somewhere a little nicer than this squalor for your wife."

The men smiled at one another.

"Do you spend entire days sat looking at this view?"

"I avoid it wherever possible," the major answered, looking relaxed for the first time today. It struck me that the major hadn't been in the company of a true friend for so very long. I knew he had maintained regular correspondence — I was sent to the post office most mornings with a stack of envelopes, but was that enough? My mind floated to our dawn rituals, the silence of our gardening, the quiet pleasure of our midmorning reading or cooking. A thought nagged for attention; had our working relationship smudged toward friendship? I flicked away the banality of the idea like a stray crumb from the table.

"James, you must be absolutely ravenous?" the major asked his friend.

"Thirsty perhaps, yes. Some light refreshments would be welcome."

The major turned to me.

"I'll take the doctor's case upstairs and bring some prosecco?" I suggested. "Would the major enjoy a *spaghettata*? Something light?"

"As always, Santina, you read my mind like an open book. I'll never convince anyone I am a quiet man of great depths at this rate."

The doctor chuckled. "Your friends gave that up some time ago."

I left the two men upon the canvas deck chairs in the garden beyond the terrace, under the fragrant shade of our lemon trees.

The smell hit me before I reached the upper landing; a putrid smack. I stood the doctor's case just inside the doorway of the guest room and edged along the corridor. I knocked on Adeline's door.

"Get away from me!" she yelled, a coarse growl from behind the heavy door.

"It's only me, Santina."

"Stay away!"

I stood in the stench for a moment. Whatever was happening the other side of this door needed immediate attention, but I was loath to pierce the peaceful bubble the major floated in with his friend two floors down at the far end of the garden.

"I'm going to open the door a little now, madam," I said, trying to sound firm yet calm.

Silence.

My heart thumped.

I eased Adeline's door open a little. The air thickened with the odor. My fingers crept around the door. I poked one eye around the edge. That's when I saw her. She sat curled into a naked ball. Her back was toward me, the bones of her spine poking through her skin, across her buttocks the smudge of excrement. She didn't hear me creep in. Didn't see me look back toward the wall by her bed. Across the painted plaster, waste smeared the floral designs. I turned toward her again. Her shoe narrowly missed my head as I did so.

"I said get out!" she spat, lunging in my direction.

I slammed the door shut. Then turned the key for good measure.

My feet percussed the stone steps, tapping under the trip of my thoughts. Could I keep this incident from the major? I reached the men, saving the clinking glasses of prosecco from destruction several times before I did so. My flushed face gave away more than I wanted to.

"Santina, whatever is the matter? You look like you've seen a ghost!" The major knew me better than I'd like to admit. "Is Elizabeth alright?"

I placed the tray down upon the small wooden table between the chairs and straightened, a talking plank.

"Yes," I answered.

The major stood up. "What's the matter?"

"It's Adeline, sir."

Now the doctor stood too. He didn't wait for the major to take the lead. When he reached the bottom of the stairwell he had already rolled up his sleeves, someone who lived on the precipice of attending to emergency situations as a matter of everyday occurrence. I didn't have a chance to explain before they stormed into her room and were enveloped by the awful sight. I stepped inside, after filling a bucket of water in the bathroom and grabbing the rags I used to clean the floor.

I didn't dare look at the major. It would break my heart to see him defeated. In his friend's first hour inside their sanctuary, the major's upheld reality frayed. The major went to Adeline, took a sheet from her bed and wrapped it around her. He sent me to draw a bath. The doctor rummaged through the medicine cabinet.

"Where do you keep the belladonna, Henry?"

"It's quite alright, James, we'll clean her first."

"Nonsense. Are the vials of Valium ready? That will sedate immediately."

"I'm perfectly capable of handling this!" the major snapped, louder than I think he'd planned.

Elizabeth ran in. She heard her father shout and she burst into tears. Adeline looked at the major and began to roar, wordless, guttural. The doctor stepped in and gripped her from behind. "Don't just stand there, Henry! Administer!"

I picked up Elizabeth and shut the door. Her sobs shuddered down my shoulder as I walked back to her room, her mother railing at the men, all the while the frustrated rumble of their voices echoing down the stairwell.

I waited with Elizabeth till she had returned to deep play. I made sure the wooden gate the major had made was secured, preventing her from entering onto the terrace, or out of the room. Then I returned to the upstairs bedroom. I opened the door. The eerie quiet prickled with tension.

Adeline was upon her bed now.

"I will see to Adeline," the major said to me, dipping some washcloths into her ceramic washbasin.

"I will take care of the walls," I said, pretending I didn't hope one of the men would volunteer. Neither did.

"Why don't you take the bath, James? Freshen up." The major couched it as a question, but we all knew the doctor was not being given a choice.

"If you're sure, Henry?"

"Quite sure."

The doctor left.

The major and I worked in silence. I opened the doors. Wide shafts of golden evening sun glossed the once darkened room. In my periphery, I could sense the tender strokes of the major over his wife's body as he cleaned her while she lay, collapsed into a Valium-induced sleep. Like a widower washing his deceased spouse.

After the disinfectant dried, I dropped the

rag into the bucket and removed my thick rubber gloves. The major remained next to Adeline. He sat motionless, save for the gentle rise and fall of his wide back. The light from the sea caught the side of his face as he looked down at her. I watched his private moment of reflection. There was no hint of resistance in his expression, nor surrender to hopelessness. His hand moved round to his wife's side by her lower ribs, as if he checked for her breathing. I watched his fingers smooth small circles across her abdomen. He wasn't searching for his wife, nor pining for what was. Try as I might, my eyes could not look away. That he hovered nowhere but in the present moment compelled me.

When we were together he would often search his memory for a poem, something that had happened to him in order to prescribe some life, or grammatical lesson. But now, he was consumed only in the physical task at hand, no more. Much like our care of the garden, or Elizabeth, both jobs required a piqued focus on the shifting present.

Where was I now? Spying on a man who loved his wife deeply. I wasn't here with them. I was prying. I watched his fingers. What was unspoken in that quiet space between a man and wife? How did it feel to caress the memory of the person he'd moved to Positano for? To hold on to the hope of his wife returning? Damaged but healed, fuller maybe in spite of, or because of, her fragile mental health. The love he described to me came floating back to memory. The way his face had softened in the morning light as he relived the first blush of love for Adeline, the dart that burned into his heart with speed. In the simple movement of his fingers, soft circles over her nightdress, I saw that unswerving devotion. It was ardent yet gentle. I thought about Paolino's clumsy kiss just outside of this door only a few days ago. That icy feeling of being conquered surfaced again. I didn't want to be fondled in deserted doorways. I wanted this adoration. I wanted to be loved like the man before me loved his wife. I tried to picture Paolino nursing me like that. The pictures were a watery reflection upon a moving sea, warped, fleeting, skewed. The major's fingers slowed down. They ceased their dance.

That's when he sensed me behind him.

Our eyes met.

I froze. Embarrassment pulsed through my veins. His sad glint gave way to something I couldn't read. Neither of us spoke.

The doctor opened the door. He caught my gaze first and then faced the major. It looked like he had interrupted something; a second person had discovered me spying on my employers. My cheeks burned a deeper red.

I grabbed the bucket and rags and fled for the silence of my kitchen.

I lit several oil lamps placed on top of the balustrade for the men's dinner. By the time they were ready to eat, the night was deep purple. The air was still. From the kitchen I could hear their conversation.

"Henry, we both know what the right thing to do is."

"Do we?"

"Who are you keeping her here for? Her daughter? For her? It's for you, Henry. You're torturing yourself. You're blaming yourself for what happened, aren't you? This is some complicated plan to exhume your guilt. But this is no one's fault, Henry. Postpartum psychosis is beyond our control. And the medical profession knows that some women simply do not recover. Why do you punish yourself like this?"

"What punishment, James? I don't believe in retribution, or contrition, or whatever man-made construct you want to throw at me."

Their talk fell silent. I saw it as the opportunity to take their plates. I had planned to offer a very light dinner, but after our start to the early evening I thought we all deserved some comfort. I worked through the adrenaline with two handfuls of cherry tomatoes, toasted walnuts, and a couple of plump garlic cloves, which I pounded with my marble pestle along with some capers, a glug of olive oil, a fist of chives, and one slim chili. I forked some salted anchovies into the mix, a pinch of fine sugar, and the zest and juice of a lemon. I let the salty citrus lift my mood, comforted by the savory earthiness of the garlic and determined kick of chili. It was a pesto of balance. Something we all needed a dose of. When the linguine was cooked, I drained it and forked the other ingredients around it, coating each strand with the savory mix. I placed the plates before them. The men breathed in the promising aroma. Their shoulders relaxed. Their expressions softened.

"As I was saying, James, what punishment?"

The doctor shook his head with a smile. "One woman elicits your heroics, the other services your corporeal needs. All under one roof. What punishment indeed!"

"Santina is a marvelous cook," the major said, flinty. He didn't look at me. I could feel his affront at the doctor's remarks, which puzzled me. Together, the major and I had shown his friend that between us we could cope with Adeline, that neither of us longed for the household to run any other way. The doctor could see I intuited what all the members of this house needed at any given time. He may not have said it in so many words. He didn't need to. I could see it in his eyes. But the way the major picked up his cutlery told me he was not best pleased; with me? With Adeline? With his friend? The afternoon's events hovered over him like a tiny gray cloud of failure. I was dismissed without a thank-you.

We ate, the gentlemen upon their terrace, me at my kitchen table. All sat facing the same azure water, but our minds floating on different currents.

That Sunday morning I expected to forfeit my day off, in view of the company, but the major would hear none of it. I stayed on a little while longer, despite his insistence, even when Rosalia's cousin arrived to take over for the day. The men departed for an

232

early swim. I oversaw breakfast, rising before dawn to make sure the lemon cake was baked in time for their return, and that the small rolls I'd left would be still warm. I came back to the table with a second coffeepot. The doctor looked up at me, his hair still wet, his cheeks rosy with summertime. "Santina, you are a goddess. I'm sure this misery never tells you that!"

The major gave an operatic sigh.

"But you have to know you are," the doctor persisted, despite the major's resistance. "This is the best breakfast I have ever eaten. It is baked with love. The view is to die for. And the panorama isn't half bad either."

"That will be all, Santina, thank you."

I returned to the kitchen, catching their bickering through the open doors.

"Good heavens, James, what on earth do you think you're playing at? She's not an imbecile."

"Really? Happy to work for one though."

"The sea air's got to you."

The doctor let out a breathy cackle. "Is that what they call it down here, Henry, old chap? Carry on — you've almost convinced yourself."

In that moment I knew I couldn't stay in the house to listen to their banter. I hung my apron upon the back of one of the chairs and let Rosalia's cousin finish clearing up. I packed a bag for the beach. I needed to be in the water today. The doctor's voice caught me off guard as I reached the main door. I had thought he had retired to one of the upper terraces.

"You always this jumpy in your own home, Santina?"

I had several answers, some more polite than others. None of them left my mouth.

"Off for a swim yourself?"

I nodded.

"Ought to have come with us! You could have translated what all the fish were talking about."

I held my breath, waiting for the awkward silence to dissipate.

"It's a ridiculous joke, Santina. Designed to stop you being afraid of me."

I offered a feeble smile.

"It's obvious I've put Henry under a little strain. He feels watched, I suppose."

Then he watched me wait for him to continue. Or finish.

"Really, I'm trying — in a very pathetic way — to say how wonderful a help I think you are. And it doesn't harm that your eyes are alive with a delectable energy to boot."

He cocked his head to one side a little as he closed with a smile. I wanted to mirror him, but the hairs on the back of my neck bristled.

I slipped outside.

The beach wasn't awake yet. I was glad. I didn't want to wade into the shallows with the throng of scantily clad bodies. The sharp black stones poked at my soles as I tiptoed in. Then the emerald cool rose up around me. My breath snatched for a moment. I dipped my whole body down into the water, washing away all the prickles from yesterday afternoon and this morning. Nowhere else in my town could I feel invisible. I bobbed up for air once again. I didn't realize quite how far I'd swum. I treaded the water between my feet, delighting in my thoughtlessness. I'd been cleansed of my week. The more difficult memories of the past few days washed away; my father, the major discovering Paolino and I alone in the house, Adeline's outburst. Out here, lifted by the gentle pull of the waves, nothing mattered. Not even my American life, still hovering over the other side of my sea.

A voice called for me from the shore. It ripped me out of my floating emptiness.

I squinted against the light. It was Marco. I swam to shore, feeling like my anchor had just dropped and I was being reeled in. How had he recognized me out here? What on earth was he doing at the beach at this hour?

"You always half naked on a Sunday morning these days?" he said as he wobbled along the piercing stones. He threw me my towel.

"I've decided that I should be, yes, as a matter of fact," I replied.

"Why you acting like them all of a sudden?"

"Good morning, Santina, how are you, my sister, may I buy you a coffee? Any of those seem like a nicer way to greet me on my day off?" I shook my hair, splashing him with the tips.

At last, a laugh.

"I've never seen you in town on a Sunday. What you up to?" I asked.

"Meeting some friends."

He shifted his gaze to sea. The reflection crisscrossed his eyes. I read something sharp. He pulled down his sunglasses as I did so. My own warbled reflection bent toward me.

"You okay?" I asked. "You seem —"

"Hungry?" he interrupted. "I'm starving."

". . . on edge."

"That's what happens when your sister doesn't visit you with her delicious picnics."

"We've got guests. It's been difficult."

"He pay you extra?"

I slipped on my toweling dress and hooked my arm in his. I never knew how to talk to someone if they were hungry. Growing up not knowing where our next meal would come from had ingrained this obsession from an early age.

We reached Pasquale's bakery near the *mulino,* where all the grain was ground. He and Rosalia were on the precipice of a delicate romance. At least that's what I could intimate through the ornate descriptions of his every look and smile shot in her direction. I couldn't shake the sense that Rosalia's plans were already formed in full and wondered if he had been party to them yet. When I did catch them together though, I loved the glow that cast over his face, rendering it even more relaxed and charming than it already was.

His bakery was simple, painted plain white, with one long glass counter. This morning it was loaded with tempting rows of *pasticerrie* ready for the Sunday feasts. Marco insisted on paying for several *sfogliatelle,* crispy, scaled pastries filled with lemon crème, others with the same pastry but named mini lobster tails, because of their shape, with toasted hazelnut crème. He wouldn't listen to me when I said that was plenty, rather insisted Pasquale sell us two slices of *torta della nonna* for good measure, a thin, short crust pastry cake filled with a thick layer of custard and chocolate.

"On the house, Santi'," Pasquale said when Marco tried to pay.

"Nonsense, Pasquale, please take something."

"Rosalia talks of nothing but you and the house you work in and the food you cook — and the cakes! I don't want any competition, you hear me?"

He placed our sweets upon a card plate and then wrapped paper around them with string.

"Buona domenica!" He smiled as he handed them over to me.

At that moment the beads of the doorway curtain flung out in all directions. Pasquale's sister flew through them. Her face was white. She yelled out.

He raced out from behind the counter. "What's the matter, Angelina?"

"You have to come quickly," she replied, panting, "It's Rosalia's brother. They found him by the docks in Sorrento. They —"

She couldn't get the words out. Her body shook.

Pasquale pulled off his apron. A colleague came out from the back. He signaled to

Pasquale that he was fine to go. I watched him fly back out through the beads after his sister. I followed them, but they were racing away uphill. Marco stepped out behind me. Several other customers followed the commotion. I turned to a lady beside me on the pavement. She squinted at me in the white sun. "I just heard about it — terrible business."

"What is?" I asked, feeling my chest tighten.

"That boy from Li Parlati. Someone told me they found him by the ships." An arthritic finger lifted to her throat and mimed a knife swiping across it.

I don't remember hearing anything after that, not the sound of the pastries falling to the floor, Marco yelling for me to slow down, the whispers along the alleys as the news spread across our town. I will never forget the look on my best friend's face as I reached her house. The way she gripped me, the tremor of her tears. The weight of her as her legs resisted their load.

My heart broke.

The home I'd known full of laughter suffocated with the echoes of despair.

CHAPTER 13

The sun dipped toward the horizon, as Marco led me out of the Rispoli house. We left tears behind us as a second wave of visitors flowed in, loaded with food and murmured prayers. He hooked his arm in mine and shuffled downhill in silence. I drew to a stop outside the front door of the villa. That's when my own sobs tore through me. I had spent the best part of the day being a buffer for my friend, letting her cries and those of her family crash against me with the stillness of our Positanese rocks. I was strong and calm for them. Now, in the quiet dusk, I allowed my grip to loosen. Marco held me tight. I must have made more noise than I'd planned because Rosalia's cousin opened the door to see what was beyond. I reached for her hands. "*Oje nè,* go straight home. I'm so very sorry." I took a breath to tell her but the words caught at the back of my throat.

"It's your cousin, Segnurina," Marco began, "we don't want to be the bearers of bad news."

"Whatever's going on here?" the major asked, stepping in behind the young girl.

Her eyes darted between the three of us, confusion streaking toward dread. I looked up at the major, eager to restore my calm, but in vain. The more I tried to speak the harder the tears thwarted my efforts to a soggy mess.

"Good heavens, come on inside, Santina." He reached a hand out to Marco. "My name is Henry, Santina works for me. You are?"

"Marco," he answered, *fratello di Santina.*"

"*Fratello?* Oh — brother — I see," he answered. It puzzled me to hear the twinge of surprise in his voice. My life was compartmentalized. It never occurred to share anything of my past with the major. I kept it hidden. It seemed ridiculous all of a sudden, impolite, even. I heard people shuffle around me, Rosalia's cousin leaving, Marco sitting down beside me. A glass was placed on the table in front of us. I looked up. The major placed a second glass for Marco.

"Now," he soothed, "you are to tell me who has done you wrong. Something terrible has happened, that much is obvious.

241

Do I need to call the police?"

I shook my head. Concern grayed the major's face. He looked at me, his eyes warm but prying; a lawyer delving in for the facts with polite tenacity.

"No, Signore, nothing like that. I'm so sorry. I feel so stupid making all this fuss. I am fine. It's Rosalia's brother. He —" The words swirled into sludge in my stomach. The major looked to Marco, then to me, impatient for an answer, for reassurance. Marco struggled through a mumbled explanation in Neapolitan. Off the major's frown, he ran a finger across his throat, coming to my rescue.

"Murdered?" the major said, his voice a whisper.

"Down by the docks in Napoli," I began, "he was involved with the wrong crowd. Or, his crowd upset another. Something like that. It's a tragedy. None of us knew."

Then the sobs exploded once again. Marco wrapped me in his arms. The major moved around to my side of the table and squatted down next to me. Marco relinquished his grip. My hand was in the major's. I didn't follow his words. I couldn't hear anything beyond the pulsating in my ears, feeling a great urge to pull my hand out of his. His skin was cool to the touch, his hand wider than I thought. Mine was couched inside his like a child's. I wanted this cradle to soothe, even though I craved to be quite alone all of a sudden. His touch steered me to shore.

"That's it, Santina. Just breathe. I'm so very sorry, my dear." He smoothed a stray hair from my face. I felt the tip of his finger trace my cheek.

"*Grazie,* Signore," Marco interjected.

The major stood.

"*Grazie* to you, Marco — please, you may stay as long as you need."

His arms were pantomiming where he lacked Italian. Marco followed his exaggerated gestures.

"Good God, Henry, you're not doing that awful thing of speaking loudly to foreigners in the hopes they'll understand, are you?" The doctor swung around the doorway, the ice in his glass clinking the gin from side to side.

We all turned.

"James, something dreadful has just happened," the major replied.

"I can see. Your acting is atrocious."

I watched the major suck in some air and lengthen, choosing not to return the retort. The doctor saw me. He took a quiet step forward.

243

"Santina — please tell your brother he is welcome to stay."

"Thank you, Signore," I replied, turning to my brother. "*Per piacere,* Marco, eat with me, I'll make us some supper."

"I don't know, Santina," he replied, shifting his gaze over the terrace, as if he were trespassing all of a sudden.

"It's fine, Marco, the major never says anything he doesn't mean — of that you can be sure."

"Only for a little while then."

I led him down to the kitchen. He sat, silent, as I brought a small pan of broth to a simmer, threw in a fistful of *pastina* and some fresh cut carrots and celery.

"Are you alright, Marco?" I asked, without turning to him.

"*Sì.*"

"You're so quiet all of a sudden — can I help?"

"No."

I watched the *pastina* float in the liquid. The image of Rosalia's tears stung my mind. I wondered who was comforting her now? We ate the soup on the lower terrace. Marco kept his head down, as if someone might steal his bowl.

"I'd like to see your home one day, Marco."

"No you wouldn't."

I let his refusal hang in the steam from our bowls. He caught me staring at him. He let his spoon drop to the rim. "Why are you looking at me like that? My God, you're acting like I just cursed our mother!"

My eyebrows raised.

"Well, aren't you?" he asked without waiting for me to answer. "You want to see the pigsty I live in? Compared to the palace you serve in? Want to compare how well you're doing to me, is that it? Go ahead, big sister. Show me how it's done. Your poor little brother, raking around the dead."

"Marco, I didn't mean —"

"I think you did. I *know* you did." He gave an angry swirl around the cooling broth. "I live with two other men. It's a hovel." I wondered if he was making slurping noises just to irritate me. "Feel better now?"

I let my spoon drop into the liquid, watching the handle slide down the rim and shift under the floating cubes of carrots, my appetite disappearing with it.

"It's late. I'm going to go." He stood up and pushed his chair under the table. "You know where to find me." He reached the doorway and turned back to me. "*Grazie* for dinner."

There wasn't time for me to answer before

he disappeared. When I reached the terrace, he had already let himself out of the front door. I stood there for a moment, a puppy waiting for its owner. Then I shuffled back to the kitchen to clear.

The major stepped in. He took a seat.

"May I get something for you, Signore?" I asked without taking my eyes off the task at hand.

"No, that's quite alright, Santina. I just wanted to make sure you were feeling better."

I wiped my hands on the dishcloth and turned to him. "I'm alright," I said, hoping the words would take me there.

He replied with an unhurried smile. "Actually that's not what I wanted to say. Preposterous thing to say really. Utterly British. I know you're not all *right*. I suppose I want to check that you're able to not be alright, without panicking. Being able to *not* be alright is a rather wonderful lifelong skill. Everyone is very fearful of fear, of grief. These atrocities are tragic. Yet so very human."

His eyes met mine. His collar was open. His hair wasn't his typical neat sweep off his face, but tousled, the red streaks deeper amber than usual.

"What I'm saying, in the most clumsy

fashion possible, is, even in the most painful scenario, there is perfection. All is as it should be." He sighed a snap of laughter with a shake of his head. "Yes, from your expression I can tell it sounded far better in my head than out."

I laughed. My eyes felt puffy and sore.

"Don't be scared of breaking, Santina."

He looked into me. The words were paternal, but his expression pinned me to stillness. I felt bare; an electric thread of liberation and terror splintered up my spine. He could see I felt broken. He filled in the cracks with mercurial words, soldering the gaps with his gaze.

"Don't stay up too late, will you," he said at last, jumping to his feet. When he reached the door he spun round. "Santina — have you ever been to Pompeii?"

The absurdity of the leap in conversation made me frown before I could control it. He chuckled, noticing the fact. "James and I are taking Adeline to the hospital a little farther up the coast from Sorrento, for some treatment. She'll be staying there for a few weeks."

He must have read my response despite my silence.

"I know," he continued. "I'm working hard on believing it myself. He's reassured me in the way only he knows how. If we reach it tomorrow and it's a horrendous prison, we shall turn around and return home directly. *With* my wife."

His face creased into a question. I could sense his struggle; he longed for some kind words from me, a nugget of reassurance, yet at the same time he knew he'd edged over the boundary of my duties. Then he performed a deft turnaround, like he always did when he spoke to me as a friend. "I have a good sense of how you're feeling right now, Santina. I hope you allow yourself to let those sensations permeate you. Don't shut them off. If it's something Adeline taught me, it was how to feel, so very deeply. Pain and pleasure make you feel the terror and joy of life."

He coughed, clearing away the thought.

"A change of scenery might do you a world of good? No, that's altruistic posturing — the change of scenery will do *me* a world of good." He looked at me, expectant. "I would love to share it with you."

Another pause.

He stepped in before I could answer. "If you'd like to. You may find ancient history dull. And I would judge you heavily on that, of course."

We both laughed then.

"Elizabeth?" I asked, steering us back to reality with reluctance.

He shifted. "I'd already made arrangements for one of our neighbors' help to cover for a few days." He cleared his throat again. If I didn't know better, I would have said he looked nervous. "Of course, you could take those days for yourself, I suppose — good heavens, I'm taking a liberty rather. Truth is, I'm dreading this hospital and I need to make the trip less torturous. I need to be peaceful for Adeline. Perhaps if I led us on a little stroll through antiquity, showed you the place that made me fall in love with this part of Italy, it would eclipse the abandonment of my wife — for a day at least."

He looked at me. I didn't feel like his housekeeper. He smoothed our bristling nerves with a tilt of his head. The expression that cast across him was elegant resignation. I admired him for standing in the awkward silence, acknowledging what he was feeling without expecting anything in return.

"I'm babbling," he decided at last, shaking his head with a sigh, "I haven't really thought this through."

"I would love to come," I answered, stopping him from unraveling another sentence.

He lit up. Then gave a stiff nod back to composure and left without a word. I turned to the sink.

"We'll be leaving just before dawn!" he said, with a sudden pop through the doorway that almost made me let go of the bowl in hand. I caught it before it slipped onto the tiles.

"I'll be ready," I said, my face widening into a smile I hoped he wouldn't mistake for mockery.

"Yes."

I watched him take a breath to speak. His eyes were smiling too. No words surfaced.

He turned and left.

The awkward bubble burst as he did.

We left the house at dawn. I packed Adeline's bag, the doctor packed all her medications. The major ran a warm bath for her. I lingered by the closed door, holding her large leather travel case. I hoped his singing soothed Adeline as much as it did me. An old English ditty, he'd called it when he had taught it to me some weeks ago. A funny word, I had decided; a staccato sound, a falling stone tapping on the cobbles. The rhythm indeed was cheery enough, but the words were thorny. The song reminded me of my own folk songs. I didn't know too many love songs from our hills that swam a merry stream of melody without some dissonance, some surprise dip into a sonorous key. Perhaps the hot blood of the Amalfitani wasn't so far from the temperate British after all. Our melodies had the power to filter through a soul's true sentiments far better than words alone.

Giuseppe met us at the bottom of the hill. Pasquale's brother had been hired as a driver for the day, something he seemed all too happy about.

"*Buon giorno,* Santina — lady for the day, I see!"

Off my glare, he changed tack. "So sorry to hear about the Rispoli boy."

"We all are," I replied, taking my place beside Adeline, between the major and I on the backseat.

As we curved out of Positano, the major slipped his hand into Adeline's. I tried to tune into her energy beneath the alabaster countenance. Her pools of blue looked darker in the suffused light. Gone were the dancing eyes that had bewitched me in London. I glanced down at her hand. Perhaps one day she might paint again. Perhaps this short sojourn would bring her back after all. I looked over to her other hand. The major ran tiny circles around her

251

wrist. The beautiful simplicity of the movement expressed more than any brash demonstration of romance. I thought about Paolino singing to me across the room at the party. How different this love beside me was. And here, a man willing to sacrifice his idea of what would be best for his wife for her sake alone. I knew the next few weeks would be tougher for him than he would like to admit.

The sanatorium just north of Castellammare di Stabia reminded me of the monasteries from the countryside where my mother grew up, farther south along the coast. It was a small building, modest in design with thin smooth columns lining the portico across the main entrance. The major led Adeline out of the car, hooking his arm in hers.

"Do come with us, Santina, you may be of assistance should we need it," the major said, turning back to me.

I followed them and the doctor into the dark cool inside.

A starched nurse welcomed us. A long corridor ran from the center of the entryway. Where we stood, we could see it faced onto a courtyard garden. At its center there were several raised beds with vegetables and, around, a spray of flowers. This was nothing like the stories I'd heard about the hospitals in Naples. I could see relief wash over the major's face too.

The doctor strung together a few phrases and a male doctor appeared, greeting him like a friend.

"Henry, this is Dr. Giacomo, the gentleman who I've been writing to. He studied for a while in England, you remember me mentioning him, don't you?"

"Of course."

"Please," said Dr. Giacomo, "I can lead you to Adeline's room. We don't advise you stay too long. It can be very upsetting for our patients, I'm sure you'll understand."

"Yes," the major said, disguising the emotions I could see racing in his eyes.

The doctor and I watched the figures of Henry and Adeline disappear down a corridor off the main strip.

"I should think we ought to offer them some privacy, don't you, Santina?" the doctor said, turning toward me.

"Yes."

We strolled back toward a bench just beyond the entrance.

"It's a beautiful place, Doctor."

"Yes," he replied, lifting his trousers and taking a seat on the bench, signaling for me to join him. "Henry wouldn't believe me of course. He loves Adeline more than I could ever imagine. He adores assembling a fierce exterior, but my friend has a molten center. Always has done. Even from when we were children. That's what all the girls found so dreadfully compelling. Never mustered that veneer myself." He shook his head with a boyish smile. "What you see is very much what you get."

He watched me smile.

"And you are a light, Santina. Thank heavens for you. I am all too aware that your town affords the kind of beauty I can only dream of living in, but even the panorama of your sea can lift the spirits only so much. Henry misses his wife."

"I know. I see it. In lots of ways."

"If he didn't have someone like you, a beautiful young lass with a spring in her step and intelligence beaming out of her, I know his life here would be a very different experience."

I felt my cheeks redden.

"I speak out of turn. I always do. I don't care. I've seen enough people die to know that life is horrendously short. I can't waste any more time not saying what I feel when I feel it. If my father taught me nothing else, it was not to live anything like he did."

"Yes. My father too, I mean."

He flashed me a warm smile and lifted himself off the bench.

"I'll take my bag from the car now. Dr. Giacomo and I will run through the plan for the next few weeks, and he's arranged transport for me to the port in Naples."

He reached out a hand. I put mine in his. He shook it.

"Thank you, Santina. Keep up the good work, won't you? Several people's lives depend on it. More than you'll ever know."

The major reappeared in the doorway. He looked tired but hopeful. I left the men to their goodbyes in private. Inside the car, Gennaro met my eye in the mirror.

"Finally locked her up, eh?"

"It's not a prison, Genna'."

"She coming out anytime soon?"

"Two weeks."

"I don't know, Santina, from what Paolino tells me, there's not much hope of a full recovery from that one."

"You always believe what other people tell you?"

Giuseppe's eyebrows lifted, then dropped into a cheeky grin.

"You sound like I'm talking about your family, not your employers," he goaded.

I didn't reply. He was angling for more idle gossip. I wish I had known the major

255

had asked him to do the job, I could have done my best to dissuade him. The major returned to the car at last. I watched the doctor disappear behind a billow of dust as we pulled away.

My feet crunched on the gravel at the entrance to Pompeii. I squinted in the light.

"Thank you, Giuseppe," the major said, "see you in the early afternoon."

The major swung his bag over his shoulder, his face alive with anticipation; a young boy waiting to show off his toys. He bought our tickets and then launched through the entrance at his usual pace, taking long strides uphill along the opening *via*. He turned back. I struggled to keep up.

"Forgive me, Santina!" he called down to me, waiting for me to reach him. "How horribly selfish. I think I'll pretend it's my first time too. Let us savor every step, yes?"

His face was golden in the start of the full morning sun, catching the blond in his red hair. The huge stones underfoot led us uphill past ruined homes either side of us. There were tourists around me, the sound of cameras clicking for posterity, but I couldn't hear them. I was dipped into the eerie silence of the stones, the quiet fortitude of them all, standing despite the terror that had shook this spot. We arrived at an area the major explained was the Forum. We walked to its center, the purple hump of Vesuvius smoking in the near distance. The columns rose high, supporting invisible coffers. It wasn't hard to imagine this place a throng of activity at the center of Roman life.

I didn't feel the major beside me until he spoke.

"Words fall short of describing this feeling, don't they, Santina?"

I nodded.

"There's much more. Follow me."

We floated through another several hundred years of history and palatial ruins. I stood before mosaics I'd only ever heard about. I etched their tiny golden squares to memory, the pools at the center of the courtyard homes, the way the place upheld a dignified silence despite the clatter of people. My mind flashed with pictures of these streets filled with people. At every turn, the major reveled in describing life as it once would have been. He drew pictures in the air with his words. He breathed life into these relics, so much so that I felt I could almost hear the chariots charging down the streets, or the roar of the crowds as the senate met.

When we reached the first, smaller theater, we took a seat and the major reached into his bag. He handed me an apple. I accepted, feeling rather stupid for not having prepared it myself. The major had insisted there was to be no need for me to do so, each of the three times I'd asked him what I ought to pack. We sat, chomping in antiquity for a moment.

"What play shall we watch?"

I looked at him. He returned the gaze with an inkling of a smile.

"Well, Santina? Some awful tragedy perhaps? Pierced with war and betrayal? Or a tragic love story? Two lovers who cannot be together, and, ignoring the advice of their parents, surrender to their undying love with dire consequences."

I laughed.

"Both!" I replied. "We can stay all day."

"Perfect."

He took another bite. His eyes landed on tourists as the steady stream rolled through, a hover of wonder in their chatter.

"What do you make of all this beauty?" he asked, before taking another bite.

"I need more words. I can't draw it like you."

"Don't try to do that. I want to hear how you feel. How you see it."

I took a breath. All nerves or insecurity of seeming stupid dissipated looking at his open expression. He made me feel like he had a genuine interest in what I was thinking. He wasn't setting a trap. This wasn't a test.

"It's a spell," I said, at last.

He didn't comment. He opened the space, urging me into it.

"That's the word, I think," I began, "as soon as we stepped in, I felt swept up in it. Like in church when everyone is singing and the sound is above you and around you and inside you. Like that."

He didn't move his eyes from mine. I could see the reflection of the white stones beneath us in them. He didn't comment. He held the quiet for me with silent encouragement.

"But there is sadness too. I feel it so very strongly," I added.

"I do too."

Our gaze returned to the stage down below.

"Tragedy left us these treasures," he said, in his Adeline voice, the one he used to usher her back into herself at the ebb of one of her fits. It was a silken scarf caressing my face.

I let his words hang, noticing how comfortable I felt resisting the need for an immediate reply. For all the beauty of his words, his stories, his pictures of this place's past, the graphic descriptions of what it must have been like for those poor souls trapped in the volcano's eruption, the most golden gift the major offered was silence. I couldn't remember a comfortable silence before him. He had couched his offer of teaching me the language as a bargaining tool for my staying with the family, but the longer I lived with him the more I came round to the idea that he was driven by a love of sharing his world. He was not fulfilling a promise alone. Today, I felt my perception was important to him. It was an art, his skill of crafting a space between us for me to stretch myself, to widen my ideas, share my feelings. I admired this gentle skill. However easy it might appear, I knew it took a great deal of selflessness, and a genuine desire to understand another, rather than projecting his ideas alone. I was not a blank canvas. He forged a space in which I was doing the painting. Not with the frantic passion of Adeline, but with my words and their colors.

"You can read history, Santina. You can list facts. You can learn from them, of course. But if you can *stand* in it, if you can let it trace through you without judgment, without analysis, just let the atmosphere course through you fully, then you are absorbing it. Much like a recipe, no?"

"A recipe?"

"Certainly! You and I could follow the same recipe and your dish will still taste different from mine."

"You think so?"

"Absolutely. Your recipe is *inside* you. You've *lived* it, tinkered with it, intuited the precise moment to stir, or not, to lower the heat, or intensify it. My approach would be academic. I would be following instructions. But I would need to surrender to the process physically in order to tune in."

He took in my unconvinced reaction.

"It's a challenge!" he exclaimed.

My eyebrows creased. How had we arrived at food when we were here to absorb history?

"You will write me a recipe. I will cook it. You will cook it. Then we will compare and I can expatiate."

"Ex . . . ?"

"A long word designed to make you admire my command of the language. An arrogant slip. And a good word: expatiate, to extemporate, elucidate, expand . . . much like my waistline if I were to eat as much as

I wanted to of your food."

He wiped a bead of sweat from his brow. All color left his cheeks, his skin at once a sudden, papery gray.

"Are you alright?"

"What's that, Santina?"

He shook his head, as if flicking off the dizzy spell.

"Yes, quite alright," he replied, his rhythm staggered. "I think the heat's getting to this Brit after all. Come on, we'll find some shade farther on. I know a beautiful spot for some refreshments."

He stood up. I followed and lost my footing. He took my hand in his. It felt colder than I'd expected. I found my balance. He let go.

We carried on past an enormous statue of a naked man at a central courtyard.

"The human form, in the hands of an artist, holds up the mirror and blurs our sight toward unattainable perfection. Such a dangerous condition."

"Why dangerous?" I asked, trying not to sound too out of breath as we climbed the steep steps along the walkway that led the crowds toward the gardens of Diana.

"It is an unattainable. It is a mind-set, not a truth."

I thought about his rows of tomato plants.

How Paolino joked he'd planted them using a ruler.

"The only truth we see here is the one the artist wants us to see," he continued.

I stopped for a moment. "It's beautiful."

"He is horrendously gorgeous. Do let's move along. I can't bear to wither in his shadow!"

We laughed.

The white sun pounded down but I couldn't feel it. I was lifted into this other world. His world. I cherished these moments to gaze through his spectrum. He made me feel like we were in a safe place despite the deep sadness he lived with. Today he had left his wife in a stranger's care. I had watched my best friend and her family toppled by grief. But the major couched these realities as the very essence of life; the real truth. His courage and simplicity in the face of these things was compelling. His mind was the gateway to a higher reality, rooted in the botany of every-day: the plants, our garden, the gentle daily rhythms, but also in the high ideals of great thinkers, ones whose passion was the human condition. How he could smudge the two intoxicated me. It felt so very real, incisive, yet full of gentle, unwavering respect. How I loved being pulled into the shaft of light through which he viewed the world.

We rode in silence till Pompeii slipped into memory. Without warning, the major ordered Giuseppe to come to an abrupt stop by a tiny roadside pizzeria, perched upon a curve in the road. "Come along, Santina, you must be absolutely starved. I know I am. Giuseppe — *mangiare, sì?*"

"No, no, Signore, *io aspetto.* Waiting."

"Can't I feed the poor man?"

I shrugged with an apologetic smile, feeling like I ought to follow Giuseppe's lead.

"I shan't dine alone while the two of you simmer in the heat, for heaven's sake. Come along. I'll get him something to take home."

We stepped inside the tiny space and were escorted to a terrace overlooking the Bay of Naples. The major ordered for us. He filled my glass with cold gold from a carafe placed on our table.

"This is a thank-you luncheon," he said.

"Thank you," I said, feeling myself scratching for a more appropriate reply, "I mean, I don't expect thank-you."

"Of course you don't. You're one of those rare breeds of people who are capable of giving of themselves without the desire for immediate repayment. But it's the right thing to do. And that's why I'm doing it."

I watched him sip his wine. I tasted mine. Its chilled fruitiness slid over my tongue. I'd never drunk with him. It felt inappropriate, yet rude if I didn't mirror him.

"It is delicious, isn't it?" he asked, unfolding his napkin.

I let the pause hover.

"I remember my first visit to Pompeii. I may have shed a tear. I wouldn't admit it to my uncle who took me, of course. He saw it as a rite of passage before his nephew left to be the officer he was always destined to be in India. And it only gets better, Santina. Pompeii, I mean, not the army. That's quite a different story entirely. For me, at least. The next time you're there, you'll discover more treasures. Your eye will have the freedom to focus on the details. Your mind won't be overloaded by the majesty. It will receive it like a friend."

"Next time?"

His eyes softened, or saddened, I couldn't decide which. He ran a hand through his hair. The luminous turquoise of the Bay of Sorrento behind him made it appear a deeper shade of red. His gaze drifted toward the kitchen where a waiter burst through the double doors and laid an enormous pizza between us. Another waiter slid a bowl of salad beside that, and a third filled our glasses once again.

"Good heavens, it's a tempest of service," he said, with a sardonic grin.

He insisted on cutting the pizza and serving me first. I ought to have felt like an imposter at his table. Yet I felt safe. The relaxed way he sat, light reflecting off the linen tablecloth picking up the darker streak of blue in his eyes, looking at me with a soft smile, could make me feel nothing but that. Cared for, even. Like the comfort of the shade of a lemon tree on a hot day.

I didn't realize just how hungry I was till the sweet tomato sauce and delicate ooze of mozzarella filled my cheeks. I may have eaten a slice without looking up. I know I did, because when I lifted my gaze, the major was laughing.

"What?" I asked, wiping my face with a paranoid swipe of my napkin, picturing awful smears of tomato across it.

He didn't stop, but lifted his glass and insisted I cheer to our health — and appetite, he added, with the warmest smile I'd ever seen.

We returned to the villa in the afternoon glow of travel weariness and full stomachs. After the pizza, he insisted we finish gelato and sorbetto, limoncello for both of us, and espresso. He ordered a calzone for Giuseppe, and had a waiter take it out to him. I lost count how many times Giuseppe thanked him along the road home.

We stepped into a cool silence.

He left for upstairs. I followed. After a few moments we met at the top of the stairwell, both changed into gardening clothes. I hadn't expected him to help me.

"I couldn't very well leave you to do all this alone, now could I?" he asked.

We walked down the stairs in silence, but for the gentle tap of our shoes on the stones.

I watched him fill a watering can at the tap. I waited to fill a second, myself. He took it from me to fill. His peculiar mood was leaking the fact that leaving Adeline at the hospital was causing more discomfort than he'd expected. I bent down to lift the full watering can. "I'll get that, Santina, don't worry!"

I lifted this can every day. He knew that. His erratic behavior started to unsettle me. I bent down to lift it again. So did he. Water lapped over the top. I gasped. My skirt was drenched.

We rose together. He grabbed my shoulders out of instinct. "I'm so sorry, Santina!"

"It's fine," I said, feeling the cold seep

267

onto my legs.

His hands didn't move. Neither did I.

The sun streamed across his freckles, catching a sideways beam over the luminous blue of his eyes. His face moved close to mine. Our breaths met. I didn't move. My heart thudded but my body didn't retreat. Neither did his. Reality slipped away with the water overflowing from the watering can at my feet.

His lips edged closer.

CHAPTER 14

A sharp knock at the door skidded us to real time. I heard my feet scuff the hot earth as I walked through the garden and across the terrace to open it, but my body felt like it hung back a pace or two, a lost shadow trying to reach its owner. My hand clicked open the catch, its metallic sound clanging through me like a peal of Sunday bells, urging me to return to the home this place was till a moment ago.

Paolino stood on the other side. He flashed a wide smile. I watched. He revealed a bunch of flowers from behind his back with a flourish, a haze of yellow, my least favorite color. I summoned sunny appreciation, but my performance slid away, spilled honey oozing off a countertop in lazy droplets.

His face fell. "Oh, Santina, I'm so sorry. I heard about Rosalia."

Perhaps I'd forgive myself for using my

best friend's grief as a mask for the time being? It seemed the kindest thing to do.

"That's alright, Paolino. It's awful."

He took my reply as a cue to take my hand in his. He lifted it to his lips. I slipped it away. I nodded behind me, indicating we were not alone. His voice dipped into a whisper. "I've missed you, Santina — I look forward to our Sundays together. The last two you've filled them with other people."

"I was with my best friend!" I replied, a little louder than I planned.

"I know," he cooed. "Can I come in?"

"The major is here."

"Yes. I want to speak with him."

"He doesn't pay the bill till the end of the month, you know that."

He ran his free hand over his slick hair. There was nothing left to smooth. His hair wax had done a good job of that already.

"It's not business. Private matter."

He wasn't speaking sense. My head spun, trying to ignore the sensation of standing a careless whisper away from the major. It was as if the furious heat of the day melted reality, a scorched, crushed plum forgotten on the pavement.

"Don't look so panicky, Santina — you're making me feel nervous!"

"You should be. The major doesn't sit

around here waiting for unannounced visits from grocers on *private* matters. Since when were you friends? You can't stand the man."

"I never said that."

My eyebrow raised. He received the arrow.

"Look, we going to stand here and talk at the doorway like a couple of peasants or you going to let me in?" He cocked his head to the side, flicking me a playful grin, which was almost resistible.

I shook my head with a reluctant start of a smile. "Don't say I didn't warn you." I didn't fear him facing the major as much as I dreaded turning to face him myself. What expression would I read there? What would he read on mine? The ground beneath me felt molten, shifting plates on the sea. Paolino edged inside and out onto the terrace. He turned back to me. "Why don't you put these in water, Santina?"

"*That* private?"

A look streaked across his face. I'd never seen it before. He always looked so self-assured, at peace with his surroundings, able to sing and smile his way in and out of anything. He reached out the bouquet, crushed at the stems now from his tight grasp. He was a grown man with the heart and energy of a boy, unhardened by any-

271

thing, in love with life and all it might offer. Who wouldn't fall into a man like that?

I silenced the answer.

Paolino reached the table and traced a nervous finger along it. The major's head appeared around one of the trees flanking the vegetable patch.

"Paolino is here to see you," I called, hearing myself shout across him. Paolino twisted around to me, as surprised at my delivery as I was.

The major strode across the garden toward us, trowel in hand, a smear of earth across his cheek that wasn't there before. He'd painted on the mask of gardener whilst I'd spoken with Paolino at the door and wore it with impeccable grace. I envied him that. He caught my eye over Paolino's shoulder. The tingle of my lips, a kiss away from his, the feel of the sunset upon our faces, these pictures swayed before me like the spiral of delicate shells on a mobile in the wind.

"I pay my bill at the end of the month, Santina," he said, without a trace of anything other than the matter-of-fact breeze he blew over Paolino and the like.

"Yes, Signore," Paolino interrupted. I'd never heard him speak English in this house, "I, come . . . message, sir." He retrieved a letter from his pocket and waved it by his cheek. "*Per piacere,* we talk? One moment" — his fingers came alive, searching to pluck the words from the air — "*poco minuti,* Signore."

The major's expression crushed into a brief frown. "Very well." He sighed. "Sit down, Paolino, out with it, and be quick. I've had a very long day and I loathe visits at this hour."

Paolino shot me a pleading look.

"You've got a hard head," I said. "I'll be in the garden if you need saving."

"What a woman," he replied under his breath. "Not sure if that means you think I can't deal with this Viking soldier or that you're more in love with me than I thought."

I smiled. It helped me ignore the thudding in my chest. Or the way the last rays caught the fierce blue of the major's eyes. I hid away in the kitchen for a moment longer than I needed to, gazing at the bouquet stuffed into the first vase I could find, feeling like I was being drawn out to sea. I left the darkened safety of the room, lured out by the need to know what mischief Paolino was concocting with the major. I walked past the table.

Paolino placed the envelope at the center of it.

The major reached for it.

I returned to the spot I'd escaped a moment ago. The major had cleared away the cans and finished the watering. He had wiped away all evidence of where we had stood, what we had thought, or failed to. The ground no longer bore witness. I couldn't shake the sensation that perhaps it hadn't happened at all. My feet traced an idle line, trying to catch the frayed ends of the conversation just out of earshot. I was behaving like an adolescent and chastised myself for it. But most of all, I resented the desire I felt to shunt time back to a moment ago. I floated to the memory of the quiet space between us. I crouched down to weed the cleared earth, sending useless twists of a trowel beneath the tomato plants, making vain attempts to bury the roots of my conflicted emotions. Their fruit and foliage was a camouflage to everything but my renegade thoughts. I craned my head at an obscure angle to see the major reaching the end of the note.

He stood to attention. Paolino lifted out of his seat. I could see the major saying something, which gave Paolino a great deal of joy. He shook the major's hand with too much enthusiasm. The major signaled for him to leave. He turned, looked as if he were about to call me, then thought better of it and stepped out onto the street. The major shut the door. I could hear him climb the first few steps up to his room. I stayed till dusk threw its purple veil over the garden. The major didn't return for supper, nor his evening drink. I could have retired myself. I could have read or written, but my mind wouldn't settle, the thoughts whizzed through me, mothlike tangents of doubt and embarrassment, flitting in and out of sense. Beyond these twists of half sense, the golden memory of what might have happened if Paolino had not appeared.

I sat and peeled an apple, the course of the knife against the skin the loudest sound in the whole villa now. I wanted the day to be over and never end. I chewed the fruit, trying to swallow the truth with it. I rinsed the knife, dried it, and placed it back in the drawer. I clung to the banal order of everything in this room, but it refused to ground me the way I longed for. I flicked the light switch. The darkness enfolded me, but it couldn't blot out my thoughts.

I was so alone.

Rosalia's brother's funeral the following morning drew the crowds of a carnival. From the entrance to the main Chiesa Nuova, a sea of Positanese flowed up the surrounding alleys. The piazza in front of the church was filled with familiar faces. Most of them cried, clung to one another, prayed between tears. The coffin was carried out. The applause began, rippling from the entrance to the church and spreading like an echo through the throng to the farthest person high up on the steps. The patter of sad hands, like a wave, was drawn into a unifying rhythm till we clapped as one, the sound ricocheting against the stone surrounding us and lifting up against the hard gray rock beyond. As the coffin slid into the hearse, a silence fell, like the thick gray humidity before a summer storm. When the door was slammed down shut, the applause rose again, defiant now, as if we alone could augur his ascent to the heavens, the sound of each palm golden cobbles to lead his way to peace. The car performed a complicated maneuver, bodies crushing against one another now to allow it through. As it left the piazza, people started the pilgrimage to the cemetery. Some sang, their notes floating down from the front, a lament, the tune strung along a minor line, frayed sails on a fishing boat's mast. Beneath the melody the constant drone of a warbled rosary, murmured and lifting, dipping like the rhythmical tumble of small waves lapping the shore.

A hand slipped into mine. I started.

"Has the major spoken to you, Santina?" Paolino whispered in my ear with a kiss I did not invite.

"Paolino! Not here . . ."

"Did he talk to you?"

The wailers beside me crashed over his words. I looked at his animated face, trying to interpret the sense of where he was headed, but to no avail.

I felt his hand tighten. The hot bodies of my neighbors pressed in as the river of people flooded into the narrow *viccoli*. We huffed and puffed up the incline now, the older women ahead stopping every now and again to rest, slowing the flow of those behind them, who navigated around the human dam on our Via Dolorosa. No one paid mind to the tourists, an official day of mourning had been declared by the mayor. It left me wondering whether the friction between the rival groups had permeated our town more than I would have at first believed. How naïve I felt all of a sudden, living in my small English bubble, watching the world around me now, the sounds a muffle of confusion from underwater.

At last, the cemetery loomed ahead of us, a resting point in more ways than before.

Rosalia, her siblings, and their parents stood by the gates, receiving incessant trickles of hands, tears, and embraces. I held my friend to my heart. She was pale. It was our turn to cry now. The family were translucent with grief, standing with much effort. Only family and close friends would go to the grave itself. Even with the combined ingenuity of all the Positanese, there would be no hope of squeezing the entire town inside the gates without further casualties. Rosalia would not let go of me.

"I want you with me, Santina," she whispered, her voice a scratch.

"Of course, if that's what you want."

"Please."

We walked through the gates. Marco wasn't inside his hut just beyond. He would be at the grave now. We reached the plot, higher up the hill above the older graves. Two dozen of us clambered around the hole. My brother appeared. I felt an oblique ripple of pride. It was an honor to see him at this precious time, ushering a family toward the belly of their grief. Then I felt a whisper of morbid embarrassment followed by the sting of self-reproach. The reality of my brother's job came crashing into focus. Perhaps there was more truth in the words he'd said in haste over the supper table? Was

I becoming the sister who would look down on her brother? Could he sense these thoughts even before I became aware of them? The idea sent a shiver down my spine.

I heard the scatter of earth upon the tomb. Rosalia's mother fell to her knees. Even three of her brothers wrenching her up would not lift her away from the son she looked down at. Rosalia bent down and wrapped her arm around her mother. I crouched on the other side. I rocked with the women. I felt her tears wet the side of my hair. I heard her muttered prayers spatter in my ear. Together, Rosalia and I eased her back to standing. It was a while before the group trickled away from the grave. I held back, caught between them and my brother. He waited for them to clear out of sight before he began covering the body in earnest. He worked without tiring, shunting the shovel deep into the pile of earth with smooth strokes. All of a sudden he stopped, caught in my gaze.

"You never see someone dig before?"

"I am proud of you, Marco."

He took a breath, wiped his brow.

"I'm sorry about the other day," I offered, "you helped me so very much and then I made you feel awful."

"Already forgotten." He walked down

toward me. "You're my family, Santina. If we can't quarrel and then forget it what are we? Nothing more than these crazy men going around killing each other for no reason. Pride is ugly."

I looked up at him; all traces of that skinny boy racing ahead of me evaporated.

"I'll wait for you, yes?" I asked, in no hurry to return home. I had no idea how to navigate communication with the major and was stalling it as best I could. The mere thought of any impending conversation made my stomach tighten.

"I'll be a little while, but yes, of course."

The family had already begun their descent toward the house, where a small army of women would keep the family fed till the sun dipped and the tears ran dry. I took my time tracing the narrow walkways through the cemetery. I let myself linger for a moment on the stone bench where I had first spoken with my long-lost brother. I looked out to the sea, deep turquoise at this time of day. I let the salty breeze remind me that all was well in the world at large. The next time I saw the major, if he did in fact ever descend from his room again, he would fix everything. He would iron away the impossible awkwardness with a deft sentence or two. He'd rationalize away our impulse.

He'd rake through it all, knotting out the weedy roots of uncertainty like a skilled gardener. Everything would return to normality. We had been tired, overwrought with the emotional day, that was all. Elizabeth would return, my duties would resume, and Adeline would be discharged soon enough.

I clung to these wisps of thought, but they flew beyond my grasp, dandelion seeds on the breeze.

I headed for Marco's little cabin by the gates. He would be finished soon enough. I took a seat on his wooden chair, from which he spied all entrants. He must know more about everybody's lives than I had given credit. His shelves were a peculiar menagerie of religious artifacts and utilitarian aids. I would have expected a little more order, but here tools hung beside small plastic Madonnas, vases rose in precarious towers, some still with dried flowers decaying inside them. My eyes traced the noise of papers, a wide radio and a much loved but ill-treated coffeepot.

That's when I saw it.

The glint caught my eye first, its metallic shimmer the brightest thing in the room. The length of the blade was the next thing to sharpen my attention. I knew an excellent knife when I saw one. I don't know why

I picked it up, or read the initials burned onto the leather handle. I don't know why the "R" would have interested me if not for the noticeable curl of the decorative flourish around it. The beautiful violence of the object was compelling. What on earth would Marco need a knife like this for? And why would he have that initial on it? The door swung open. I dropped the blade. It ricocheted on the stone, spun once, and landed, facing Marco.

"I'm so sorry!" I uttered, reaching down for it.

He grabbed my hand, a little too tight.

"My God, Santina, do you know what harm you might have done to yourself? Christ, what were you thinking?"

"Nothing! Nothing at all. I just —"

"Just what?"

I didn't recognize his expression for a moment. He saw me note it and softened.

"You gave me fright, *oje nè,*" he soothed.

"Sorry."

We looked at one another. He opened the top drawer of his desk, aching under the weight of a collection of more glass and paper, and placed the knife toward the back. Then he straightened and reached out his arms. I walked into them. I felt a great need to unload the strangeness of my day onto him. Perhaps, another day, I could paint Pompeii for him, take him on my travels, he could be my confessional. But as I lost my thoughts into the quiet of the embrace I knew that would be impossible. I imagined the look on his face if I confided in him about the major and me in the garden, standing a breath from one another, saved only by a knock at the door.

He lifted my chin. "I love you, Santina. You're the only person I have in this world now. Sometimes it makes me jumpy. I'm afraid of losing you all over again. I see people come in and out every day, mourning the empty space where their loved one stood. It breaks a person. Slowly. Like the sea lapping up to the rocks, you know, eating away the hard stone, so slowly no one notices. Then, one day, I find my sister and the thought of losing you tears me apart."

"I love you, Marco. Nothing can change that. Ever."

He kissed my forehead.

"Go to your friend now," he soothed.

"I think I will go home first and pick up some food I've made them. Besides, the crowds will be there for a while yet. I want to go when I can be of some use."

"One day, you will make a man a proud wife indeed."

I shrugged.

"Come see me, yes?" he asked, squeezing my hand.

"You can count on it," I replied.

I stepped into the villa. The unaccustomed sound of a cello concerto wafted up from the lemon trees. At the far end of the garden, I caught the back of the major's deck chair, the tip of his panama hat poking over the top, beside him a squat wooden table with a jug of lemon water. By his feet stood his gramophone whirring out the seductive strings. The door closed heavy behind me. I walked across the terrace toward the kitchen. His voice stopped me halfway.

"I have a glass for you here, Santina."

I stood still. He looked back at me over the side of the chair.

His expression put me at ease.

"I think we need to talk," he said.

I walked toward him. He gestured for me to sit down on the deck chair beside him. As I sunk down onto the canvas I allowed myself to acknowledge how my legs ached. I realized I had been on my feet since early this morning. He filled a glass, handed it to me, and watched me drink.

At last he spoke.

"Your gentleman friend," he began, "took great pains to meet with me."

I could feel embarrassment claw up my cheeks. I didn't feel ready for what he might say. I wanted to wind our way out of this conversation before it began, stepping through sea thistles by the water's edge.

"I had no idea quite how serious your relationship was. You kept that a well-guarded secret. That much is overwhelmingly obvious."

My eyes lowered. I longed to summon the courage to be honest with him, with myself. Ours wasn't a relationship. Ours was a dance. Paolino and I were brief partners, no more. I had followed his lead. When it had become serious escaped me. Why was the major even having this conversation with me?

"And choose, if you can, not to look as if I were speaking a language of which you have no understanding. I have been teaching you these past few years with what I considered deliberate dedication. With passion. Now I think my love of sharing all I know with you has been an utter waste. You are a bright student, Santina. Have the courage to not use the mask of stupidity as a frail device when you don't want to confront something!"

His voice was rising now. I was back on the mountainside. I heard my mother pleading with my father. The crack of his belt, the sound of her falling, wailing, streaking the floorboards with blood. The pictures pummeled my mind. I cried stupid, fat tears.

"I am a good student. You are a good teacher." I felt the warble of more sobs in my throat but clamped them down. "I don't know why you speak like this."

His face fell. "Santina — forgive me." He stumbled over his words, tripped through his search for them. "Please. I shouldn't . . . I didn't mean that. I just —" He let out a deep breath.

We floated on this stilted silence, a rowboat with its oars lifted. I longed for him to steer us back to normality and resist control at the same time. Perhaps we could stay on this watery expanse, nothing but the two of us and a sapphire horizon.

My tears began to ebb. Our eyes met.

I watched his fingers reach over to mine. I watched him trace a gentle line over my open palm. A wave of electricity raced up my arm. He lifted my wrist to his lips. The soaring resonance of the strings beside us scored through me. There was no afternoon breeze, no lap of the sea, no birdsong. He slid off his chair and lowered himself onto his knees before me. Our faces were level. I felt his hands cradle my face, gentle, craving permission. A sliver of light was between us now, no more. We held the complicit quiet. I wanted nothing more than the taste of his mouth on mine. I ached for the feel of him.

But I pulled away.

I shouldn't hide in his arms.

My tears weren't an invitation.

"We can't do this."

His voice was a murmur. "You are right. Of course. I'm sorry."

He looked into me. I felt naked.

He lowered back onto his heels. His gaze left me, fixing on a point on the horizon, beyond the inviting mountains of Capri, a place this garden begged you to linger on, rolling downhill toward the seascape, as if the answers to difficult questions lay in full view yet out of reach.

I watched him search for words. I couldn't remember seeing him at a loss like this. The man from Pompeii sank in confusion or desire or despair. I couldn't decide which. His expression pulled between them like a riptide.

At last, the words slipped out, insipid; a saltless soup: "It would seem, Santina, that you are to be married."

CHAPTER 15

I stopped listening to the major's words as they lapped over me. He could sense my retreat and slipped the letter into my hand. The words were a jumble before me, my eyes skimmed across the sentences written in a hand I did not recognize.

"Would you like me to read it for you, Santina?"

I looked up from the paper. He was sat back on his chair now.

"I don't know," I replied, annoyed at my dithering.

He reached out his hand. I placed the note in it.

It was a declaration of love from Paolino, written in English but with the flowery singsong of the Neapolitan lover he'd decided to be. He spoke of lifetimes, he compared me to both a nightingale and a lark. He spoke of sunshine and moonlight and stars. He declared his intent for us to be married, his desire to ask permission from the major, the closest male to me other than my father, whom he could not reach. I don't know what I loathed more, the clumsy writing or the idea that he believed the major had the power to oversee my personal affairs.

When he finished reading, the major folded it with care, slipped it back into the envelope, and handed it to me. I wanted the setting rays to ease me back to the delicious warmth of a few moments ago. I wanted a peaceful close of the day to steer me back to familiarity.

Paolino's proposal felt hapless. A boy pretending to be a man; a note from someone who was in love with the idea of love.

"Who wrote this?" I asked.

"I think that much is obvious."

"No, who wrote it for him?"

"Our new neighbor, I believe. An American, Paolino led me to understand. I'm sure she was all too happy to do it. A romantic, from what I can tell. Met her new husband on a holiday here and married him a month later."

Another woman's words. My chest tightened. The whole thing was awkward. No less than two foreigners had pored over this declaration before me. I felt like exposed chattel.

The major stood up. Time was trickling out of my control, water streaking through a tiny crack in a vase base. I wanted him to reach for me, pull me into him, and hated myself for it.

He looked away from me toward the coast. "I'm sure you'll give the matter a great deal of thought."

"I'm sure everyone will decide what I ought to do without asking me first."

The words tumbled out before I could stop them. He turned toward the sharp brunt of them.

"What on earth is that supposed to mean?"

I shook my head, biting back my tears. We stood motionless in the punishing silence.

"I'm sorry," I muttered.

"For what?"

For craving his touch. For retreating from his kiss. For loathing the great ache inside me to never be anywhere but close to him.

No words surfaced. We looked at one another. His shadow reached me, streaking across the parched grass between us.

"I will prepare your supper and, if it's alright, take a delivery of food to Rosalia."

"Of course," he replied, with the honeyed

tone I might have mistaken for genuine care once.

Had he expected me to crumble? To melt into him like a lost child? Did he need me to be that for him, after all? Was he drawn to me because of my apparent weakness? I had believed the opposite for so long. These past years, while we did so much side by side, complicit, comfortable, all this was nothing more than a professional engagement. The sense of friendship I had come to rely upon was an illusion. Perhaps I craved to be looked after more than I thought? The weakness smarted. I wasn't a mountain goat after all: self-reliant, unafraid of challenges, determined to reach any tricky nook unaided. I was a local servant girl, nothing more. I was another cog in the working of these foreigners' lives, oiled like machinery, running with predictable consistency. Our almost kiss — nothing more than a man threatened by another's declaration of love. If I married Paolino, he would lose his trusted aide. No more than that.

I turned and walked back toward the kitchen, crisping across the garden, feeling his eyes on me and hating it. Inside, I found the basket for Rosalia I had prepared earlier. It drew me out of my present. Beyond these villa's walls there was deeper grief to attend to. My problems paled in comparison. It was time to be a true friend.

The mood in the Rispoli house was fractured; stepping inside was like crunching over a floor of glassy shards. I had avoided the onslaught of visitors from earlier in the day. I found Rosalia in the kitchen. She looked exhausted. I took a seat beside her and reached for her hand. She squeezed it. I looked across at Pasquale on the other side of the table. He forced the start of a sad smile.

"I don't think I've got any tears left, Santi'," she murmured.

I ran my thumb over the top of her hand, not rushing for an answer. "Where's Mamma?"

"In her room. Doesn't want to leave it. Won't eat. Will barely drink."

I let her words hang. I didn't have any desire to hurry her sadness away. I longed for a memory of people around me when my mamma died to allow me to grieve. I wanted people to hold the space for me, to give me permission to wail or sit silent, feeling the incessant numbness cloud me without a fight. The feel in this house was familiar to me. I felt the stark realization that a shadow of death trailed me. The thought was a tiny pebble rippling into a well, sending watery echoes spiraling skyward.

"I love you, Santina. Thank you —"

That's when her sobs began again. I held her. Pasquale brought over a cup of chamomile tea that a cousin had brewed for her, the comforting sweetness lifting up scented steam.

"*Tesoro,* why don't you get some rest now?" he asked, his voice warm.

"I'll come with you," I offered, much to the relief of Pasquale. She hooked her arm in his and rose to her feet. He planted a soft kiss on each cheek, and I led her down the corridor to her room. I placed her tea upon her side table and drew back the sheet. The shutters were still half closed against the early evening light, sending wide strips across the white walls and across the crucifix above her bed.

"Will you stay with me a little while?" she asked, slipping on her nightdress and sliding herself into her bed.

"Of course."

She sat, sipping her tea, asking me to talk to her, to let her mind wander anywhere but to the picture of her brother that terrorized her dreams.

"And the major? How is he?"

I wanted to say beautiful. I wanted to say the kindest person I'd ever met, with the gait of a young boy and the wisdom and care of an older one. I longed to describe the way the light played across his freckles, making them look different depending on the time of the day. Or the width of his palms into which mine fit to perfection. Or the way he knew about all our plants and cared for each in their own special way. That I was mesmerized by him from the moment I met him and, only now, having stepped into the intimate space where one person ends and the other begins, could I admit I may have even fallen in love with him. But the words stuck deep in the center of me; a fog in a box, hissing out in wisps, murky thoughts swirling within. Then I remembered the awful expression on his face after my reaction to Paolino's letter. My cheeks reddened in spite of myself.

"What's wrong, Santina?"

"Nothing."

"Please tell me. I want you to let me be as good a friend to you as you are to me."

I needed to say something. If I upheld this guilty silence, she would know something had happened that shouldn't have. Rosalia had a feral sense for these things.

"We went to Pompeii," I announced at last.

"Tell me everything."

I did. But I left out the detailed flecks of our colorful day. The way he laughed at me inhaling the pizza, his eyes dancing, making me feel free. I described the ruins and the stories but not how we sipped *limonata* under the shade of the curling pines surrounding them. I imagined her expression if I'd revealed that we had slipped back into the villa and almost into one another's arms. Part of me longed to. My feelings were fast becoming a burden. Who was I to involve her in my near deceit? The first tear traced my cheek.

"*Tesoro,* you've caught my crying," she said, laughing into some more of her own.

"I'm sorry, Rosali', I didn't mean to —"

"Don't apologize."

"Paolino asked me to marry him," I blurted, surprising myself as much as her.

Rosalia burst into laughter, released for a moment from her sobs. She wrapped her arms around me. We cried together. She mistook my tears for the happiness of a blushing bride-to-be. A girl overawed by her lover's intentions. I had no idea how to unpack my feelings now. How to say that Paolino's letter lacked true intimacy. He had asked permission from the major, someone who had no right to decide whom I ought to love, yet the person I had come to orbit like my sun.

"I am so very happy for you!" she exclaimed, wiping my face and then hers. "Life is so very short, my *tesoro* — you find love? You treasure it, whatever it takes."

Her well-meant words prickled. I daren't let myself hear them.

Besides, whatever the truth may be, at this very moment, my news had offered her a much-needed escape.

"I hope someday I can share such happy news with you, Santi'. You've been here for me today in so many ways. My best friend. If you'll let me call you that."

I smiled. "Of course."

She sank back on her pillow. She didn't move her hand from mine. After a while she released to sleep. I watched her chest rise and fall. My mind returned to Adeline's room. To the major's tender hands tracing her back. I felt those same hands on my shoulders now. I was back in the garden. I felt his lips on mine. My stomach tightened. I couldn't ignore the dreaded return to the villa any longer.

I said my goodbyes and left the house. Pasquale met me at the top of the steps that led up from their front door to join the alley that ran down to the villa, stubbing out his cigarette.

"*Grazie,* Santina, I wish I could have soothed her as much as you."

"I think she needs time to feel."

He nodded with a half smile. Then he shifted, anxious to tell me something but not knowing how to begin.

"I really love her, Santina."

I replied with a smile. "It's beautiful to watch."

"I've asked her father for permission. Now I have to wait."

This time my tears were genuine happiness. "Your secret is safe with me."

"You're the only person I can tell. No one in this town can hold secrets. You know what it's like, sisters, brothers, neighbors, everyone takes a crumb and before you know it the loaf is devoured."

I smiled at the way his face creased into an embarrassed half-grin. He took a breath, struggling to find the right words for the thoughts racing in his eyes.

"I knew about her brother."

"What do you mean?"

"The same people who were after him, look after us, *capisci*?"

I shook my head, willing him onward.

"My family and I, we are struggling. A lot. The bakery is forced to buy its flour from certain providers. If not . . ."

He trailed off, his eyes darkening.

"Are you in danger, Pasquale?"

"Not if I behave."

I watched his eyes moisten with anger and fear.

"It's making my father sick. Doctor says his kidneys aren't working like they should. He says it's old age, but I know it's because of them."

It was hard listening to this admission. However special I felt having been entrusted with his confidence was eclipsed by my helplessness. Was he really telling me because I was trustworthy or did he believe I could be of some actual help?

"I'm so sorry, Pasquale. Is there nothing we can do?"

"Close it. Move to America like everyone else. Or buy our supplies at twice the price."

"Rosalia knows?"

"No. That's why I'm telling you. It seems so selfish to start talking about our future together now that her house is in mourning. But I need to know we have a future together, you know? Outside of this place. Now she sees what living here means. I want her to know, I suppose. And I don't."

He brushed away his stumbling thoughts with a shake of his head. "I'm sorry. I shouldn't have burdened you. I don't know, I've heard about your plans to go to America. Rosalia tells me all the time. She doesn't want you to go. I don't think I want to stay."

"You must be honest with her, no? Perhaps a little time. And in the meantime, you tell me anything you need to, promise me that, *sì?*"

"I wish my own sisters were more like you!"

The light shifted toward the deepening purple dusk.

"It's getting dark," I said, not intending to cut off his conversation before he was ready.

"You need company?"

"Only my own thoughts, but thank you. Please take care."

He nodded and straightened. I watched him turn back and follow the steps down to the house. Once he was inside, this conversation would evaporate. I thought about his expression as it rippled through a childlike panic and the warmth of a man in love. How mature was his declaration in contrast to Paolino's note. I thought about the American scribe, hoping the excruciating meeting I would have to face at some point could be delayed as long as possible.

The shadows wrapped around me along the narrow alleys. The sound of my footsteps echoed against the back walls of the houses. Tumbling vines of bougainvillea softened their white stone, the gray silhouettes faded memories of a summer's day. At last I reached our door, a gateway to a very different world now.

Inside the quiet, my eye flitted toward the garden. I was thankful to find it void of chairs, gramophones, or employer. The moonlit stairs welcomed me with stony silence. I reached Elizabeth's door, she would return tomorrow, but out of habit I was drawn inside. A wide moonbeam shafted across the tiles. My eyes darted to the parted double doors, both sides swung open onto the terrace. I watched the linen curtains dance on the night breeze.

And I saw his silhouette.

I could have shut the door and retreated to my room on the opposite side of the hallway. I could have crept into bed and forced myself to sleep, knowing he stood on the terrace. But I didn't. I couldn't tear myself away from the spot. I longed for him to turn toward me. To invite me outside.

He did.

I walked across the darkened nursery. He was swirling a drink. I watched him place the drink on the ledge of the balustrade, then lean onto it, looking out toward the lulling moonlight upon the sea.

"Apologies are painful, are they not, Santina?"

I took a breath, determined to tap into some semblance of courage. "It's an important part of an apology, I think, the pain."

He turned to me then. All embarrassment and anger from the afternoon melted away into this quiet, darkened space between us.

"I think you have a wisdom beyond your years. And a smile that makes me believe that all is well in the world. And an insatiable curiosity for things beyond these walls."

I smiled in spite of myself.

"I apologize because . . ."

I knew what I longed for him to say but could scarce admit it to myself. My silence urged him on.

"Because in spite of the promise I made myself, I have come to have very strong feelings for you, Santina." His voice dipped into honey. "Because at this precise moment I want nothing more than to feel your body against mine. And that is unforgivable. Not just because I sound like as much a brute as your grocer, but because it puts you in a dreadfully awkward position. Most especially because, as I suspect, your feelings are quite different than the ones I have for you."

I knew the reply I longed to give, but the words ricocheted in my mind, sealed shut with fear. I couldn't move.

"I've rattled around this house all afternoon, with only you on my mind. My feelings aside, you must decide what it is you want from your life."

"What *I* want?"

He shifted, rejected in some way. His movements became angular.

"After our years together, I foolishly assumed that you would absorb everything I gave you, the knowledge I offered you for the sake of your freedom. Is that something you want to throw away for a life in the local *salumeria*? Because if that's what you want, then that's what you must have. True freedom is having the liberty to decide such things. I've wanted to give nothing but that."

The ocean's scent was on the air. "I don't feel free."

"Because I've cornered you with the possibility of a better life than the one you would have had here if it wasn't for me? I'm so sorry!"

I could feel the anger rise now. His words seemed pompous. He was wounded and lashing out at me. Perhaps his feelings were far stronger than I would have liked to admit.

"I have always done my best for you!" I cried, defensive.

"And I you! And now we face your future being nothing more than retreating into the back alleys of a small fishing town that a few poets have decided to make the center of the Italian bohemian scene. Is *that* what you want? I thought you needed more. Your mind is vast, free, insatiable. Your passion for learning is a wonder to behold. Have you any idea the delight I've felt watching you chase every flourish I have challenged you with? How wonderful it has been to watch you yearn for more? You've given my life new meaning. I'm learning things afresh, and it is exhilarating. Now you seem willing to walk away from that. It breaks my heart."

I hovered in the angry silence, terrified of what I might say if I opened my mouth.

"For heaven's sake, Santina! Don't stand there mute. Did we or did we not embark on your education just for you to run into the first local lover to set eyes on you? You want a pedestrian life serving others?"

"I spend my life serving *you*! What's the difference?" I blurted, not pausing to regain control. "If I'm his servant or yours, what is the difference? At least with him I will run my own business. I will be part of a family, not paid to pretend to be one. Not paid for friendship!"

His eyes streaked with defense now too.

"Is that what you really think of what's been going on all this time?" I watched him deepen his breaths, forcing his voice away from anger. "Tell me we both couldn't tell, while we gardened at dawn, in the food you cooked with such care, in the times we shared a space doing nothing but watching Elizabeth. Tell me, with your hand on your heart, that you couldn't feel something more than an employer and his employee? Tell me I'm a deluded man chasing childish fantasies. Because as I stand here looking at you now, not saying a word to the contrary, I'm wondering if that isn't the truth after all."

I stood motionless, wielding a stubborn shield against his words. Not wanting to admit that of course I had felt it. That it slipped through my every action. That it trailed me in the silent reliving of my dreams. How could I stand out here and allow him to see the passion that stirred in me? If I did, there would be no turning back. If I did, how could there ever be a future for me in this house? How could I carry on working here if I didn't? And then where would my path lead me? Down a narrow street into Paolino's arms and a life I never wished for myself.

"Then go to your grocer! Walk away from your future, Santina."

"What future? I am your serving girl. No more. And you stand there, saying things that aren't real because you know you can. Because you know you've trapped me. That's what a man like Paolino does! You are no different!"

"Of course we're different!" He stepped closer to me now. I'd pricked his pride. It smarted.

"You both pour out your feelings over mine," I continued, not allowing him to interrupt. "There's no space for me! You've both made me a puppet. Neither of you have any more feelings for me than you do your own shadow!"

He looked into me. I knew my words were brittle and untrue.

So did he.

That's why he didn't move. That's why he held the space for me to hear what I'd said. That's why he waited to watch me surrender to my instincts. I looked at his face, streaked in the moonlight. I saw the familiar intelligence there, an ardent desire.

To win the argument?

Or to hold me?

He took a breath, searching for a way to unfold the truth, his voice lowered into a murmur, the unhurried glow of a dipping sun. "My feelings overwhelm me."

We breathed in the quiet. A ripple of laughter rose up from the bay.

"That was what I want to apologize for," he said, at last.

Nothing but shadows between us now.

"I've fallen in love with you, Santina."

The words were light and terror. Flight and obliteration. He stepped closer. I had no fight in me. He looked through me. His hand reached for the side of my neck. His gentle fingers rested there, waiting for consent. His lips pressed onto my skin. I left so many thoughts somewhere in the sparkles of starlight streaking across us, as he raised me up, as I wrapped myself around him, as we gave in to what wasn't ours to articulate. I felt his lips hot and tender on mine. I felt the moonlight twist around our knotted silhouettes, casting guilty shadows along the tiles.

I left my conscience somewhere on that terrace.

CHAPTER 16

His hand reached for mine. I followed his lead through the shadows to my room. He turned back toward me, lifted my hand to his mouth, and kissed it.

"Is this the part where the servant girl gives in to her master?" I asked.

My hand slipped out of his.

He sunk down onto the edge of the bed, his hands clasped, head bowed.

I resisted my instinct to apologize for my bluntness.

"Yes," he said, his head shaking, "this is exactly how it must seem to you."

"It's not how I feel. But it's what I need to know."

His eyes met mine. Every fiber wanted the touch of him. Every ounce of self-respect I had protected from the moment I left the mountains begged me to hear reassurance from him.

"I watched you arrive in our home, barely

out of childhood, Santina, but with a swagger and pride to your gait that revealed your intelligence. Your sense of self is compelling. Your self-reliance. That's the woman I took in my arms on the terrace, not a subordinate who will do as I ask because I pay her."

I had never heard anyone describe me, let alone in these terms. Tears pricked my eyes. I refused to let them fall.

"And now you stand there, swallowing back those tears because you can't bear to hear how beautiful I see you are. How many young women would have done what you have, Santina? How many would have grown into a mother for another's daughter? How many would have set their hearts on a life beyond their tiny town whatever the cost? How many would have taken on their education with such an open heart, with such a drive to know more? Open themselves? Search out who they are supposed to become?"

"Many, I suppose."

"No. Only those with fire. Adeline saw it too. That's why she insisted you come and work for us."

"And we betray her."

"Do we?"

"Please be honest now. You've taken time to earn my trust. You've laid knowledge at my feet and the world you've opened to me is more beautiful than I dare admit. You chose to do that. Nobody forced you. And you lit up. And you lit me up too. I want to let my tears of gratitude fall right here but I can't, because what we speak of will break that trust now. Every gram of it. And for what? A moment to satisfy your pleasure?"

"And what about yours, Santina? What about how you feel? Let's both be honest now. You and I are made of strong stuff. We're not fainthearted. But we can't control every aspect of ourselves. Why would we want to? To half live? To feel less?"

The answer smarted, pricking the pause.

"The woman I married disappeared a long time ago, even before you came to us, perhaps. I will never stop loving Adeline, but I don't know how long I've been without her. Or if I'll ever know her again."

I held his gaze. My breaths quickened. I felt weak, scored with a spectrum of sensations I'd never felt before.

He stood up and walked over to me.

I watched as he moved in to kiss the base of my neck. I felt his lips brush my dress by my stomach. I saw him kneel down before me. He kissed my calves. His fingers traced my thigh. I stopped him with my hand.

"We can't do this."

"Santina," he began, looking up at me, his face lit, ardent, "this is bigger than either you or I. You know that."

"I think you like being in control."

"I do. And I'm not. This is me surrendering. I don't want to conquer you, Santina. Let me love you. For one night. Please let me show you how I feel."

I loosened my grip on his hand. He smoothed the back of my wrist with his thumb. I felt his fingers reach farther up my thigh. My muscles clenched in defense.

He wrapped his arms around my legs and held me. I felt his heart beating against the top of my thighs. I knelt down to face him.

"I've never been here before," I said, sinking into vulnerability, wondering if that proved me brave or a coward.

"I know," he murmured, tucking a strand of hair behind my ear, "let us be gentle with one another. The night is as long as we need."

His lips found mine. The smell of his skin was woody, mountain air and salty, pine-toasted breeze.

"Take all of me, Santina," he whispered into my ear, brushing it with his lips.

My hands ran up his neck toward his hair. I let his tongue find mine. Neither of us led. We searched together, molding the moment between us, two children working clay; wordless, playful, complicit.

Then he stood and lifted me up, laying me down onto the bed without force or hurry. This night would be our lifetime of love. This was the one moment we could express what wasn't ours to share. My body opened as he traced his tongue up my thighs, as he eased away my underwear, as he gazed deep into the heart of me.

I'd never felt so bare nor so safe.

"You are perfect."

That's when the tears came again. Involuntary, brutal. The words were never gifted to me like that before. Not even my mother had couched her love like that. Hers wasn't a verbal love. We had an unspoken bond. My father had always made me feel like I was nothing but a yoke around his neck. An unloveable. The feeling hit me like a boulder.

The major raised himself on top of me and wrapped his arms around me.

"Cry as you need, Santina," he whispered in my ear. "I want to cry too. I want to let my tears fall with abandon. I've kept them locked away for so very long."

"I'm not crying because I feel guilty," I sputtered. "I'm crying because no one has told me such a thing. Not like this."

"I mean every word."

Every moment of what followed is etched in my mind, a dream a person is sure passed through them but which cannot exist beyond the shadows. In that nebulous place, his fingers traced every curve of my body. His tender touch was gentle questions, probing for consent, uncovering the hidden wisdom of my body. It intuited every shift within me. It eased me into myself so that at last I relinquished all control and allowed the sensations to light through me, to the will of our bodies without judgment. And as we moved into one another, as we filled each other, the moon shadows played with our spirits crumpled in the sheets.

My body scored with electricity. My tears flowed. I felt his hands around me. He didn't stifle my cry. We ebbed to stillness.

He propped his head up with one hand and gazed down at me.

"Thank you," he whispered.

I turned my tear-streaked face to him, warmed by his startling openness.

"I don't want to apologize for my tears," I said, my breaths deepening at last. "There's bitter happiness inside them."

He didn't rush to answer. He wanted me to fill the space.

"I'm not a girl anymore."

"You're radiant."

He kissed my bare breast. Out of instinct I reached for the sheet to cover them. An absurd gesture, I realized, bearing in mind what we'd just done.

"Are you cold?" he asked.

"I don't know."

"Then let me adore you some more."

I sighed a laugh. He silenced it with a kiss.

"I feel afraid," I said in a whisper.

"We surrendered to something beautiful, Santina. These moments are fleeting in a lifetime. We paid reverence."

"You make it sound like we were at church!"

He sat up now. His chest was wide with tufts of blondish hair. I rose to my knees and followed the impulse to run my fingers through it.

"You are a special soul, Santina. Never forget this."

I kissed his chest. I let my lips find the base of his neck.

His hands smoothed my hair.

The feeling ached.

He eased me down onto my back. His hands wrapped around my knees. They fell open to him.

I knew there was no other place I'd rather be.

He moved himself lower, till he was kneeling upon the tiles, then drew me toward his mouth. His kiss wove inside me, a golden thread rooting me, sending splintering light through the top of my head. He pulled away for a moment, his gaze questioning whether I was comfortable. There were only two of us left upon the edge of our Positano cliff; just us, our sea, our canopy of stars. Waves of pleasure rose through my limbs. I let the tide carry me.

He rose back up. His face was level with mine again. Our breaths mingled. He traced his nose down mine. "Santina," he murmured in my ear.

"Yes?"

"I'm ravenous."

I frowned, feeling a sudden pang of embarrassment. He felt me stiffen.

"I mean, may I cook for you?" he asked, lighting up, adding even more absurdity to the unfolding of our evening.

"It's night," I replied, a feeble stalling. I knew there would be no stopping him if he had decided it to be so.

"Yes."

I opened my mouth to offer some reply but none came. He leaped off the bed. I watched him retrieve his shirt. He gave it a shake and spread it open for me to slip my arms into. Off my frown, he cocked his head with a smile.

"Yes, in order to fit into this garment you will have to arise and for a moment enjoy your nudity."

I didn't move. He waited for a moment and then squatted down beside the bed.

"Santina, it would break my heart if you thought that after all this time I hadn't learned at least one dish from watching your artistry. You've gifted me your trust in the most beautiful way I could have imagined. Surely allowing me to cook won't be that painful?"

I laughed at that.

"Don't tarry, I've been practicing my *acqua pazza,* in my mind at least, but I should be delighted if you'd sip wine and oversee the proceedings."

I don't remember how I slipped into his shirt. I think I've erased all the memory of him closing each button with a kiss. How he took my face in his hands once again and planted his warm lips upon mine. We charged toward the ridiculous midnight feasting plan.

He opened the kitchen doors onto the lower terrace and pulled out a bottle of wine from the refrigerator. We clinked. I felt like an imposter for a moment, an amateur

315

player saying the lines in the wrong order, moving through awkward gaps in her memory, trying her best not to crash into the scenery.

"Look at me, Santina."

I placed my glass on the counter, noticing I left my hand there as if the slab of marble might steady me.

"The world can wait until tomorrow." His eyes shifted a melancholy blue. I couldn't decide if we were running away or unpacking the truth. It was a frenetic sensation; a delicious escape and an ugly truth. He raised me up onto the counter. Raced his hands over my breasts.

"I'm looking forward to your dish," I replied at last, returning his kiss.

Reality could wait after all.

He insisted I sit doing nothing but keep a watchful, judgeless eye upon him, as he lifted two fish from their paper wrapper, bruised a clove of garlic, and slipped it inside each of them, dipping them in seasoned flour. He set them to crisp in a pan with hot butter. After a few minutes — I marveled at his innate timing but would scarce allow myself to admit I'd noticed — he set them aside upon a tea towel–covered plate to blot the excess fat. I watched him tip a further two smashed cloves into the warm pan, adding several handfuls of cubed vine tomatoes from the garden and a generous grind of salt and pepper. He splashed the pan with water. The scented steam filled the room with savory promise. Out of instinct I stood up, sensing he ought to add a little more liquid for the *acqua pazza,* or crazy water as he called it. Whenever I made it he declared it appropriate for his household. The joke sat at an awkward angle for my taste but delighted his sardonic sense of humor.

"I know, Santina," he said, waving me off, "that was just to help scrape off the crunchy bits at the bottom. I'm pouring in some stock now."

"Stock?"

"I picked up some shellfish when you were gone. I practiced what I've watched you do many times. I can't be sure it will taste the same, obviously, but I followed the recipe to the precise instructions."

He lifted a lid off the pan on the back burner and dipped a ladle into the thick coral liquid. The scent deepened and grew more complex, the deepening syrup of the softened garlic muddled with the tangy intensity of the shellfish broth and the concentration of heat-sweetened tomatoes. My mouth watered.

"And before you ask, yes, I passed it through the *passatutto,* or, as we say in the gray country, food mill. And yes, it does alter its texture and intensifies the taste."

"And yes, you ought to pay more attention before your tomatoes are burned *passata,*" I replied.

He switched away from me and focused on the pan. My stomach rumbled. When the smell of anticipation became almost unbearable, he placed each fish on a plate and spooned the fragrant red sauce over it. He took both plates out to the terrace.

"I'm not dressed."

"You're wearing an enormous shirt," he replied, walking past me. I stood inside the doorway. "You and I both know this is the only house in your entire town that is not overlooked. I cannot see out. No one can see in. This grand prison is the seat of true liberty, Santina."

He set both plates down and beckoned me outside. I was barefoot and giddy. I sat down.

He took a deep breath. "I meant everything I said."

I held his gaze.

"It's cruel," I replied.

"The truth can hurt. It's a cliché most people subscribe to."

"I don't want to be a cliché. Another employee who falls under the charms of her employer."

"You know that's not what is happening."

"I sense it isn't. But I can't know."

He resisted replying.

"Tomorrow? We live with this aching guilt? Who do we hurt more? Us or Adeline?"

He turned his head a little, listening to the cicadas applaud the moon. "Tonight we hurt nobody. Tonight we belong nowhere."

He turned his steel blue eyes toward me.

"I want to believe you, so very much," I replied.

"Maybe you won't. But it is the truth. My truth. I long for it to be yours too."

A whisper of breeze lifted the shirt off my back a little.

"*Apetito,* Santina."

I smiled, hoping I would convince myself.

Hoping the thorn in my chest might ease out by morning.

We slept in a knot at the center of my bed. He'd carried me upstairs after our dinner, lain me down. We creased the sheets with more lovemaking until the dead of night swallowed us into slumber. My head rested in the nook by his shoulder. Delirium eclipsed my guilt, until the doorbell clanged, sending a charge of panic through me. I leaped out of the bed, dashing to the door. I was halfway down the stairs when I realized I'd run out without a single piece of clothing on me. I dashed back into the bedroom, letting the door swing open with a bang. The major stirred. I whispered apologies and grabbed my dressing gown. The bell clanged again. I rushed downstairs, swinging open the door before asking who was there.

Paolino's expression was one of horror.

"*Dio* — what's happened?!"

"*Buon giorno,*" I replied, sweeping my hair off my face, the sudden realization of being stood barefoot in my dressing gown in the middle of the morning seeping down like a cold trickle of water.

"You unwell? You look . . ."

I rubbed my forehead. "Terrible headache."

"You look like you have a fever, Santi'."

"Yes."

I stood looking at him.

"Can I take these into the kitchen?"

"Oh yes, sorry, go ahead."

He stepped in, unsure. As he reached halfway to the kitchen I remembered the debris we'd left there last night. The major refused to let me clean up. We'd left an adulterous dinner for two strewn upon the counters.

"Wait!" I yelled out.

Paolino turned. I grasped at fictions and hated myself for it.

"It's a terrible mess. Please, leave the box here on the front table."

"I really think you should rest, Santina. You want me to bring some soup for you maybe? I can bring some pasta for the soldier too, save you cooking?"

"No need. I'll be worse if I do nothing."

He placed the box down and stepped toward me. He took my hands in his and lifted them to his lips. I wanted to cry.

"Rest today, my *tesoro.*"

I nodded. Then he shifted, took a glance out to sea, and straightened.

"Did the Englishman talk to you?"

"Talk to me?"

"Did he . . . mention anything . . . unusual?"

My stomach tightened. I longed to be swallowed up into someone else's reality. My mind dashed to my mountains, to the cool of the forest, to anywhere but here.

I shook my head so I didn't have to hear myself lying.

"We'll talk when you're better."

"*Grazie,* Paolino."

He kissed my forehead. We looked at each other. I felt cruel.

He left.

I turned back toward the kitchen. Perhaps I could clear away the gnawing inside me with each dish. My guilt was wrapped up like a tumble of prickly sea thistles, thrown on the wind along the rocky bay below. The mechanical motions silenced the tide for a brief respite. When all evidence of what had happened was dried and cleared, I set a pot of coffee upon the stove. I took a bowl from the cupboard. A batch of *crespelline* would force an escape from my awakening. I beat all my worries into those four eggs and milk. I sifted the flour into it, watching the powder snowflake over the liquid. I whisked it all together, each flick of my wrist sending me closer to a place of control. I lit a ring and set a large pan to heat. I watched the butter swirl in the warmth, and the picture of the major stood here but a few hours ago filled me. I ladled a spoon onto the hot iron and flipped it once it had browned. I continued like this until the mixture was used up. They would cool until I was ready with the filling. With each addition to the stack I inched away from the turbulence in my stomach.

I placed another thicker slab of butter to

ooze into liquid in another pan. I added flour. Watching the wooden spoon smooth into a béchamel did quiet my mind. I cut a slab of ricotta and slipped it in to melt. I ground a generous amount of salt. Concentric circles of warmth soothed me. Now I sped up, smoothing the mixture until it was an even consistency. I removed the pot from the stove, set it upon an iron pot holder and tipped in a mozzarella, roughly torn, and finely sliced salami. I looked at the mixture and the pile of *crespelline.* Later I would fill and bake them. Order had been restored. Today was like any other.

The major stepped in.

I turned toward him.

I wanted to pretend last night was a myth. Yet I ached to touch him.

"Your kitchen is alive, Santina."

My lips creased into an unsure smile.

"A glorious torture to wake up to the allure of delicious food. I suppose you're going to tell me I am to wait until lunch."

I stood wordless. His utter mastery of apparent ease left me unsure of what I ought to say. Who was I today? He intuited my shift.

"Elizabeth returns this afternoon," he said, steering us toward what we were supposed to be.

"Yes," I said, longing for reality to stay stalled somewhere beyond us.

"I'll take my coffee outside."

He lifted a cup from the cupboard, filled it, and left.

Perhaps it was best not to talk about last night at all. Perhaps this was what we ought to do. He spoke of one night. Perhaps I ought to summon the strength to shelve it, sift through it like flour, let the thoughts fall away without effort.

It was absurd. And impossible.

The sun was starting to peak. I needed to get water to the garden before it became too hot. I ran upstairs and jerked into my gardening housedress, ignoring the sheets, ignoring our creased shapes of lovemaking, breathing in the scent of us still lingering in the closed room. I found the major already in the garden, crouched down, examining the morning's crop. Beside him were several zucchini and a small pile of their flowers.

I didn't know where I should be.

"You look haunted, Santina," he said, looking up at me.

"I'm . . . lost."

He nodded, reaching into the thick tubular stems for another zucchini. He placed it with the others.

"I don't know this place either, Santina,"

he said, lifting his face up toward me.

The dappled light cast lemon shadows over it. He looked radiant.

"Let us just go about our work, shall we? I'd really prefer not to talk just now. If that's okay with you?"

I nodded. I couldn't believe that any amount of words would ever patch over our wrongs.

I filled a watering can and began on the farthest row from him. I watched the earth guzzle the liquid at the base of our eggplants. I tried to let their lustrous purple skins ease me into normality, like I would of a typical day, hatching what I might prepare, what voyage I might set on in the kitchen. But their luster glared in the sun and filled my head with nothing but the memory of the weight of him. I carried on with each trip to the tap, hoping the perfume of the melon plants might lift me away from the awkward vise around my middle, to no avail.

Then I felt him behind me.

I felt his breath on my neck, a whisper of him.

I stood there, allowing him to unzip my dress. I stood feeling the sun all over my body. I gave in to the maddening sensations as he knelt before me and led me far away from myself and into the heart of me. I relinquished to every touch. I folded into his arms as he lifted me under the shade of the lemon trees. As he pressed me against the trunk. As I welcomed all of him inside me.

He took my face in his hands. "There is only ever now, Santina."

He pushed deeper into me. My breath caught. I let the taste of him fill me.

We were nowhere and everywhere.

CHAPTER 17

The next afternoon ebbed toward early evening when the bell clanged and the parcel named Elizabeth was returned. I hadn't let myself acknowledge how much I missed her till I breathed in the oat scent of her hair. The young woman who delivered her looked wan. "She was up in the night calling for you. Broke my heart. Then my eardrums. Got a temper for something so small too!"

I scooped Elizabeth up into my arms. "You wreaking havoc up on the hill?"

Her eyes lit up with the sharp blue of her father's. His face blew into my mind.

"Grazie," I began, turning back to the woman, "her father is indebted to you. Please, take this."

I handed her the envelope the major had set aside, filled with notes as an extra thank-you. Only after my third insistence did she accept it and leave.

I placed Elizabeth down, and she slipped her hand into mine. I laid her small suitcase by the top of the steps that led down into the garden. We tackled each one with unhurried feet. We reached the ground; she squatted down onto the grass and picked up a stick to trace the blades. The sun was a spotlight on the golden glint in her red hair.

"*Cucino la pasta,* Santina!" she exclaimed with a giggle. I couldn't remember her stringing a full sentence together in Neapolitan before. Her laughter was infectious.

"Welcome home, *fanciulla!*" the major called down from the upper terrace.

Elizabeth looked up. Her face widened into a grin. She waved both her hands into the air. "Papà!"

She ran away from me and toward the stairs.

"She left a Brit and returned a local, Santina," he called down to me. "How did you manage that?"

His smile reached me like a flying ember. His skin was bronze in this light, as he faced out toward the sea, the sun on its final dip toward the horizon. He held my gaze. How were we supposed to navigate these straits? We were still threading through the story we wove. But even in this reassuring light, the ease toward the dusk, the pleasant shift

328

from the scorch, I couldn't shake the feeling that it would all fray before I was ready, like parchment on the breeze. All that was left of what happened between us would be an unfinished paragraph, a scrambled ending. I wasn't ready for that ache.

We slipped back into a semblance of normality that first night. I fed Elizabeth and laid her to sleep. I could have curled up next to her then and there, tiredness lapping over me. I resisted, prepared the major a light dinner, and laid it on the terrace beyond the kitchen. The evening was balmy, one you could steep in for hours. He stepped into the kitchen and closed the door behind him.

"I don't know where we go from here either, Santina."

"Nowhere at all, I think," I replied, noticing the words tripped out stickier than I had intended, hot licorice.

His expression clouded. "I have a strong instinct that you deserve a little space. From me. Paolino will come here soon enough. He'll be expecting your answer."

He looked down at his hands for a breath. "I suppose in my very clumsy way I want you to know that you must choose whatever is best for you."

The hair on the back of my neck prickled.

"You talk like I should choose between the two of you."

"Nonsense — I'm trying to explain how I . . ."

"How you talk of feelings for me and then ask me to give myself to another!" I replied, not caring that I interrupted. "I was a fool to think you wouldn't need to control everything."

"I'm trying to say that I don't want what we did to affect your life. For the worse."

My cheeks were hot. I wondered why he chose to broach the subject like this, clumsy strides of thought at odds with the lover I discovered last night, the same who held me just that afternoon. The change was brutal, a winter storm whipping in from the sea. It made me think of Adeline. My heart was nettles.

"What we did?" I asked, louder than I'd planned. "I thought we gave in to something bigger than either one of us? We didn't *do* anything. It *took* us. I stand here now feeling like you want me to be ashamed of it all."

"Of course not. If anything, I'm insisting you shouldn't be. We shouldn't be."

"I can't listen to how you think my life should be. I don't want to think about anything other than what I have to do in the next hour. Don't force me to brush everything away. I can't do that. I won't do that!"

He stepped closer to me. I fought so hard to hold on to my resolve. I bit down my tears with all my strength, but the feel of his hands upon me, the warmth of his embrace was more than I could bear. I let go. I was crouched in a tiny rowboat tossed on a churning sea. I hated myself for clinging to him, grasping for an anchor.

"I don't know how to let go," I sobbed, horrified at my dismantling.

"I don't know either."

We held the silence, our breaths in unison, softening. I'd never had a sense of the fluidity of time until that moment: the seconds sapped, oozing in different directions. And we stood in the warm mess of it, gazing into one another, answers drowning where breath took their place. One day I wouldn't be able to stand here like this, inside him a little. One day I would not invite him into this quiet. And the feeling crushed me. How could I ever leave this place?

It didn't surprise me to find he had made the decision before I could. I woke to a folded note upon the table inside the kitchen, beside a small package wrapped in tissue paper. Elizabeth and I had revisited her startling dreams somewhere in that mercurial sliver between night and dawn. I'd held her as she'd cried them away, drowning the memories with cold tears until sleep wrapped her up into the dark quiet once again.

I'd sat there pretending I would give in to sleep, thinking only of the major on the floor above. I wanted so hard to not behave and feel like a young woman who had just given the most private part of herself to another, caving in to the panic of having laid too much bare. I tried to intuit the strength inside that vulnerability. In all those glorious poems the major read to me, line upon line searching out the wonders of the world, exploring that powerlessness that makes us all human, this was the thread that those writers returned to time and again. But I lay in my bed, tossing under my sheets, and the feeling of comfort within doubt eluded me. And it made me feel ashamed. I'd thought myself stronger, but it was naïve bravado after all. This is what hurt the most.

That morning as I shuffled through the whisper of dawn, tousled from my lack of sleep, I almost didn't see that letter. My first thought was that it was my termination of employment. Somehow it was easier to imagine myself hating him for his turfing me out without a second thought, than to sit with the feeling that his passion might indeed last more than our night together. If he turned me away, I could despise him at a distance. If he felt love for me, I would have a great deal more to turn away from. Joy and loss were tempestuous dance partners after all, smoky silhouettes, entwined, an intoxicating floor show, taking turns to lead.

Inside there was a poem. His script like spun sugar. Tennyson's words ran the length of it. We had studied this one together. He'd pored over each line, encouraging me to pull away the words of Ulysses, dive deep into their meanings. My favorite line shone, as it always did:

"I am a part of all that I have met;
Yet all experience is an arch wherethro'
Gleams that untravell'd world whose margin fades
For ever and forever when I move."

This was the line that he had taken special care over. I'd watched him that afternoon when he first presented it to me. I listened as he'd drawn a parallel to Ulysses' restlessness and my desire for a life beyond my bay. And now I let the memory wash over me, that feeling of needing to escape my town, realizing it was never born from hate, but because there was simply nothing here for me. My eyes traced the words again. The untravell'd world was closer than I thought. Inside me even. Inside him. Which path was the bravest? Following the trail inward or outward?

On the other side of the paper he explained that he would be away in Naples for several days conducting some business errands and would spend some time with Adeline. There was an envelope with extra money to cover any incidentals, which I was to use at will. He urged me to invite my brother to stay with me rather than remain alone. He mentioned nothing about what had happened. No explicit reliving of that. But his true sentiments were couched inside that poem. He was urging me to map my own course. That's when tears coursed down my cheeks; no braver expression of love than the desire to set another free.

Elizabeth and I went to surprise Marco at the height of the midmorning sun, heat rising in zigzags from the blistering stone beneath the startling cloudless blue sky. An invitation to the cool of the villa and a refreshing lunch looked like the very thing he needed. We didn't stay to distract him from his work, and I took the chance to stop into Rosalias on the way back.

Elizabeth sang to the yellow budgies chirping in their cages along the shaded wall leading to the main door, calling out their song toward the turquoise sea far below. One of her brothers opened the door. Rosalia and Pasquale were sat with two policemen at the kitchen table. Even Elizabeth slipped into silence along with the group as our eyes adjusted to the dark.

"So this is how to contact me, Signorina," one of the policemen concluded.

The second, a smaller, rounder, older man, turned and spoke to the whole family. "No matter how small. This is the time to find courage. Please don't keep your doubts to yourselves. We're taking this very seriously indeed. We wouldn't have come all the way from Napoli if we weren't. We know someone in this town must know something."

My eyes shot to Pasquale. His expression was as serene as it always was. My heart tightened.

"*Grazie,* Signori," Rosalia's mother said at last.

The men stood up and shook hands with the family. Rosalia moved around from the other side of the table and squeezed Elizabeth.

"Now that's the nicest view I'll have all day, *fanciulla*!" She planted a warm kiss on either cheek. "Thank you so much for stopping in, Santi', those men have been here all morning. It's turning into a full murder inquiry. My mother refused to move. She wanted to hear everything. Come on, let me walk with you, I need some air."

"It'll cook you out there."

"I don't care, Santina. It's like a prison in here."

We climbed the narrow steps up from her door, passed beneath her fragrant lemon and kiwi canopy, then strolled along the white stone alley toward the villa, bougainvillea cascading celebration over the wall each side from the flanked houses, and beyond, my slate mountains looming up around us, closing in.

She took my hand. "My mind is a sea, Santina."

I looked at her, wishing I could tell her why I felt the same.

"An awful thing happens and it makes you know how short this all is. And it's ridiculous and selfish maybe, but truly, one of the first things I thought was don't waste a second. I want Pasquale to be my husband,

Santina. I want to share whatever time we have together. And now I know that in any moment things can change. Is it wrong to be thinking these things?"

Her eyes shone with their familiar warmth now. She looked like the Rosalia I knew. It was a comfort to see her luminous despite, or maybe because of, the anguish her family were in.

"I think mistakes don't happen if we truly follow our hearts. And I don't care how sappy that sounds," I replied.

She stopped and turned to me, against the blanched white of the wall behind her, scorching in the sun; her skin looked a deeper shade of olive. A palm from beyond the garden wall behind fanned her outline. It reminded me of the Madonna's crown of stars. She pinned me with the same direct stare as the first time I met her.

"What's happened?" she asked.

"What do you mean?" I replied, feeling my cheeks deepen, pretending it was the unforgiving beams from above.

"Santina the mountain goat has softened at last. I turn to you for sensible truths. Now listen to you. From this I know your answer was 'yes'! Tell me everything! What did he say? How did he say it? What did he look like?"

Elizabeth took off at a sudden pelt, allowing me to escape the answers. We called out to her and reached her just as she was about to negotiate the steepest length of steps. I took her hand despite her protests.

"Well?" Rosalia asked.

I couldn't shunt the truth for long. "I haven't seen him yet."

"Why? What on earth are you waiting for? If Pasquale asked me, I'd be dancing on the streets."

"You're always dancing on the streets."

"Beside the point."

"Does Pasquale know how you feel?" I asked, steering the conversation to safer ground. She blushed at that, which caught me off guard. Perhaps I had misunderstood her confidence all this time. At the mention of his name, her expression streaked with a childlike vulnerability.

"Rosalia, I'm sure it must be difficult for him now with everyone grieving. He wouldn't ask you now, would he?"

She shrugged, intimating that it wouldn't be wrong if he did.

"And your mamma? How would she react if you blurted this out right now?"

"That's what I mean, Santina. Time. It's so precious. It's so fast. Am I supposed to stand by and watch it all trickle away? Why?

To be proper? How can I believe in that anymore? My brother is dead. All the rules have been broken."

That's when her tears shuddered through. I held her. My tears fell on her shoulder too. She pulled away and held her hands around my face.

"I don't want you to cry too, Santina. I'm so sorry."

"Don't ever apologize, Rosalia," I replied with snatched breaths, feeling like my tears were a lie. I longed to let her in on everything that had passed in the few hours we were apart, but it was more than I could burden her with.

We pressed our foreheads together. Soggy laughter. I felt the heat rise up from below, in that narrow stony *viccolo* where we stood.

"I love you, Santina."

"I love you too, Rosali'. We look like a couple of witches, no? Standing here with our wet heads together."

A belly laugh frothed out then. We wiped our faces.

"Then let's cast a spell!" she boomed, dancing her hands like she always did. "For love and courage and not wasting time!"

I smiled. In spite of everything she was still a sunbeam. My first true friend.

■ ■ ■ ■

Marco arrived looking cooked.

"Food or a bath?" I asked, opening the door.

"Both! So the cat's away?" he asked, skulking into the terrace. He looked up at the vines. "Impressive! Does he ever let you sleep?"

My stomach tightened with guilt. I wondered if my face hid it as well as I hoped.

"Why don't I throw in the pasta and you go ahead upstairs and have a wash?"

"You really taking to this lady of the house thing, no? Comes a little too natural if you ask me."

I forced a giggle.

"Well, if you twist my arm," he said, "I'll swan around here like a lord, what the hell!"

I didn't love the way his eyes surveyed the major's belongings. He took inventory. My memory pierced with our last conversation here.

"How's he have the time to read all this lot?" Marco asked as we walked past the bookshelves beside the stairwell.

"Every day a little. He's taught me too."

"Doesn't he have a job like the rest of us?"

I rolled my eyes at that and led us up to

my floor. I showed him the bathroom, laid out some extra towels, and explained that he would be staying in the guestroom toward the back of the house, just near mine. He stood in my doorway and leaned against the wooden frame.

"Just look at this, Santina." His eyes rose toward the ceiling. "Do you ever really see where you are anymore? These ceilings, look at all that work. And the colors make me feel what I think people go to church to feel."

His eyes lit up. It was wonderful to see him like this. Yet the fleeting happiness soon slipped into a more familiar sarcasm. "We all end up the same place though, eh?"

He turned toward the bathroom, humming to himself.

Downstairs I set to lunch. I laid a dish with several handfuls of fresh vegetables: cherry tomatoes, lengths of cucumber, a small head of cos lettuce. I chopped a *radicchio* into quarters and set it upon a griddle pan to wilt. When its skin became charred, I slipped the leaves onto a plate and drizzled it with olive oil and a sprinkle of coarse salt. Meanwhile the spaghetti swirled in a steamy simmer, a handful of fresh anchovies melted in several glugs of warming olive oil to which I added some paper-thin slices of garlic and one of our homegrown chilis to infuse. When the pasta tasted done but not soggy, I forked it into the warm oil, coating each strand with the sweet-salty taste. The smell earthed me. For a moment I could escape the sensation of standing at the precipice of a deep hole. For a moment I was safe in the daily order of the world.

When Marco returned, Elizabeth and I joined him on the terrace. His hair was wet and fragrant, swept off his face to reveal his high cheekbones and the reddened apples of his cheeks. That's when I noticed his shirt.

"Marco, put that back this instant!"

His eyes took on a childlike gleam. "What do you mean?"

"That's not yours."

"Obviously. I never have my shirts monogrammed. It's like he's terrified someone's going to steal it. I'm impressed you noticed. You know all his shirts by heart?"

I could feel my cheeks turn crimson.

"Touched a nerve, did I?" He laughed. "Seriously, it's just for lunch. I'll hang it back in his wardrobe after. Alright?"

I shook my head in resignation. "You're a liability."

"I'm starving is what I am. And this, my darling sister, smells like I died and went to anchovy heaven!" He poured a glass of wine for me and made me *salud* before I could press my point. We sipped the chilled wine. He teased Elizabeth for her lack of table manners. Then he inhaled my spaghetti and vegetables.

"So, he says I live here to guard the place, eh? Did he talk numbers?"

"Stop it, Marco! You're here to look after me. You're not working."

"You don't need looking after. That's what other people ask of *you.*"

I smiled and twirled another forkful of the spaghetti, noting that I'd timed the softening of the garlic to perfection. "He wouldn't trust anyone other than my own family in here. I won't let anyone in past the front chairs usually. People have greedy eyes around here. I don't need to tell you that."

"What's that supposed to mean?"

I received his affront and let it slip off me without defense. "I mean, look at the people living down on the *viccoli.* Barely enough to eat, Marco. And we sit here, sheltered like kings. He knows that. I do too. I also know there are roving hands all over town."

"Speaking of rovers. How's lover boy?"

I blushed in spite of myself.

"That bad, ha? You've turned into a to-mato."

"Nonsense."

"And you're denying it too. I didn't realize it was so serious!"

"It's not."

Marco looked through me.

"I've heard rumors, is all," he added, with a twinkle in his eye I chose to ignore.

"Rumors about what?" I was stalling. We both knew it.

I never longed for Elizabeth to command my attention more.

"Santina, you may live in a fairy tale, but around here, if a man follows a scent he usually expects a little something in return."

I was counting the strands of spaghetti now.

"I would guess it wouldn't be long before he either asks you to do something you're not ready to do, or beg you to put a ring on, so he can."

"That's enough!" I blurted.

He rested his fork on his bowl. I sipped my water. My swallow was loud.

"I'm sorry, *sorellina*. I'm teasing, is all." He reached for my hand. A gentle squeeze threatened the start of my tears. I swallowed them.

"Seems like it's everyone's business but mine," I answered, trying not to replay the slew of memories.

Marco's face lit up. "See, I know things when I see them."

"Ready for some fruit?"

"You don't get to change the subject now. I want to know if he's going to be my brother-in-law."

"I want to know why it's so important to you."

He leaned in toward me now. His face was a moody sky, fast moving clouds passing over the sun. "You say you want to be family. You say how important it is that we've found each other. Well, Santina, the harsh truth of that is you actually have to say the things that are hard, because in the end family are the only ones you can trust around here, believe me, I know. I had no one, just like you, and I learned who to trust. I found my family where I had to and I stick to them because they have my back. And I have yours. And if you think you can't trust me to tell me the things you're going through, then we're not family at all."

My face froze.

"And it's fucking scary. But until you stop behaving like a sanctimonious island you aren't ever going to know what it means to love. Not really. This is your brother asking you to trust him, for chrissakes!"

I ignored the way he spoke and clung to

his meaning. He was right, of course. I did hold him at arm's length. I was happier knowing about his life than revealing anything about mine. His delivery was brusque, aggressive even, but I knew that it came from a passionate place. His words were of a kid who'd grown up as an orphan. This was new territory for both of us. I wondered how many conversations I could have at this intensity over the next few days before it broke me.

"I'm so sorry, Marco. I didn't mean it to feel like I was shutting you out. I just don't know which way my life ought to go right now."

He watched me for a moment. I let him read me in the silence.

"You're not in love with him, that much is clear."

I stiffened.

"It's okay, Santina. Please, trust me. Does your master know about it?"

"He's not my master."

"Pays you, teaches you, has you be his child's mother. That's pretty much a master."

The bell jangled.

"Who comes at lunch hour?" Marco asked, irritated.

I walked down to the door, unlocked it.

A hopeful lover stood before me. A tray of sweet pastries eclipsed his sunny smile.

CHAPTER 18

The knots in my stomach tightened. A dusting of vanilla sugar powdered the space between us.

"Buona sera, tesoro," Paolino said, his eyes lighting up with the familiar gleam of mischievous affection.

"My brother is here," I answered, realizing there were several hundred other more appropriate replies. He registered my unease, then stepped in anyway.

"Buona sera, Signore!" Paolino called out to Marco who sat at the head of the small table at the far end of the terrace, the two huge terra-cotta pots framing him like pawns to their taking. His expression tipped into an oblique smile.

"Please, I'm only her brother, not her father." He lifted his wine glass then and gestured for Paolino to join. It was my place to do that, not his. It felt like excited adolescents had overtaken the villa. "You can call me Marco if you must."

"Piacere," Paolino said, balancing the tray of pastries in one hand, strolling down the length of the terrace, reaching out the other for Marco to shake. "We met last year, Ferragosto. On the beach."

"I didn't know I was so memorable."

I shot Marco a look.

"We've just sat down to lunch, Paolino, have some with us, yes?"

We performed a perfunctory polite rally of insistence and refusal till he sat down at last. My spaghetti would be getting cold. I took the pastries into the kitchen. For a breath, the small room skidded back into my night with the major, the sweet smells of that midnight feast filling my mind, our hushed thoughts and words, his gentle fingers on mine, his mouth. Marco's voice, calling out for me to not keep them waiting, wrenched me back to the present; how different these voices were, bouncing across that table, a world away from that night. It was no longer the tiny altar at which we paid reverence for a secret, our culinary delights. It was fast becoming Marco's chessboard, in which he might corner Paolino, that much was clear. I stepped back outside with a bowl, cutlery, and a linen napkin. Paolino watched me fork several generous swirls of pasta onto it. His face lit up.

"Won't the major mind us eating out here like this?" he asked, flicking his napkin out onto his lap, sitting between Marco and I, opposite Elizabeth. He didn't wait for an answer but dove into the bowl, twisting his fork at speed.

"Master is out of town," Marco replied. "My sister doesn't waste any time getting all sorts of riffraff around her table." He grabbed Paolino's glass and tipped in some wine.

Paolino laughed a little too loud. My appetite clamped shut.

"What's wrong, Santina?" Marco asked, filling his mouth with a final twist of pasta, emptying the carafe of wine into his glass, then raising it as if I ought to go back to the kitchen to refill.

"Nothing," I lied, standing up, feeling my eyebrows crease together.

"Why the look? You want us to enjoy the fruits of your labor or not?"

I walked to his end of the table and snatched the carafe from his hands. I stepped back into the kitchen and tipped the demijohn to fill it, only halfway this time. I had no desire to be sat upon that terrace with two drunk men sullying it. The liquid swirled into it and the major's face rose into view; his lips, salty with our dinner, sweet with this wine. I returned to my seat. Would I be a coward and pretend I hadn't read Paolino's proposal?

"So, Paolino," my brother began, a swagger in his voice, as if intuiting my reticence, "when are you going to make an honest woman of my sister?"

I stiffened. Marco noticed. Paolino slid him a wry grin, as if he knew the answer. Perhaps his written proposal was a formality and nothing more? How different this childish expression from the flowery words he'd asked the American to write on his behalf. His whole demeanor a world away from the major, my tentative lover who had lost himself with me, who had cradled the heart of me, tasted me, searched me. I ignored the prickle at the base of my neck.

Paolino's expression fell. He glanced back at me, a man betrayed. Had my thoughts streaked my face?

"You talk to him about it before me?" he asked, letting his fork drop onto the rim of the bowl.

"What do you mean?" I stalled.

Paolino shot Marco a look.

"Santina and I have no secrets," Marco replied.

My embarrassment bubbled toward rolling boil. "Paolino, Marco is teasing — and you're letting it work."

It fell flat.

"And you invite me in here, to sit at the table to make a fool of me?" Paolino replied, his words poking up like little thorns.

"Most people don't need others' help for that," Marco replied, cool. "There are exceptions of course." His glass touched his lips, and he swallowed the contents.

"Are we ready for fruit?" I asked, a feeble attempt to rein in the battle of pride combusting before me.

The men weren't distracted that easy.

"I think I'll come back another time," Paolino said, running a tense hand over his hair.

"It's fine, Paolino, really," I replied. His clothes looked at once too tight, the heat fighting to escape somewhere around his suffocating collar.

"Thank you for lunch, Santina. I'm not going to impose any longer."

He stood up, let his napkin drop onto the tablecloth, pushed in his chair.

"Food that good, eh?" Marco chirped.

"Please! That's enough," I called out, my own temperature rising.

The men stared at me. I was navigating

down a narrow gorge. My breaths quickened.

"Elizabeth will be taking her nap soon," I began, determined that their little game would not conquer my feigned calm. "I will have lots to do. We'll come to the shop later, Paolino? Will you be there?"

"Of course."

He reached out a hand to Marco, which he shook without hesitation.

I followed Paolino along the terrace, beneath the vines and the trailing wisteria, which did little to soften the atmosphere. I closed the door behind him.

"You never told me he actually asked you already," Marco said in a sarcastic slur.

"You're right. I didn't," I replied, twisting back to face him, watching his body language slip toward inebriation.

"Why so cagey? Shouldn't you be waltzing around with flowers in your head?" he asked, as I walked back to the table. "Isn't that what all girls want? A rich grocer on their arm. I mean, this palace is all well and good but living in luxury as a servant isn't all it seems, no?"

"I'm not a servant." I rearranged the cutlery upon the table, fretful lining up of inane objects to regain futile control of my frustration. "I don't know why you spoke to him that way."

"Because I don't think he's good enough for you."

"You don't know anything about him!" I replied a little too loudly, stacking the plates, yearning for this space to be returned to the stillness with which it usually hummed. I returned with a bowl of peaches. Marco grabbed one. I watched him peel it with a deft knife. His movements were precise, methodical, surgical almost. I was observing an autopsy.

I confided in the coroner. "He's a good man."

"Says who?"

I rolled my eyes. "And he has asked me to marry him, yes." I reached for a peach, feeling glad Marco wasn't hurrying for a retort.

"But you don't want to," he said at last.

"We've known each other for so little."

"And you don't want to."

I found his gaze. The peach drizzled its sweet juice down my finger toward my thumb. The major loved this fruit. He blew into my mind like ribbons of smoke. The sensation of his fingers tracing my body seduced my thoughts.

"You see, Santina," Marco began, his sermon yanking me out of my waking dream, "you either love someone or you don't. People talk about time. Rubbish. They've never loved. Love is an instant. A flicker you can't ignore. Time fans the flames, or extinguishes them. But love? Powerful and brief. It's an instant — our first and last heartbeat. Don't tell me you don't know this."

"I don't," I lied, easing myself beneath the crumpled sheets of lovemaking, back to the major's face rising from my hips to meet mine, the scent of me on his mouth.

"You're a shitty liar."

"And you're only happy when you're fighting," I replied, happier to argue than relive the thorny memory. "Wonder where you got that from? Besides, what makes you such an expert, baby brother? Where'd you learn all this wisdom on love?"

A flock of memories flitted across his expression, fitful shadows, till he returned to what I now understood was a studied, not innate, calm.

"I've felt it power through me like lightning. I know the destruction it leaves after the fire. Why do you think I love the solitude of tombs?"

"I think you like to paint your life differently from what it is."

He didn't rush for a reply.

"And I think I have a hard time remembering you're not just my little brother," I added.

His eyebrows raised into a smirk. "Amen. Back to work then," he said, straightening. "Your food was delicious. Your lover was clumsy. Your brother was rude."

I waited for him to remedy his actions.

"And he apologizes."

A reluctant acceptance furled the corner of my lips.

"I feel protective over you, Santina. Allow me that. Someone's got to make sure you do the right thing, no?"

"You seem to think so, yes."

He held my gaze, searching. And for the first time, I allowed myself to agree with what he had said. Every piercing syllable of it.

Elizabeth and I reached the shop just past the final scorch of the afternoon. I hadn't been down here for a while, and at first the blaze of color draped on the tourists, the giddy frolic of their passing conversations, overwhelmed me. There was a bubble of summer to their gait; their feet skimmed the cobbles with buoyant steps, lilting to the seaside rhythms of our bay. They walked around unhurried, drinking in every stone, every storefront, gazing wide-eyed at the mountains that encircled us, looming reminders of antiquity. They cooed at the quaint flowerboxes, the men in starched white overalls, too ready to serve, accommodate, inviting a sprinkling of glamour to their quotidian lives.

Elizabeth and I wove between the onslaught of linen beach dresses, the bronzed beauty of the outsiders, basking in their snippet of vacation in the molten light, slipping us toward evening. Outside Paolino's shop, some tables were laid out, edging toward the triangular convergence of several boutique-lined alleyways. Paolino leaned against the doorway, chatting with a man I didn't recognize. I watched him for a moment, letting the stream of people brush past me. I looked up at his well-maintained shop, the care with which he nurtured the blaze of geraniums and hibiscus in huge pots beside the entry, spraying the welcome with their coral, fuchsia, violet, and lustrous amber blooms. In the window hung legs of prosciutto and huge wheels of cheese, garlands of shallots and garlic woven around them, and beneath, wooden crates tipped at jaunty angles, laden with eggplant, zucchini, and lush green-purple heads of *lollo rosso* lettuce. He was an artist. He had flair for such things. He knew how to attract people

357

to him, and I was torn between feeling like I was just another who had been lulled into the buoyant haze of him, unable to decipher what it was I felt for him in all honesty, beyond the apparent joy of basking in his luminous energy.

I watched the young women stroll by. Several took time to send looks his way. He was handsome after all, without an aggressive swagger. His face was open, an invitation, a spring song; uplifting, well rehearsed, yet intangible, fleeting — the precursor of greater heat. My heart ached. I ought to love a man like this.

He saw Elizabeth and me. His brief smile rippled toward awkward.

We crossed over to him, weaving through the sun-toasted beachgoers.

"You, Signorina, look like you need some chocolate, no?" he asked, beaming at Elizabeth. He took her hand and led her inside to his treasure trove of delicacies. She breathed in the salty sweetness of the shop, her eyes dancing over every shiny wrapper of candied fruits, sugared almonds, jars of pickled vegetables, olives, oversized barrels of olive oil, and a large glass urn of fresh lemonade.

My mouth watered.

He handed her a small basket of *gianduia,*

soft praline wrapped in red foil, then led us back outside.

"And for the love of my life?" he asked.

The words smarted.

"I'm fine, Paolino."

"Please, I insist. Lemonade perhaps? Some *stuzzichini*?"

My resolve wilted. He returned with a plate of delicate strips of prosciutto, a few hunks of bread, a large ball of buffalo mozzarella drizzled with dark green olive oil. He poured each of us a glass of lemonade. Elizabeth and gluttony made messy acquaintance beside me in the shadow of his culinary seduction.

"I'm sorry about lunch," he said at last, crisping through the pause.

"So am I," I replied. My chewing sounded clumsy in my head. "My brother is, well, he doesn't spend a lot of time with people. Well, he does, but they're mostly dead or grieving. It affects a person, you know?"

Paolino nodded, but it didn't underline agreement.

We slipped back into silence; the destruction of the softening mozzarella distracted our thoughts. It melted in my mouth. My guilt swelled. I longed to intuit how to steer them. I wished for one moment I could be Rosalia. She would breeze through these stilted thoughts. I longed to navigate them like a mountainside, judging rock by rock at lightning speed, deft, poised, trusting my balance and confidence to adjust with implicit skill. It would be better to stop considering his feelings and offer brutal honesty about my own — the very thing that had attracted him to me in the first place. I didn't play games like the others. Now I watched myself swaying around my mind, an affected dancer, not so much the ballerina as the failed tightrope act. I could see Paolino would be the husband most girls would want, but the truth ached; I needed to forgive myself for not loving this man the way I longed to feel for a lover.

"Paolino," I began. He met my eyes. I hung in the hiatus, almost able to resist the warm chocolate of his gaze. Almost able to convince myself that I would never be happy creating a life with him. Almost able to acknowledge that to live and work amongst this stream of strangers, this incessant reminder of other lands, creating tempting displays to progress his empire would leave me unfulfilled in immeasurable ways. I longed for the solicitude of a life the major had unfurled. I longed for a partner to pore over words and thoughts with, who would gain as much pleasure from this as eating the finest dish I could create, or eating the first matured peach fresh off the tree.

I remembered the feel of Paolino's lips on mine. The way he looked at me with a tender sparkle, as if he intuited more about me than he let on. A twinge of pleasure, followed by a swell of guilt; my night with the major still pulsed through me like a heartbeat, incessant, unstoppable, thudding for life. The entire escapade wrenched like a torrid dream I might never wake from while sending the caramel shivers of a treasured memory to the tips of my limbs.

"I received your letter," I said. The words flopped onto the table in a clumsy heap.

A ray streaked across us. He squinted. It made it hard to read his expression.

"The major read it to me."

Sun glow, near kisses, his hands, his weight.

Paolino swallowed. "And I meant every word, Santina. Your neighbor was so kind to help me. She told me I had talent for poetry. See what you do to me? I was a boy till you came back. I chased after pictures. A pretty face, a nice dress — I was gone. A child. But you're the person I want to be old with. You're the one I want to hold my children."

Time skidded around us. Smudged pictures of a certain future cluttered my mind. The words closed in on me like static. And beyond, the steady underscore of bodies strolling to and from our bay, their feet scuffing the cobbles, bubbling sea-soaked conversations of delight.

"Are you going to make me the happiest man in Positano, Santina?"

He led me to the precipice. Perhaps we could teeter at the edge a little longer. There was no hurry after all. In a few days' time, my mind would be clear once again, the dreamless sleep with the major would be a past, no longer trailing my periphery like a sun-bronzed haze. Soon I would be able to give the answer I knew both he and I longed for.

"You sit around like that all day, boy?! You should make a mother proud!"

I'd never been happier to be bludgeoned by Signora Cavaldi's sarcasm. We twisted around to see her charging toward us. In a few words I was back in their corridor, huddled in that cot. A familiar panic rippled through me.

"Mamma! You should follow my lead! Let your son spoil you for once!" He signaled for her to sit with us. I balked at the idea of this conversation becoming a group discussion.

Elizabeth burst into sudden tears. I looked down. Hazelnut *gianduia* streaked her dress and slid in muddy tracks toward the floor where it disappeared into mucky destruction.

Paolino ran in for more napkins.

"He fusses over you and that English child like you were his already."

Elizabeth's face contorted. I envied her lament.

Signora Cavaldi's face looked older, but her gait was as stiff and bombastic as ever. Paolino returned, fussing over the stain by Elizabeth's hem. I urged his hand away.

"Leave the child to the girl who's paid to do that — and serve the *americana* who just walked in," his mother piped, flinging her hand into the air.

Paolino caught the final tip-taps of the beaded curtain as the young woman swayed inside. "Don't go anywhere, Santi', I'll be right back."

Elizabeth took her time to return to peace, all the while attracting bemused and disgusted looks from the passersby. I felt the hot glare of the woman Paolino would make my mother-in-law. My throat scraped dry. The fishmonger on the opposite side of the *viccolo* called out to Signora. She stood and marched over to him and they began an animated discussion on the catch that morning.

Rosalia's face emerged from the crowd, a buoy bobbing amongst strangers. Her dimples deepened into a warm smile. She reached me and gave me a squeeze.

"I'm meeting Pasquale for a *passeggiata* along the sea, *lungo mare,*" she said, her face gleaming in the burnished rays. "Mamma said it was okay. My sisters weren't impressed. Today they can go to hell."

"You don't mean that."

"Don't I? They make a prison up there. I can't breathe."

I admired her defiance, her resilience, her courage, qualities which shone even as her heart broke, streaking light through the cracks. Meanwhile I stood, feeling like a paper decoration fraying in the wind, repetitive cutout patterns in faded pastels.

"You're especially beautiful today, Rosalia," I said, watching her capture the attention of several passing tourists.

"I feel completely lost. You make me feel that the world has order."

"You make me feel like your accountant."

She cackled then. I hadn't heard her laugh in too long.

"So, how is your husband-to-be? Beside himself with excitement? I knew you had no chance once he decided it would be you."

Decision: a final word, a brick wall, a declaration of camps. I'd never struggled with it before. Now the idea penned around me, a stable door slamming shut.

"He's inside. And he's not my husband-to-be." A young child squeezed into a smart shirt and pressed shorts darted around us, followed by another screaming out in chase.

"Stop dancing around your words, Santina — he told my brother that he was going to speak to the priest at the Chiesa Nuova."

The idea of me standing at the steps of the biggest church in town waving to crowds of his family clawed at my stomach. I lifted Elizabeth off her chair.

"We'd better get going, Rosali', Marco will be home for dinner soon."

"Thank you, Santina."

"Stop thanking me. It's like you're chalking up a debt."

"And that's why I love you!" She twisted away, straightened her shirt and swayed her hips downhill toward the man she loved, swallowed back into the throng of well-dressed visitors waltzing downhill to their evening entertainment.

We stepped into the cool of the shop. It took a moment for our eyes to adjust. When we did, the figures sharpened into focus.

The woman was tall, slim, with hair that lulled down her back in gentle waves. Paolino's face colored through his well-practiced spectrum of charm. Her head was cocked to one side. I don't think I'd ever seen an exchange of prosciutto look so romantic. Something ugly sludged my stomach.

They said their final goodbyes. She walked by me, leaving a fragrant mist of rose, a flowery memory hovering between he and I. I felt a sense of her being someone familiar, a face sparkling in a crowd, but the picture wavered, a watery reflection in a puddle underfoot. I turned back to him, disorientated by the infantile whisper of envy snaking through me.

Would I make him the happiest man in Positano after all?

CHAPTER 19

Paolino's eyes found mine. He came out from behind the counter, wiping his hands on a dishcloth, flopping it over his shoulder as he reached us.

"I didn't plan to have this conversation surrounded by legs of ham, Santina."

I smiled at his surprising self-awareness. A frank discussion in the middle of his shop seemed at once the most sensible idea. I longed for the courage to do so. He looked at me, expectant. I felt like he needed me to step into the outline of a wife he had drawn in his imagination, to add color and depth to his half-finished sketch.

I didn't long for romance after all, the dreamed-up version of a lover or what love should look like, feel like. I ached for intimacy. A quiet complicity. Standing there surrounded by the paper garlands advertising the latest confectionary, the wooden boxes of coffee beans, the stacks of labeled tea boxes shipped in for the foreigners, I could imagine Paolino and I hovering in that spark of silence between two lovers who know one another's completeness. Then the intimacy of my night with the major conjured into view. Around me were the abundance and displays of romantic love. Yet I yearned for a lover who would unwrap himself and shine light on the hidden parts of me. I wasn't sure I would ever allow Paolino to do that.

I felt his hands around my face. His lips kissed mine. Guilty tears pricked my eyes. I didn't let them fall. He mistook them for the kind of love he sought, which made them smart even more. He looked deep into me. Perhaps he too could sense there would always be a part of me I could not share with him? His love was a beautiful panorama, serene, a mountain lake sheltered by trees. What I felt for the major was an unknown sea, stretching beyond what my eyes could fathom, unknown, powerful, profound. Impossible. How could I stay in that house living under the pretense of normality? How long would I hover in this limbo?

"Paolino, everything feels so very fast," I said at last.

"Life is the blink of an eye."

I felt the knot around my middle tighten.

"Santina, when I heard about Rosalia's brother, it just made me think that we shouldn't waste time. Over anything. And I know how I feel about you. And I want to share everything with you."

"And I feel like we don't even know each other yet."

"That's like saying you need to know the ending of a story before you read it."

Embarrassment flitted across his face for a breath. I watched him make a conscious decision to retract his impulse. "What I mean is, I don't know all there is to know, I don't know all of you, I don't know all of me, for heaven's sake! But I don't care. I trust my gut. Always have. In the end that's all we have. Look around us — none of this was built from logic alone!"

He swung around at his precious displays, the embodiment of his courage, his ambition, a self-professed disciple to apparent beauty. I might have felt attuned to him more if we'd been standing upon my mountains, if he'd been gazing or paying worship to the dense forests, the damp air thick with earth and dew and the hum of wordless wisdom deep in my rocks, my craggy paths tangled with roots and moss and memories. I stood before him knowing that if I carved a lifetime beside him, the shadow of the major would trawl me forever. The realization was a sharp white ray of sun, a shaft of light cutting through storm-filled clouds like a blade.

"I need to get back, Paolino."

"Are you alright? You look gray."

His acute observation caught me off guard.

"I feel gray."

His expression fell.

"I want to make you the happiest woman in town, Santina."

Conversational quicksand pulled at me.

"I need time, Paolino. I've promised the major to stay until Elizabeth leaves for England."

"He doesn't own you, Santina."

The words were a stone dropping to a pond's muddy bed. He did. A part of me was already his. And the feeling was woven golden threads that stretched out over the hills toward wherever he now sat beside Adeline, or lost in his thoughts, of us perhaps, or delving deep into his favorite book of poetry, lines that skimmed the luminous tip of what we had shared. Surrendering to the sensation was the cusp of liberation, not imprisonment.

"You are a beautiful man, Paolino. I don't

know if I am ready to be a wife."

"Not any wife, Santina. *Mine.*"

"And what kind of wife can I be to you now? With someone else's child on my hip, living up at the house? You're asking me to leave everything that has given me the chance to follow my dreams, beyond this town."

"To chase what, Santina? Imagined lives? You don't hear what life is really like for us over there? You think these rich *americani,* all smiles here, treat us fishing folk like equals back home? You're living a daydream if you do."

I could feel his feathers of pride start to ruffle, but I wasn't ready to walk away.

"I'm saying I didn't picture becoming a wife."

"So you want a life of loneliness? You expect me to believe that with all my heart? Look at yourself — you look after this girl like she's your own. You're born to care. It comes naturally. It shines out of you like a sun. And I love this about you. I can't believe that that's the same person who wants to live alone in a stranger's city."

And just like that, a gulf widened between us. The delicacy of a minute gesture described the truth of our friendship. Standing there that late afternoon, it felt like

Paolino would always keep me in this cozy mold; the dutiful caretaker, an obedient worker, qualities that would make a perfect wife to him indeed. The flicker of apparent compliments left me empty. He described the woman he wanted beside him. I wanted to have light shone on who I could become.

"That sounds like an ultimatum, Paolino."

"Do you love me, Santina?"

His cheeks were flushed. I couldn't decide whether it was because the conversation was steering out of his control or because he was indeed laying himself bare before me. My heartbeat thudded in my ears. I longed for the words to come to my rescue, but I was giving in to panic, splashing around in the deep, hoping a passing ship would throw me a buoy. He registered my indecision before I could mask it.

"I thought you felt the same way, Santina."

He held my gaze, searching me for truths.

"I'm scared, Paolino."

A nib of honesty, at last.

He wrapped his arms around me, then lifted my chin and pressed his lips against mine. His eyes softened. "There is no hurry. But if you are telling me that the idea makes you want to jump on the next boat to New York, we stop this right now. And if you're telling me that you need more time to get used to the idea of the life I want to gift you, then I will wait as long as it takes. I don't want you to be a picture frame next to me, Santina. You understand that, don't you?"

I wanted to. I had come from poverty, that much we both knew, but I longed for a different wealth than what he laid before me. I didn't have the means to articulate this. Not then, not there in the softening hum of the early evening, with the streams of people passing before the shop, holiday chatter frothing like a cloud above them, marveling at our picturesque nook of the world. I didn't want to be the dutiful wife in a photographed delicatessen, stilted clicks of another life to be gawked at by strangers, trophies of a foray to Positano to savor for years to come, for the neighbors to salivate after, envy even. What ached was the sensation that I ought to want it, that I ought to be satisfied. The thoughts filled my mind like smoke.

The beads clicked open and a family shuffled in, committing every nook of his shop to memory. The children ran to the baskets heaving with bags of *gianduia,* the mother hovering close behind, snapping their hands away whilst drinking in the details of the appetizing display of ceramic bowls laden with charred vegetables, swimming in olive oil. The father lifted a bottle of wine from the shelf, studying the label with a scientific eye.

"We'll talk another time," I said, feeling I was leaving the conversation unstitched, frays of thoughts in a messy pile.

He nodded, his smile papering disappointment.

Elizabeth and I stepped out into the dusky atmosphere. I squeezed her little hand in mine, hoping the feel of her skin would ground me. We climbed the steps with unhurried feet, visitors wading through the start of the evening beside us, tumbled conversations of where they would dine. It was like strolling through the warped memory of a dream whose ending I sensed but couldn't picture.

As Elizabeth and I reached the final curve of alleyway that led to the last set of steps toward the villa, a familiar silhouette stopped me dead. I squeezed Elizabeth's hand, thought about slinking back into the doorway of the house nearest us till the person I wanted to meet least in the world got tired of waiting for me and left.

"Too late to hide," my father called down to me. He looked more haggard than the last time and the dipping sun cast streaks of shadows across his stubble.

"What do you want?" I called up, as loud as I could, hoping someone in the near houses might come out and witness our conversation. I hated the wry grimace creasing over his face as he stared down at us, several steps below.

"I want to know why my daughter is hanging around her loser brother."

I held a defiant silence.

"Santina — what a fitting name your mother chose — 'little saint' indeed. Hears no evil, speaks none either. Least that's what she thinks."

"I don't need to stand here listening to you."

"No, you don't. But you should. Because your darling brother is keeping a lot of dirty secrets from you, little saint. Ever ask him what he's been getting up to while you were swanning around town, around London?"

"This is your son you're talking about. The boy you're supposed to love. What would you know about that?"

"Raise your little voice all you like, Santina, no one will come to your rescue. Nor his. Just you wait."

He shuffled down several steps toward us so that the stale whisper of alcohol and garlic reached me. I lifted Elizabeth up and clasped her to me.

"And when you've found out, and you refuse to believe it, and you can't decide what to do, I'll be there, receiving kind donations from the servant girl to make sure Marco stays a free man."

He nodded his head with a raspy cackle. I wanted to hear the smack of my hand across his face, but it closed into an involuntary clammy fist.

"Go now, get to work, little saint. And don't forget to ask your brother to tell you some bedtime stories about the docks."

And with that he shifted by me. I watched him zigzag down the alley, inebriated footsteps leaving the whisper of doubts obscuring my better judgment. Though the dying sun warmed our faces, I felt an icy shiver scissor down my spine.

An eerie quiet greeted us inside the villa. I had the awful sensation of being watched. My father creeping up on me left me vulnerable, and I hated myself for it. I tried to focus on Elizabeth, hoping her blissful lack of awareness of my feelings might shift my own preoccupation with them. I tried to dream up something special for dinner, for when Marco would return, but I couldn't bear to be inside, I felt insecure leaving Elizabeth wandering the garden like she always did. I looked up at the crescent outline of the moon, only the fading glow of the sun remaining now, bronzed streaks across the horizon. I stayed by Elizabeth until the creeping dusk dipped us toward darkness. I led us inside with reluctance, all appetite diminished.

A knock at the door. Elizabeth ran toward it.

Marco called out from the other side. A great wave of relief swept over me.

"You been looking for ghosts again, Santina? You look like a sheet!" He laughed, stepping in past me with dirt-encrusted boots.

"What took you so long?"

"This how lover boy is teaching you to be the dutiful wife? Interrogation by the door?"

I brushed off his remarks with a shake of my head and stormed toward the kitchen.

"Santina! Don't be like that — has something happened?"

"No!"

He pinned me with that razor stare from the far side of the terrace.

"Yes."

He walked toward me.

"Papà. He was outside waiting for me."

That's when I let the angry tears fall. I didn't want them to eat at me any longer. He wrapped me into his arms.

"Look what he does!" I sobbed, fighting for breath, for calm. "I want to be free of him, Marco. He is a disgusting person. And look at me. Crying like a little girl. I hate how he makes me do that."

Marco lifted my chin and wiped my tears away with his thumb.

"So don't let him."

"It's not that easy. Has he come to see you at the cemetery?"

Marco's expression wavered in that familiar studied control, though if I searched a little deeper, I could see where the edges of the performance frayed, minuscule lifting furls revealing a mild panic beneath, a bit like tipping the lid of a boiling pot and watching steam fight out through the gap.

"He knows best to stay away from me," he answered, his voice metallic.

"He was speaking nonsense about you this time. Asking me to ask you to tell your stories from the docks."

"He's a sad old man, Santina. He's got word we've landed on our feet. Can't stand to see anyone happy. God knows he did his best to ruin our lives, no?"

A faint smile painted over my frown, a

watercolor washed away before it dries.

"Come on now, Santina. Leave him to his misery. You ever heard of a drunk knowing how to look after his children?"

"Not ours."

"You're shaken. Let me clean up and I'll make dinner tonight, yes? Pay my way somehow, no? Why don't you take a bath or something, relax?"

The idea was alluring, however impossible. A hungry Elizabeth was starting to trace circles around my legs.

"Let me give her some dinner and then get her to bed. A bath would be wonderful — if you don't mind?"

"It's the least I can do to thank my sister."

He kissed my forehead and crouched down to pinch Elizabeth's cheek between a couple of gentle fingers. She giggled. I watched him go inside. The darkness swallowed his silhouette.

After a simple broth for Elizabeth and some warmed milk with bread, she looked ready for bed. It wasn't hard to convince her to head upstairs. I turned on the lights of the dining room to reach the stairs.

That's when I noticed the walls.

Several paintings were missing.

My eyes darted across the space in panic.

They landed on the large Jacobean dresser

in the corner. Half the silver was missing and the doors swung open on their hinges. I looked back toward the library, noticing the door ajar.

"Marco!" I yelled.

No reply.

I lifted Elizabeth. I called him again. Still no answer.

The library lay dark. Light from the dining room bulbs spilled inside. From where I stood glued to the spot, I noticed that several piles of books were overturned.

My heart pounded.

I didn't hear Marco come down the stairs.

"What's the matter?" he asked.

I jumped.

"Look!" I signaled toward the library. "The pictures, Marco! The silver! It's gone!"

Marco followed my gaze toward the library. He stepped inside and flicked the light on. A mess of the major's prized books tumbled across the floor. The desk drawers were pulled open. Papers were strewn across it.

"Who's done this, Marco?"

He shook his head in horror.

"What do we do? This is all my fault! I should never have left the house empty. We never do that. That's why he asked you to stay. I can't believe I'd be so stupid."

I was starting to babble now. Elizabeth rubbed her eyes and fidgeted.

"Santina, calm down. Get the child to sleep and I'll clear up here, alright?"

"No, Marco, the major likes everything a certain way, let me."

"You are in no state, Santina. Please. Look to the child. Leave this to me."

On any other day I might have insisted, delayed bedtime, but my panic was roiling, and the horrid sensation of a stranger trawling through the home sent nausea through me, rancid regret. If I hadn't gone to see Paolino, this would never have happened. I would have been spared my father's creeping visit, I would not have left the house vulnerable. It wouldn't have taken long for it to get around town that I was there alone. I knew better. I could have stalled my meeting with Paolino. I might have spared us that awkward conversation. My duty was to the major first and foremost. I had let him down.

Marco caught me standing frozen in panic.

He placed a gentle hand on either shoulder.

"Clear heads, Santina. You've had a difficult afternoon. And I think I'm in part to blame, especially for how I spoke to Paolino over lunch. Now this! We get one thing straight, yes? This is not our fault."

I wouldn't have assumed him to take any blame. That much was obvious. Why would he have even entertained the idea of me considering him at fault? Was I that hard on him?

"The child is exhausted," he soothed. "You're in shock. Go. Let her rest. I'll make some chamomile tea. We'll tidy up."

I nodded, a marionette at the will of the puppeteer.

"Is everything alright upstairs, Marco?"

"Yes — no one is here, Santina" — he looked into me — "you want me to come with you?"

I did and was disappointed in myself for it.

He took my hand in his and led us up-stairs. He stayed with me while I settled Elizabeth. He even sat next to me on my bed as we waited for her to drift into sleep. In the quiet of the shadows, he whispered in my ear, "You're doing such a wonderful job here, Santina. Promise me you won't tell yourself this is your fault."

"I want to promise you. But I can't."

"Santina, this town is full of poor people. I hear about these things happening on all these villas. Count yourselves lucky it hasn't happened before now. A few things go missing, it won't harm this family, not in the long run."

"But it's my job to look after this place!"

His expression was impassive. Why wasn't he as surprised as me? Something about his demeanor intimated that he considered this a rite of passage, bound to happen to the rich foreigners. If I didn't know better, I'd say he gleaned a warped sense of justice from it.

"And it's mine to look after *you.*" And with that, my doubts flickered out, snuffed candlelight in the dark.

We stepped out into the light of the hallway and wound down the stone steps, our shadows creeping along the walls before us. At the bottom, we reached the now bare walls. My favorite painting of Malabar had been taken. I walked into the library to survey the debris. That's when I noticed the small safe inside a far dresser had been tampered with. It looked like a crowbar had been used to try to prize it open but without success. Some respite. But there were people at large who now knew of the major's secret hiding spots. Terror crackled through me. A stranger had fingered this room, the major's beloved possessions. I watched Marco reach down and start to replace the books into their haphazard towers, some onto the shelves. He stacked the papers into neat piles. I watched him take control of the situation, envying his clear head, stifling my disappointment and dreading delivering news of this to the major on his return.

I would do well to mimic my brother's behavior. At the bottom of the hill was a kind man who loved me. Beyond our surrounding hills was a man who was my lover for one unforgettable night. A shadow; the brighter Paolino's sun shone, the more distorted the major's silhouette grew. I didn't want to dance alone in the dark.

CHAPTER 20

I watched the water trickle down from my watering can onto the toasted earth, soaking into the thirsty ground. I willed the dawn birds' chatter to etch me into the garden, to root me in the task at hand, but my mind was a tumble of weeds. Marco wouldn't hear of me going to the police this morning. He'd insisted I stay at home with Elizabeth rather than leave the home empty once again. I stood in the white haze of the morning, listening to the droplets rain down onto the roots of the major's beloved vegetable patch. I pictured his face on hearing the news. I imagined the scalding brunt of his disappointment.

I crouched down toward the base of a pepper plant, twisted off several fruits, and placed them inside a basket. The house felt empty. The garden swelled toward the height of summer harvest but an air of abandonment hung like a mist. The major was this place's sun and everything and everyone within orbited around him, attracted and repelled by his unseen magnetic pull. It ached to admit it, but the tangle of these past few days made me feel like I was spinning on a shifted axis.

"You never give yourself time to sleep, woman?"

I lifted my face up to the house, where Marco was shuffling across the terrace in a fresh white shirt, his hair still dripping from a shower.

"There's a pot of coffee ready to light," I called back up to him, "the box beside it has some lemon cake inside."

"Of course it does!" He smiled down at me, a man without a care in the world. I was glad of his breezy mood, for once, but irked that he seemed so ready to move on from the robbery. It was his way of steering my own sense of shame, but it felt clumsy, bombastic even, as intrusive as his sarcasm somehow. I stayed in the garden a little longer, reaching in to pick off some tomato flowers. Their scent earthed me. A grapple of cherry tomatoes caught a crescent of sun along their lustrous skin. I picked them off the stem and laid them on top of the peppers.

When I reached the kitchen, Marco was

already pouring both of us a cup of coffee.

"When in doubt, murder a pepper?"

I slit my eyes toward him.

"Don't play the big sister with me, Santi', you're glad I'm here talking pig shit and you know it. Don't tell me you'd prefer the convent atmosphere?"

"I'm just amazed at your ability to switch polarity at a whim."

"Big words for a small woman."

"Nothing a cup of *caffe* won't cure — for you, I mean. Perhaps you'll understand me with a bit of caffeine in your blood."

He cackled at that and cut himself a brick of lemon cake. "This smells like a grove! All is well in the world. And seriously, once I've reported this at the station you can put the whole episode to bed, yes? Stop walking around with that sour look."

"Your reassurance sounds like mocking. Besides, I've been thinking, I'll go down and speak with them directly."

"You've never seen how police listen to women? You want that for yourself? Honestly, if it comes from me, they're going to take it a lot more serious. Sad, but true."

He picked up his cup, slab of cake in the other hand, and headed back out to the table on the terrace. He sat and took a deep breath, looking out toward the sea.

"Still, this hovel has proven to be the perfect weekend 'away' for me, all said and done."

"Too much said, not enough done," I barked back, bringing a chopping board out to join him and begin the dissection of the peppers.

"You know how to handle a knife, *sorella mia.*"

"Not just for boys after all, no?"

My flyaway remark seemed to zip around my brother like an unwanted mosquito. The sooner he got to the police, the better. He stood up and wiped his mouth.

"You'll tell me what the police say, yes?" I asked, laying down the knife and scooping the seeds into a smaller enamel bowl.

"I know what they'll say — list what's gone missing and let them do the rest. What they say to all the sons-of-whores who have too much money around here."

Off my look, he beat a jagged retreat. "You're gray, Santi', can't blame me for trying to be the clown, no? Anything to see the sister I know."

Elizabeth called down to me. I jumped up from my chair.

"No rest for the wicked!" he called back to me as he heaved the heavy main door open and disappeared onto the steps outside.

Elizabeth and I filled our morning with chores; she swept and dusted in my shadow. I propped her up on a small stool beside me, and she watched me with an eagle's eye as I stirred the thin slices of pepper around shaved, softened onions and garlic in warmed olive oil. I let her pour in a little of the vinegar to make them easier to digest, sending tangy steam that smudged into their sweet scent. She liked throwing in a pinch or two of coarse salt too, then ripping basil leaves between her chubby fingers and launching them into the wide pan to wilt off the heat. Her utter absorption in the task at hand was a comfort. I pretended to ignore the clock but each time I passed the tall pendulum on the opposite wall of the missing pictures I couldn't help but count down to when Marco might return for lunch with news; they'd found the loot abandoned somewhere, return it even, the major needn't know, perhaps.

A knock at the door. I raced over to let Marco in. Rosalia greeted me.

"You don't look as happy to see me as I'd like!" She beamed, the lunchtime sun tracing her thick black locks with a sheen.

"I'm sorry, Rosali', I've been like this all

night, please, come in."

"Where's the boss?"

"Gone to the hospital to see his wife."

"He finally committed her? Thank God."

Off my look, she pivoted. "I don't mean to be so cruel, but the woman needs full-time help."

"What am I? A salted anchovy?"

She giggled at that and took a few steps into the terrace.

Then she switched round to me and reached for my hand. "It's happened!"

I searched her eyes for the explanation and saw the answer streaming out in rays. "Pasquale?"

I didn't hear her yes. I just felt her arms wrap themselves around me, squeezing her excitement through me. I pulled away and placed my hands either side of her face.

"You are beautiful, Rosalia. You deserve this. Now, more than ever!"

She nodded, tears catching the light dappling in through the vines overhead, burnishing her brown eyes a deeper ochre. I wiped her cheek.

"Will you walk with me? On Sunday?" she asked, her voice a *tarantella*. "Will you come with me up into the hills? Everything is happening so fast, in a way, I want to go up high so I can look down at our little lives and keep it all in perspective! Do I sound crazy to you?"

"I miss my hills every day. I'll bring food, yes?"

"I was hoping you'd say that."

Her face dimpled into a grin, and, after crushing me in her arms several more times, she left for home.

I laid Elizabeth down for her afternoon nap, pretending I wasn't disappointed Marco hadn't shown up by lunch. I took longer than usual clearing our plates away, mine untouched, Elizabeth's *pastina* inhaled, only a smidge of butter and parmesan licked the plate.

The heat beat down, a dazzling silence percussed by the rhythmic drone of the cicadas. I made to retreat to the cool of my bedroom, pretending the idea of surrendering to sleep didn't make me feel uneasy. I tried my best all morning to resist these threads of panic, but they kept twisting around my middle like tentacles of minuscule translucent jellyfish, tugging at last night, of what Marco might be telling the police, of what they might think of me.

I heard movement at the door. It creaked open.

The major and Adeline stepped inside.

She was whiter, wan, gazing in watchful wonder at the terrace, as if it were the first time she'd set foot inside the space. I knew that expression from the occasional delivery porters who'd stopped by. Her eyes raised toward the vine.

The major looked at me. His polished calm shone, as always. "Good afternoon, Santina. The travelers return. I will see Adeline to her room."

It wasn't the time for me to begin an explanation. Adeline was a paper cutout beside him, delicate, intricate, expertly modeled. I was thankful of the windless air. I watched him lead her inside.

They were swallowed into the darkened quiet.

A little while later he appeared at the doorway onto the terrace. I sat at the table with a pile of freshly picked beans before me, topping and tailing ahead of dinner.

"Hello, Santina."

His eyes were steel blue.

"Hello."

His expression softened into the memory of a smile. Our night together felt at once like a book, delved into, adored, then shelved.

"I have some bad news," I began, my

stomach a tight knot, "there's been a robbery."

"I gathered. Either that or you had taken
it upon yourself to remove the pictures to
clean beneath them."

"I'm so sorry."

"I hear this is something happening all
over town. I've already checked carefully.
Nothing irreplaceable has been taken."

"But your favorite picture —"

"Just that. A picture. I'll carry it with me
whether the canvas follows or no. There's
the beauty of memory, you can commit as
much or as little to it as you choose."

He looked through me, but his gaze didn't
feel invasive — quite the opposite. "I'm sure
you've had an awful time of it. I hope you've
managed to sleep. You look white."

I felt it.

"What did the police have to say?"

"Marco went on my behalf this morning.
He didn't think they would be as good
recording the information from a young
woman as they would him. I wondered that
it might not be the best place for Elizabeth
either. I hope you don't mind. He hasn't
been back yet."

He nodded. I registered ordered thoughts
tripping through his mind.

"I see. It won't do me any harm to stop

393

by there myself. I'll go a little later."

Relief washed over me. I wondered why I'd expected an emotional outburst after all. We followed an improvised script to perfection. Between us, in the honeyed height of afternoon rays, deepening the heat and red undertones of the brushed pink of the villa's façade, we upheld the weighty silence of unspokens. I yearned to close the chapter of our confusing, delicious dance but lacked the expertise; a dancer pushed out onto the stage without a whisper of a lesson beforehand. A garish dream. One that only stopped if you woke up with a start.

He stepped toward me.

"Thank you," he said, in the amber tones I'd committed to memory, "for everything we shared."

I felt my cheeks crimson.

"I want you to know that things can and will return to how they were. We've shared something exquisite. My feelings remain unchanged. And will always be so. But you have a life to live, and so do I. We each have our responsibilities. Let us be kind to one another?"

I looked at him now, allowing myself to be seen. I felt a thorn of fear but stepped forward regardless. "I value your friendship beyond anything."

"Then stand here, now, and tell me we can carry on here. Together. As we were."

I took him in with courageous eyes. I found the strength to enjoy his élan, the effortless way he delivered his honest confession. I read his posture, poised, lengthened, void of fear. I allowed myself to fall deep into the gentle expression washing over his face, a glassy sea at dawn, his eyes alight with the initial timid rays of sun.

He was beautiful.

"The thought of losing you now shreds my heart," he said, his voice simple and clear, the peaceful private of a wave curling up to the shore without a fight to return to the deep.

"Mine also. That truth is terrifying. It's freedom and prison."

His smile was contagious. We stood a table length apart, but inside we were upon a precipice, his hand wrapped around mine. Neither would jump first. We hovered, the will powerful to leap in unison toward our new unknown.

"Your courage astounds me, Santina. Fearless and clear headed. I feel like I have so much more to lose if I don't assure you there is space for you to live your own life here. For us to fulfill our duties as we must."

"Thank you. I feel I've let you down."

I saw him hold back his impulse to touch me. I was looking down at him lying on the bed of the shore, a watery reflection, rippled into fragments.

"If you're speaking about the robbery, I can assure you it is no one's fault. Unless you're telling me you let the thieves in the front door!" He laughed then but his eyes were clouded.

"I'm sorry."

"I don't want you to be."

I let his words eclipse my own. It could have felt like an ending. But as we stood there, for that moment equals in the unknown, we made an unspoken promise: freedom and friendship.

"I'm so grateful for that dismal day in London when our friends introduced us to you," he began, "it has changed my life. But I refuse to let it strangle yours. Do you hear me, Santina? Do you accept that I honor what passed between us? And that we must move through the traps of doubt, embarrassment, recrimination, suspicion? Can we do that?"

It was a true question. No rhetoric here. He wasn't my lover, ushering me toward an answer or an insight he'd already had and wanted to share.

"It's what I want. More than anything." My voice came out clear, warm, free. It surprised me. Him also.

I heard Elizabeth calling.

"Let me see to her," he said. "Take a little while to rest. I'll prepare to walk down to the police, yes? Today is a new day, Santina. They can take all the things they want. I have everything I need. Always."

We drank each other for a breath, inhaling the peaceful moment for one more stretched second.

Then he was gone.

Paolino met me as I stepped out of church. Our Sundays had become as sacred as the rosary I'd just intoned myself away with.

"There she is. *La bella* Santina. I'm full of sun and song today, my love!"

"You always are."

"No, today is different."

"Your mother gone out?"

He kissed my cheek then with a giggle. "My lover is funny too. I need to tell everyone."

He swung his arm out, heaven bound. I feared he might start yelling across to the rest of the congregation streaming out of the tiny church.

I slipped my hand in his and felt his

fingers reach around mine. We strolled in silence for a moment, down the narrow alley toward the beach of Fornillo. Our feet scuffed along the stairs that led down to the water. The blackened stones crunched underfoot till we reached the shore. The morning was luminous. The villas perched on the verticals had terraces blooming with geraniums and hibiscus, bold bursts of oranges and deep pinks. The sea was a swirl of cerulean and emerald, sparkling in the hopeful rays. I turned my back against the sun. His face was spotlit, the mischievous dimples deepening as he gazed down at me; behind, the vast jagged rocks loomed.

"I want to be your wife, Paolino."

He looked at me, at once wordless.

The sudden simplicity of my decision caught me off guard. A crisp clarity drew everything around me into sharp focus. Before me, the person who would make a life alongside me of which I knew I could be proud. His verve was a force to be reckoned with, his insatiable optimism infectious, however long I'd tried to be unaffected by it. As I took in his beautiful face, suntoasted on the salty breeze, I knew this was where I wanted to be, at last.

"Unless you've changed your mind, of course," I added, bristling with something I wished was further from doubt. "Since the letter, I mean."

I didn't finish my sentence. His wet eyes were laughing and crying. My feet left the ground as he swirled me in his arms. We landed. His hands wrapped around my face. I felt the reassuring heat of them. The tip of his nose rested on mine.

"No man can ever know happiness but me," he whispered. His lips traced along mine. Then his kiss pressed deeply onto them. I let the sound of the water, the budding babble of the tourists arriving for their sea day, the thick silence of the mountains around us, ease into the distance. My mouth opened a little and he wound himself inside. Our tongues danced. Then our laughter erupted. His forehead pressed against mine, our voices mingling, crisscross currents of my mountain creeks trickling their way to the ocean. I surrendered to the promise, to the belief in a future that had always lain beneath my feet but which I'd been too fretful to admit.

Now, by the water's edge, it all made me want to cry with relief, hope, and gratitude. My hot tears traced a thick line down my cheeks. He kissed them dry, then knelt down before me.

"Santina Angela Guida. I, Paolino

Cavaldi, promise to be the best man I can be to you. Today, tomorrow, and always."

"You practicing for the service already?"

He smiled, squinting in the light. "I'm loving you. With every fiber."

I looked down at him, his body so open, his wide chest filled with happiness that he'd never be scared to share, entice, elicit. I filled up with sunshine and brined air.

"And so am I, Paolino."

CHAPTER 21

Rosalia clanged the villa's bell just as I filled our picnic basket with one final peach wrapped in brown paper. Her expression was muted, in shadow somehow. We began our climb up the first set of steps from the villa, winding through the narrow stone stairs toward Nocelle, passing the cemetery first and then turning into the ravine between the mountains. We stopped for a moment at the lowest point, and let the shade of the olive trees dapple over us. The cicadas were at their height of celebration at this time of the afternoon.

"Are you alright, Rosali', you seem quiet."

She shrugged. Her jerky movement unsettled me.

"You feel dizzy? Need something to drink maybe?"

Her back bristled with my prodding, a whispered ripple along the skin. Imperceptible almost.

"Come on, let's get up onto the path," she replied, "we can picnic like tourists."

The trickle of her usual humor set me back at ease. We walked in soft silence for the next leg of the climb. The percussive scuff-taps of our feet underscored the thick stillness of brush to either side of us. Beyond the cluster of Nocelle, we joined the Path of the Gods. I knew the trail like the back of my hand. Sharing it with my friend was like reading a diary entry out loud to her. The narrow pass curved in toward the rock, and led us under the shade of thicker forest. The familiar damp air cooled me. I dodged the sharp rocks underfoot with lithe steps, pictures of my mother lifting into focus like they always would when I passed through these old routes, slipping my child's feet into her adult shoes.

The rumble of running water rose as we followed the bend. Beside us, a small waterfall gushed down the boulders, weaving underfoot and down the sheer rock face on the other side of the trail. I stopped in front of the water, welcoming the cleansing white noise as it obliterated any thought. Standing here at the mouth of its energy, we disappeared into stillness. I looked over at my friend. Sadness misted over her. She was a portrait of the woman I knew that had been blanched for being left in the sun for too long. Her eyes met mine. A wan smile began to unfurl, then faded; a fern wound shut in the shade.

She tore herself away. I followed. The path grew steep now; we took turns to carry the basket until, at last, we reached my favorite spot to picnic. I followed Rosalia up the grassy verge to a flattened patch. She sat and let her whole body sink back onto the earth. Her arms spread wide. Her eyelids closed.

I laid out a cloth and unpacked the basket. The smell of fresh mozzarella and prosciutto roused her to sitting.

"I was beginning to think you weren't feeling well."

"So was I," she replied, pulling out a scarf from her pocket and wrapping it around her forehead, sweeping her thick curls away from her shoulders. She gazed down at the sea, onyx blue in the afternoon rays. From way up here, its texture was burned sugar, sunlight gleaming in toasted flecks. My coast snaked out in defiant curves, mountains rising to meet their sky in stubborn peaks.

"I haven't been here in too long, Santina. It's just what I needed."

I sat beside her and reached into the

basket for a peach. I could feel her watch me take a hungry bite.

"Apetito!" She laughed.

I wiped the juice from my mouth and echoed her.

We munched in settled silence, she nibbling at some fresh rolls I had cooked that morning before church, me lost in the tangy sweetness of my fruit.

I turned my gaze away from the compelling view of the water stretching out to Capri, the Galli islands rising up out of the water, stories of those sirens luring sailors to their deaths there floating in my mind.

That's when she started to sob.

"Rosalia?" I reached for her hand. She squeezed it.

"Santina, I should be the happiest woman in town," she whispered through snatched breaths, trying to hold back her tears and failing. "I didn't think I had any tears left. Look at me! A stupid mess."

I watched her drop her head onto both her hands. Her sobs juddered down her back. I wrapped my arm around her shoulders. I'd felt her cry like this before, but I knew these tears weren't for her brother. I held the space, resisting a need for words, for consolation, for questions. I let the waves roll through her, like watching a summer storm blow in from the coast and knowing the rain would disappear just as quick.

Her breaths deepened.

"I am to be his wife. I've dreamed of this moment. I was full of it all. I was bursting with love. Now I know I'm about to start my life as a fiancée with a lie."

I restrained my confusion. She filled the gap.

"I can't face telling him the truth about me, Santina. I can barely tell you. No one knows. Only Mamma, and my eldest sister. They were with me when it happened."

"You can tell me. If you want to."

"They ripped out my womb, Santina."

She looked at me square in the face, her despair wrapped around a steel of defiance I'd not seen before. It made my heart ache.

"You can trust me, Rosalia."

She took a breath to speak. Her tears cut through the thought, her sudden collapse into painful memories at odds with the startling beauty around us. Perhaps that's why she wanted to come up here. See our little world for the speck that it was, yearning for the majesty of our mountains to pale her woes into insignificance.

"I'm sorry, Santina. I wanted to stay strong. Then it all crashed down around me. This is the man I want to grow old with.

But I know I will never give him what will make him the happiest man in Positano."

"You're the person who will do that."

"No. Not when I start life together with a lie. I can't tell him, Santina. I can't tell him the truth. It will break us."

"And a lie?" I asked. The question was a lick of bile. I was in no place to offer such questions. "Do you want to tell me what happened?"

She nodded, then took an unhurried breath. "I was sixteen. I thought it was just a really bad cycle. I was doubled in pain. My mother told me to stop fussing, but when a fever struck and didn't break even by the morning, they eventually took me to Sorrento. The doctors found a cyst on each ovary. Any longer and they would have burst, and we wouldn't be having this conversation at all."

Her eyes filled. I watched her clamp down the tears.

"They operated but weren't able to save my womb. It's all gone, Santina. I'm half a woman."

Her words were ash. She had buried the pain well. I ought to have sensed it. I ought to have intuited that her sunny smile was all the brighter for having felt such brutal loss. It made perfect sense. It made me love her even more.

"You've carried your loss well, Rosalia. Like a warrior. I can only imagine what you must have gone through till now."

"Maybe you can. Most girls can't. It's like inside I'm an old woman. It's like the life has been spent already. There's no glow of the future. I just don't know if I can tell Pasquale. He'll find out soon enough. Perhaps I'll just wait for nature to take its course."

Her face turned toward the sea. I watched her feel the breeze caress her skin.

"You are a beautiful, strong woman, Rosalia. Pasquale loves you for that, not for what might be, but for who you are, right now."

"You and I both know men don't marry the person in front of them. They marry the person they've planned us to become. And maybe that's romantic, their idealized versions of us as perfect mothers and lovers. I used to believe that. With all my heart. Maybe more so because I had to hide my truth. But now I feel he's sketched me and I'm a poor impersonator. Like I've been wearing a costume of me and dangled an illusion under his eyes. That makes me weak. And cruel. And selfish."

"And living the only way you know how. You are more than that illusion. Surely?"

"I don't know. What do you do all day? Take care of a child. Feed a household. Run it, for heaven's sake. All these things I will never do."

I looked into her eyes, glistening with a vulnerability I now understood had been locked away for so long.

"I can see you are hurting. A great deal."

"I'm about to ruin my one chance at love, Santina. Could you do that?"

The question smarted. "I can't be sure there's *one* chance. That seems so final. So desperate. Like we have to earn it and grasp it before it slips away. Is love that ethereal? Isn't that storybook love? I think two souls either fit or don't."

Paolino's kiss flirted into my mind, followed by the whispered silhouette of the major, him drinking in the moonlight, reading to me, cooking. The memories tangled like the crispy mess of seaweed wafted to shore along a November bay.

"I want to believe you, Santina."

"I think Pasquale will love you however brutal the truth is. You two are made for one another. I watch him with you and you with him. There's a haze of happiness, a quiet electricity that hums about you."

She looked at me, willing me on, needing me to throw down anchor.

"But it is your choice. Always. You want to keep this from him, then you may. That is your right. But if concealing the deepest secret is going to break you, then you must find the courage to test his love. Lay the naked truth between you." I could see Rosalia filled in my sentiments with pictures of Paolino, and I knew I would never be able to tell her that I had learned this from what the major and I shared, from our last tender exchange upon the terrace before we laid our memory of that night to bed. "I don't know what is more intoxicating than a lover laying themselves bare, granting permission for another to see their vulnerabilities whatever the outcome. Isn't that the greatest expression of love? Inviting your lover to shine light on all those secret crevices you've kept hidden? From yourself even?" I was back on my bed, easing myself open to him without fear, feeling courage score through me, marveling at my body, at his. "And if that doesn't draw two people together, surely they do not love one another after all?"

"You speak like a poem, Santina. It's beautiful. And terrifying."

"And that is love, Rosalia. It's not perfection. It's nature. Life bursting out despite the random mess and order of things. It's the plants that grow in shade and those that gasp for sun. You can't rein it."

She let out a sigh, an autumn breeze lifting the dead leaves with the first chill of winter.

"You're hurting now, Rosalia. You have the right to feel that. You have the right to mourn."

Her lips unfurled toward a teary smile. I smoothed a trickle off her cheek, then squeezed her into me. In the safety of my arms she surrendered to a second wave of grief. I felt her body shake through me, pummeling my chest.

"I should have left after all. I should have just gone to the convent like they told me to. Never listened to anybody. Now look at this mess!"

"You are braver than that, Rosalia. You didn't let them crush you. You're terrified now. That's normal. But my Rosalia is strong enough to feel the pain and smile like it was the best day of her life. I know she isn't scared to cry and shout and grieve and know that joy and sorrow are woven of the same thread."

She straightened.

I'd never seen her so beautiful.

There was something compelling about her vulnerability.

The apricot light glinted her hair with a halo.

She was luminous; bare, true, fierce.

"How did you get so wise?" She sighed through a wet smile. "It's like you've lived a whole life before you came to town from the mountain."

I knew it was the major, not my start in the mountains, who unraveled my life, drew me to its molten center, then ushered me back to the cool, blistered yet bolstered.

"I could say the same about you, no?"

"I wanted to tell you for so long, but I didn't want you to share the burden."

"Your secrets are your truth. I'm inside you now. And you, me."

"I love you, Santina. There's no one else here I could have even thought about telling. Sometimes I believe just *thinking* something sets gossips' tongues clicking."

"You may be right," I said, with a smile she mirrored. I reached for her hand and squeezed it. "I'm here. Always. You know that, don't you?"

She nodded, tears pricking her eyes that she refused to let fall.

"You promise me something?"

"What's that, Rosalia?"

"I don't want you to stop yourself sharing the gory details when you and Paolino make babies just because of me."

I shook my head with a smile.

"You can't go all bashful now, Santina. Not after the way you just said your little sermon about love. I know he's a catch, but I never thought Paolino would make a girl speak like that! Those words from someone who's been whisked away by a sheer force of nature. Something you're not telling me, Signorina?"

"You're twisting my words, now."

"I'm saying you spoke like a goddess — didn't know you had it in you!"

"There's Rosalia!"

She grabbed my chin and squeezed it, planting noisy kisses on each of my cheeks. She smelled salty.

I watched her flop back onto the grass, legs and arms wide with abandon.

"And then there's the sky," she said, her voice a dance again. "All this whirrs around and inside, but the sky? It changes. It threatens us with storms. But it never goes away."

I rolled back onto the grass beside her. The earth rose up to meet our bones. I let the weight of me sink deeper into the grass, dizzy with my friend's anguish, the tired quiet after tears. We watched a cotton fray of cloud lazy across the blue above us.

"Only one saying that will save me now, Santina."

"What's that?" I asked, turning my head to face her.

She looked back at me, squinting, tearstained, luminous like the glint of a dark crystal. "Always look up."

I returned to the villa satiated with fresh air, my friend's tears and laughter. The familiar quiet enveloped me like an embrace. Despite the stillness, the distinct energy of the house being once again full dipped the silence into a welcoming ochre rather than purple shadows. I placed the basket upon the kitchen table, knowing that there was little time before the Sunday sitter would leave after settling Elizabeth to sleep.

I reached the vegetable garden. Amongst the crunched arches of *cavolo nero* and the proud spiked leaves of the artichokes, I saw a crouched Adeline. She looked up as I approached. She started. I would have liked to shake the sense of disturbing a young deer in the woods.

"Good evening, Signora." My voice powdered like confectionary sugar, I hoped she wouldn't receive it as patronizing, the help condescending as if she were a wild animal to be lured away to safety.

Her blue eyes bore into me. Languid pools where once lights shone. If I looked at the world through her prism, I might once see shards of red and orange in there if, as she had tried to persuade me, the vision of color was as much about the feeling a subject elicited than the actual shade the naked eye saw. It had taken me a while to understand this concept, but as I watched her now, her reddish blond hair tumbling in distracted waves down to the middle of her back, her nightdress hanging on limp strands over her bony shoulders, I could only see her painted in swirls of blues and grays, struck through with purple bolts.

"It is heaven here, Santina! These leaves. I can't stop touching them."

I watched her fingers reach for the base and caress them up to the tip, as if she were stroking a cat's chin.

"We can pick some, for dinner. If Signora would like?"

"I would. Don't call me Signora."

I nodded and walked to the potting counter for some secateurs. When I reached her again, she was wandering around the proud sprigs of chard. The major had insisted we plant all colors, alternating them in a pattern of purple, yellow, then white. Something that wasn't lost on the arched humor of my brother.

"And their smell, Santina. It's like wet earth and vanilla. Iron and sugar."

I watched her bury her face into them, hoping she wasn't bruising the leaves, one of the major's many pet peeves.

I reached down and began to snip at the base, sensing which were the most mature, mindful of leaving the smaller leaves at the center to grow further. With careful incisions the plant would keep sprouting throughout the summer and into early autumn. She walked over to me and snatched the secateurs from me. My hands itched.

"I can taste them already," she said, snipping with haphazard strokes, leaving the plants butchered. I trailed after her, trying and failing to judge the appropriate time to ease the tool from her. She spun around to me with a sudden movement, the tip of the secateurs almost skimming the front of my blouse.

"And how would you cook them then, Santina? How will you make it even more delicious for me?" She waved her hand around with the open blade.

"I would begin with a little garlic, I think," I said, trying to still her erratic movements along the patch by holding her attention. "No, I would warm a pan with the *cavolo* and chard in a little bit of water, *a vapore,* Signora, steaming them. Just as they start to wilt, I'd pour some olive oil and paper slices of garlic, you know?"

I edged closer to her with each description, slowing my language to lull her away from her unpredictable harvesting. When I felt her ease to stillness, I crouched beside her. "Here, may I show you how they like to be cut best?"

I reached a gentle hand toward the base of the tool but she whipped up to standing at the same time, slicing the blade across my finger. I looked down. It wasn't until I saw the thin strip of my blood that I felt the sting.

"Oh, Santina! You are hurt! You're bleeding!" I could sense the panic bubbling beneath her words, which forced me to stifle my own.

"It's fine, I will see to it," I said, walking toward the water spout.

"No, not fine!" she called back, trailing in my shadow. "Do let me cover it, we must wash it, we must disinfect it, there's all manner of deadly things to catch from blades. This is awful, this is just awful. I've hurt you, haven't I? It was me, wasn't it?"

416

Her words switch-bladed across one another, as she swirled her tool in the air. I wished it away from her paper skin, the faded beauty of her face, a marble bust at the cemetery, features worn from weather, smoothed and faded with an age of elements and neglect, frozen in a faraway soulless expression.

"Please give me the secateurs, Signora."

She froze. Her eyes darted down to the blade.

A thin outline of my blood traced the tip.

"A crushed pomegranate red," she said, looking down at it with the hot gaze she once reserved for her painting.

"I will wash them, Signora. Please may I have them?"

"A bleeding heart. A garnet in the dark. Squashed blackberries in my hand."

I reached out and wrapped a firm hand around the base of the tool. Her grip loosened. I ignored the pounding in my chest. My arm hooked into hers. I felt the empty weight of her thin arm rest upon mine. We began to retrace her steps back up to her room, her bare feet imprinting an earthy trail up the steps to the terrace and onward through the house, leaving the rugged pile of snatched leaves to soften in a purple-orange dusk.

CHAPTER 22

Adeline and I stepped into her room. The double doors that led onto her end of the upper terrace were open wide, the full-length wooden shutters swinging back and forth on the intermittent breeze. Wires ran across the space, hooking onto the wooden cornice, webbing above us like the washing lines down in the *viccoli*. The draft wafting between the open window and the doors on the adjacent wall lifted the ends of the paintings that hung along the wire. The space above our heads was a blaze of color. Frantic explosions of hues, hurried splats, scrawls of charcoal created a noise that together with the bold vermillion, ochre, and cerulean of the painted wooden ceiling above made the whole space sing, a choir's furious crescendo.

Off my look, Adeline stopped short. "Yes, Santina, I have been busy these past few days. Does it terrify you so?"

418

"No," I stumbled, stripped by her arrow of truth, "I'm glad Signora is painting again."

"So is Signora. Do stop calling me that foul name, my dear, it makes me feel like I'm living on a plantation. Or worse, one of those ghastly women who swan about in India sipping gin all day."

My eye darted to her wash table and the three glass tumblers where day-old ice cubes of her gin and tonics had melted over crushed limes, browning at the edges in the heat.

"You know the sort," she barged on, oblivious, "the ones who brought up Henry. I use the term lightly. They wouldn't know mothering if it slapped them in the face."

She darted to the terrace. I followed her out of instinct. The major refused to raise the balustrade, even though echoes of the doctor urging him to do so rang in my ears. She leaned on the edge. It made the vise around my stomach tighten. The desk from her room now stood there, fading in the sun, the leather top spattered with paint, tubes of the colors twisted and crushed by her frenetic fists, some with the lids off, color oozing out in bilious gloop. I began to trace the lids to their pairs and twist them back on.

"You are an angel, Santina. Yes, that you are," she called to me, wrapping her hands around the canvas upon the easel beside the desk. She turned the square several times, viewing the swirl of blues from opposing angles.

"I suppose it doesn't really matter which way. I think whoever buys it can choose, don't you, Santina?"

I placed a tube of ruby back on the table, rubbing the paint between my two fingers, noticing it was almost the exact shade of my cut.

"I think it's beautiful, Signora."

"Well, no it isn't. Not really. It's merely my opinion. It's what I saw as the sun came up this morning, you know? People don't want to buy beauty. They buy a chance to see the world through my eyes."

Her gaze darted down to my finger.

"Good heavens, I completely forgot about the gash! Yes, the injury. That's why we're up here in the ward, yes? Henry!" she bellowed, leaning over the top of the terrace balustrade. I stepped forwards knowing it was only a matter of a slim overbalance that could send Adeline over the edge.

"Henry!" she cawed.

"Signora," I interrupted, placing a gentle hand on her back, "I am fine, really. I shall go downstairs and see to it myself."

"Nonsense. With one hand, child? How can you do that with one hand?"

She marched back inside, for which I was glad, only to start rummaging in her dresser. She tossed underwear out behind her, some missing my head, others tapping against the overhead papers. The wire began to swing with the rippled movement, setting the papers alight, a flock of birds shaking their feathers before lifting up into the sky.

"It's here somewhere. You know the injection they do. It will make it hurt none. Yes, definitely take the pain away. And infection. Don't be infected."

She opened a second drawer. That's when I heard the rattle of glass vials and started to give in a little to burgeoning panic.

The major appeared at the doorway.

He looked at me. Then his eyes darted to his wife, now launching a full assault on the contents of a third drawer.

"Adeline, my darling, whatever are you doing?"

"Santina is injured, Henry, can't you see? I cut her, Henry, she's got a gash, yes, her finger might be infected, Henry," she replied without altering her manic speed. The major reached for her hands and wrapped his fingers around them.

"My love, let me help you. No sense throwing everything onto the floor, is there? Lots of useful things in the bathroom, yes? Do let me see to it. You've so much work to do here."

"Will you, Henry? Yes, you see to it. To her. She's not an 'it,' for God's sake. She's a person, Henry. Who feels pain. Look at her — she's pale as a ghost, or a sheet, or a cloud. Yes, a January cloud. No, not that heavy. Not so gray. No, a wafting cloud. Spring sun. Spring sky I mean. Not the sun, because that would be bright white, not faded white. That would be sparkling with streaks of gold and silver, red even, faint red, a lick of vermillion maybe?"

The major wrapped his hand into hers and led her to the edge of the bed. They eased down to sitting. He wound his arm around her. I watched them sway for a moment, then turned to leave.

Adeline called back to me, "Santina, don't go anywhere, you'll get an infection, won't she, Henry? Outside in the garden lots of things can get in there, you know, to the wound. Give her a vial, Henry, or an injection. Do something! You're just sitting there like you don't care about the child."

He kissed her gently on her cheek.

"Alright, Adeline. I'll do that. Why don't

you attend to the blues outside? They're rather magnificent."

Their eyes met. Her smile was a watery reflection of his. He waited as she returned to her easel. We watched her for a moment, the dipping light streaming over Capri toward our cliff turned her body into a bony silhouette through the threadbare nightgown.

"Thank you, Santina," he said.

I looked down at him upon the bed. His linen shirt hung in crumples along his shoulders. The blanched white creases intensified the deep red of his hair, a few stray longer lengths falling in distracted waves over his forehead.

I felt a bristle of guilt.

He stood up.

"Let me see your war wound."

"It's just a scratch."

He reached down for my hand. The touch of his skin against mine sent me to our moonlit sheets in a blink. I washed the river of pictures away to the back of my mind. It would take longer to forget the delight of his touch than I realized.

He studied the scrape. It was small. The blood had already stopped flowing. His gaze was fixed, unhurried, committing every crease to memory. His eyes followed the tiny

lines with distilled concentration, an astron-
omer mapping an encrusted sky.

"Come with me," he said, his voice coated
with a clinical veneer, a brittle mask I saw
through. He left the room for the bathroom
along the corridor. I followed. He opened
the cabinet above the large ceramic sink. I
took a reluctant step onto the marble tiles.
The showerhead dripped forgotten water
into the deep bath. The sound filled the
stone room with tinny echoes.

He lifted my hand. I watched his fingers
reach for the tip of mine. He unfurled it,
teasing it open with the softest of touches.
I'd watched him reach for our plants in the
same way, placing leaves between his inquir-
ing fingers, careful not to damage the
surface, interrupt its growth, nor the private
seclusion of its world. The tips traced the
side of my finger. A whisper of invisible
needles ran alongside his delicate touch,
prickling in toward my palm. My hand was
hot, expectant, at once I felt dipped in the
pitch black silence of the villa, alert to its
every sigh and creak.

He looked at me. I chose to hold his gaze.

He placed my hand on the side of the sink.
The stark cold shunted me back into the
room. He reached inside the cupboard
above and placed a small bottle of powdered

424

iodine upon the ceramic, beside it a roll of gauze and crepe. His movements were slow, deliberate, unhurried yet purposeful; a lover smoothing the sheets.

He twisted the small lid off the iodine and lifted my hand once again. We watched the powder fall, mesmerized, as if we were side by side on the balcony, watching the first flurry of a bitter December's fall.

Next, he cut a length of gauze. A tremor scissored along the back of my hand, a fault line betraying my slipping grip on calm. He took my finger between his two, the sides pressing against mine, and began winding the gauze length around the cut. The awful familiarity of his touch wrinkled a minute electric pulse toward the tip of my nail. He raised my finger with the tip of his and then back down again.

Our eyes fixed upon the dance, our digits performed their spiral, winding down an invisible staircase, each step at once firm yet tentative. We watched the revolutions, impossible to sense which led or followed, the cranking of a tiny handle as a mechanical music box's teeth tweak a metallic tune.

He brought the silent lullaby to a pause, lifting a finger of mine from my other hand to hold the wrapped gauze in place. The weight of his hand sighed an invisible draft up my neck. I observed myself count the tiny square spaces between the threads. My absurd cling to order achieved little to that effect.

He reached for a small length of tape. His movements were legato, his hands still in the gentle sway of our secret tune. He placed the tape onto the gauze. It smarted the sensitive tip of my cut.

My breath snatched. His hand clasped mine.

"I'm so sorry," he whispered.

I shook my head.

I watched his lips lower toward my hand. I didn't move as he unfurled my palm. His lips were inside the nook where the lines crisscrossed, intersections to nowhere and everywhere, my short life etched within my grasp, memories embossed and hidden. Among those frays, his kisses, our balcony, our moon.

He didn't kiss it.

His eyes met mine. "Can we do this, Santina?"

"Do what?" I replied, in the same hush as his. To utter syllables felt more a betrayal than the choking sting of our finger ballet.

"I'm not entirely sure how to stay away from you," he said.

His eyes ignited with the fierce courage I

once saw in Adeline.

"I want you to tell me everything is as it should be," I replied.

"I want to tell you that too, Santina."

The narrow space of air between us crushed with hushed memories. In that sliver of time, I understood a kiss was not a physical act alone. Because as we stood in the damp shadows of that bathroom, the light from the window withering through the frosted glass, we returned to a secret place. Neither spoke. Our lips didn't part, nor touch, nor lead the other inward. But for a breath we left that tiny gray space. All was remembered and forgotten. A puff of smoke from fading embers.

"Is it possible to make space for our feelings? Can we just let them hover?" he asked. "Like a tuft of dandelion seeds on the breeze? Is that strong or selfish? Careless even? I don't know." He searched me for an answer. My thoughts remained hidden. I wasn't ready to trawl them now, a fisherman casting a hopeless net toward retreating fish beneath the weedy bed.

"I only know that if you bury something," he continued, "it has an awful knack of rearing its ugly head when you're least expecting it. I don't want to bury us. I don't want to crush you either. Or me. Or Adeline."

"I have no map," I said at last, filling the pause, a dying wave as it grieves the shore.

"Neither do I. Perhaps that's the point. I've always been so very much in control. It's the first time I've felt utterly limbless. Liberated beyond comprehension. And lost" — his voice wavered — "so dreadfully lost."

I watched his eyes fill. I wanted to take my hands to that face, to feel his heat against mine, but it hurt too much.

"You are an angel. Even in this dreary light," he said, fighting a smile to fence in his tears.

I sighed a laugh then, a solitary tear streaking my cheek.

He reached toward me and kissed it dry.

Then leaned his cheek against mine.

We breathed in the quiet. Warmth against warmth.

Inhaling this moment. Exhaling it to the past.

"Signore, the baby is asleep."

The young woman's voice clipped our open-ended silence, a gate lock snapping shut.

We turned toward her with a jerk.

Off her look, I wondered if we appeared as awkward as I felt.

"Very good," the major replied with his characteristic smooth shift. "Santina will see you out. Have a good week and we'll expect you next Sunday, *si*?"

"*Grazie,* yes," she replied.

Our footsteps echoed down the stairs, a percussive beat beneath our silence. I closed the main door behind her, wishing the memory of her expression would fade from mind, a translucent watercolor sketch rather than a vivid depiction of an Adeline.

With the new week, the major instilled a refreshed morning routine for Adeline. It involved waking her to join in with the gardening rituals. I knew it came under the advice of the doctor in the hospital. He was the one responsible for encouraging Adeline to pick up her brushes again and therefore earned the major's respect. The staff at the hospital had relayed how therapeutic the gardening was for their patients and the major witnessed it himself during his own visit.

I silenced the vague whispers hinting that her joining us provided some mental barrier between the major and me. It was the perfect way of turning the intimate place where we had first fallen toward one another into a new, sacred, shared space. Our gardening became Adeline's treatment to which we both committed with verve; an artful way to disperse any final remnants of guilt, those memories were now dug out weeds, upturned roots burned by the sun.

While the major undertook the supervision of Adeline, I could get on with all the other tasks. That day it involved an eager Elizabeth, who ran the length of the tomato plants with glee, her toddler limbs getting longer and stronger by the day, picking off the reddest fruits and loading our baskets with their lustrous bounty. When the sun rose toward its punishing peak, the major led Adeline inside for her rest. Elizabeth and I set to work in the shade of the terrace beyond the kitchen, where I'd covered the table with a waxed tablecloth and clamped a tomato crusher to its edge. Below, upon a low wooden stool, I set a large enamel bowl. Elizabeth stood beside me, feeding the fruit into the wide mouth above the clamp and together we cranked the metal handle as she watched the flesh crush through the teeth and drop into the bowl below. When she seemed to tire of it, I set another bowl beside me into which she stirred some of the fresh *passata* and tore in basil leaves. She held a wooden spoon and took to the preparation with impressive professionalism.

"Pomodori!" she announced, with jerky

mixing, her red curls dancing down to her shoulders.

"*Sì, pomodori* — tomatoes. We are making *passata.* What do we use this for?"

"Spaghetti marinara!"

"*Brava cuoca,* Elizabetta! You will be a fine cook one day."

"I will," she declared, and with that disappeared back into her thoughts.

The door shook. It startled both of us. I wiped my hands on my apron and went to open it. On the other side stood two gentlemen dressed in smart clothes. One was tall, wan, wiry. The other, his polar opposite. The latter spoke first: "I'd like to speak with the housekeeper."

"That's me," I answered, suddenly aware of the red finger stripes along my apron. "May I ask who you might be?"

"I thought as much. Told you she spoke English," he sang up to his partner, "you even sound English when you speak Napoletano. All posh. You are Santina Guida, *sì*?"

"And you are?"

"Sorry, where are my manners? Just because you're a *paesan,* doesn't mean I should take liberties. I'm police officer Antonio Sant'Angelo. This is my shadow, Giancarlo. We will come in now and ask you some questions."

I nodded, taut.

"About the robbery."

"I see," I replied, stepping backward to allow them inside. They followed me toward the front table. We sat. I watched him commit every nook of the terrace to memory, his eyes lingering awhile on Elizabeth, her hands dripping with red, a diminutive butcher.

"That's the *fanciulla* you look after then?"

"Yes."

"Not a woman of many words, no?"

"No."

He nodded with reluctance. He took his time to retrieve his notebook, buried somewhere deep inside his trouser pocket beneath the folded flesh of his abdomen.

"This won't take long." He smiled.

I didn't reply.

"I'd like you to tell me where your brother Marco was on the day of the robbery."

Glassy fingers traced my spine.

"Marco?" I asked. "He was at work. He works at the cemetery."

"Can you be sure of that?"

My eyes darted to the taller policeman whose eyes were spent. How would someone so vacant be of any possible use to the stout guard dog growling beside him?

"I can. He works mornings and afternoons. We had lunch. I left for town, he left for work."

"Did you see him leave?"

"Yes."

"Can you be sure he reached work?"

"I'm not sure what you're asking my housekeeper exactly, officer, but from where I'm standing it sounds a lot like leading the witness."

We followed the voice.

The major stood in the doorway.

He walked across the terrace and reached a crisp handshake to both of the officers who stood to attention.

"*Buon giorno,* Signore," the round man spluttered, "just eliminating suspects at this stage. Following on from our conversation at the station, sir."

His command of English surprised me.

"I understand," the major replied. "May I offer you some refreshments?"

"No, no, honestly, we're fine, don't want to impose."

"I would," the blank one said, a hint of energy twitching the corner of his lips.

"Certainly," the major replied, nodding toward me. He was granting my escape, bolstering my solo team to match the duo. I placed several glasses upon a metal tray and lifted the jug of fresh lemonade from the fridge and placed it on top. The idea of Marco being implicated made every sound ricochet echoes of doubt in my mind. The memory of that day darted around my mind like a jerky colt, limbs flailing in opposing directions without control.

I placed the tray upon the table with a clumsy clang.

The major shot me a look.

So did the small man. He was sweatier now. I had the major to thank for that.

"Thank you, Signorina. I hear you're to marry the Cavaldi *impresario,* no? When's the happy date?"

I could sense the major's polite turn of his head. I felt the warmth of his questioning gaze without turning toward him.

"Oh, no decisions on that just yet," I flustered, watching the lemonade swirl up the glass. "I don't have anyone to give me away. It will be a very small affair."

"Not if his mother has anything to do with it," he replied, wiping the salty drips across his brow.

The skinny man chortled.

"You snigger, *imbecile,* but you didn't know Cavaldi when she was a young catch around here! Men buzzing around her like a honey pot. Chose a bad egg though. Women do that. They see the shine, like a magpie, peck at the treasure but don't look deeper. Caught up in a bad crowd Paolino's father was, that's for sure, God rest his soul."

I bristled off the look he shot me.

"I'm sure Paolino is a different bucket of anchovies though. Seems like he's got ambition. Vision. I've watched the tourists flock to him. Quite the setup. Signorina is going to be quite a wealthy woman, no, Signore?"

The major's smile was clipped. It made the sweaty man understand that the lemonade didn't invite conversation or comment on my personal affairs.

"Are you finished here, gentlemen?" the major asked as they took a final gulp.

The fleshy policeman loosened the second button of his shirt. A little more chest hair clawed out for air. "I'd say so. I leave my card for you, Signorina. If in the next few days things jolt into your memory — it happens that way sometimes; you know? — I'm not saying your brother had anything to do with this, we just need to understand the exact timing of things, you can understand that, no?"

I nodded. Any possible words cleaved to the sides of my mouth.

A clatter turned us toward the kitchen.

A soaked Elizabeth looked over at me.

Passata traced the entire front of her apron, the odd chunk of tomato hanging onto the fabric. Her face was smeared red.

"Looks like you have your hands full over there, Signorina," the officer commented with another unwelcome observation, just as her wailing erupted.

I reached her while the major led the officers back onto the street. Half the *passata* from my bowl had also tipped onto the tiles. It ran in tangents across the decorative yellow and turquoise swirls, trickling into small rivers of wasted food. On another day I might have kept my patience in check.

"Santina — see to the child. I'm happy to help you here."

"My brother had nothing to do with this!" I blurted before I had a chance to clamp the thought.

"I never mentioned anything of the sort."

"But that awful man did. Marco's a loner, yes, sarcastic, yes, rubs people the wrong way — I see that. I know he's no angel. But this? I'm supposed to sit and listen to someone talk about my family like that?"

His face eased into a quiet acceptance, his eyes warm, seeing through me.

My embarrassment crushed my cheeks red. They matched Elizabeth's.

I lifted her up in one brusque swoop.

"Let's go and clean ourselves up, yes?" I asked, masking my indignation with a forced breeze I knew the major saw right through.

I reached the doorway and paused. I turned back to apologize.

The major had already gone.

CHAPTER 23

The next morning Elizabeth and I left the house soon after watering the vegetable patch. The artichokes stretched up their proud crowns, their purple-dipped leaves reaching out to the sun. Before Adeline had been with us, the major and I would have collected them together, judging the ones ready and those we'd allow a few more days to mature. Now I did the task alone, my employers on my periphery, muttering by the *cavolo nero,* sometimes harvesting the lemon trees. This morning Adeline chose to sit beneath the vine that sprouted overhead along the entire length of the lower terrace. The late-summer sun beat down. She insisted on lying upon the ground, much to the major's frustration. From her prone position she babbled through a stream of consciousness, which she then channeled through the charcoal that charged across her notepad with vengeance. The major sat with her for a while. As she lost herself deeper into her drawing, he withdrew to the quiet sanctuary of his garden. It teetered at the height of maturity. The proud geometry of the Romanesco cauliflowers stood to attention, zucchini lengthened; the chard splayed its foliage, a peacock fanning for attention. The patch was a celebration of our efforts, ablaze with color and inviting produce.

I let Elizabeth run down the *viccolo* ahead of me a little, noticing how her limbs were no longer rolled with tender baby fat but muscular, lithe with our daily climbs up and down these steps. Her body looked longer too, beginning its stretch toward childhood, leaving her toddler days to fade like a receding shadow. It wouldn't be long before the major began preparations to send her to England to begin her formal education. The thought was like bruised petals between rough fingers.

We wove down the alleys, Elizabeth counting the steps as we did as far as her first ten numbers of Neapolitan would allow. We reached Paolino's shop, and she ran in to greet her old friend. I followed soon after. I found her resting up on his hip as he showed her off to unsuspecting customers.

"My favorite customer right here, Signora!

Look at that face!" he announced, taking her little chin in his two fingers and giving it a wiggle. "An English girl from the hill but Positanese through and through."

The customer twisted round to see who she presumed was the mother, but my dark hair and eyes threw her into confusion, a world away from the redheaded beauty of the child in Paolino's arms. My polite smile was well rehearsed. The customer left with several paper bags loaded with Paolino's fresh sliced meats and cheeses.

"So my beautiful Signorinas! What can I get for you today?"

"We're just taking a walk, getting some air before it's too hot."

"Mamma has spoken to the priest. We're to see him this evening."

The statement landed with a pebble's plop.

"This evening, Paolino? I'm to be at home."

"Once Signorina is asleep you come and join me at the Chiesa Nuova."

"I can't just announce I'm leaving for the evening. My day off is not until Sunday."

"So bring her if you have to, I'm sure Don Vincenzo won't mind."

"Why the urgency?" I asked, a prickle at the back of my throat.

He looked at me and cocked his head. "Why the questions?"

The beads tapped the entry of a new customer. Paolino sprang into action. He was so at home in his spotlight. I watched as the new tourist succumbed to his honeyed patter. It made me feel proud and foreign at the same time. I was so comfortable not seeing another soul but for the major, Elizabeth, and Adeline for days at a time. Paolino craved company, this incessant performance. Brilliant as it was, I felt a sudden hesitation whether I would ever be able to maintain his stamina before a crowd.

"See you after seven, Santina!" he called to me as Elizabeth and I left his shop. I reached for her hand; the crowds were already forming at this time of day. My cut smarted. At once I was back in the bathroom, fixed in the ardent gaze of the major. I knew he would let me go to church this evening if I explained why I needed to return to town after Elizabeth was asleep. I could also picture his expression; a genteel masking of his disappointment, a tender fight to hide his feelings. He'd look at me from under his hooded gaze, a half smile in spite of the inappropriate pact we had made, two people reading the same page of a book in silence, waiting whilst the other completes a paragraph before turning for the next. My marriage would go ahead, whatever illicit daydream we had drifted through. The feelings clung to me like the sticky strands of a tiny web, invisible to the eye yet spidering the skin nonetheless.

"Of course you may leave this evening," the major replied after I'd broached the subject. Adeline had retired to her room straight after the meal, as always. The major liked to enjoy the temperate gold of the late summer evenings. "I understand that Catholics must perforce breach an insurmountable length of confession before committing to their partners. Isn't that so?" He ran a hand through his hair and leaned back on his chair a little, his eyes streaking past the terrace and out toward the sea.

"Thank you. I won't be long."

I brushed away a few last crumbs. Off his expression, I paused before I returned to the kitchen.

"Santina," he began, meeting my eye, "my sarcasm is a feeble mask. You of all people know that. A lifetime of British habits dies hard. You'll forgive me."

I mirrored his grin. "I might."

As I closed the main doors behind me, I saw him turn to look toward me, a figure framed by his vines, flanked by the tall smooth columns of the terrace; someone half remembered from a moth-eaten dream.

The vestibule was smoky with remembered incense. I watched the dust motes dance in the shafts of light flinting through the high arched windows. Paolino looked over at me and reached for my hand. I slipped it in his.

"You're freezing, my love. How'd you manage that?"

"This place reminds me of Adeline's hospital."

Perhaps it was the stone floors, the pallid yellow of the plaster, or that vague sense of impending procedure about the space. The clock pendulum marked every breath, echoing its summons. At last Don Vincenzo walked in, a flight of robes behind him. We rose to shake his hand. He had a kind face, welcoming even, but his smile was distracted, like an unnecessary indulgence.

"*Buona sera,* youngsters. Please, do sit down. Thank you for coming this evening."

He took a breath, but before he could launch into what felt would be nothing short of a sermon, there was a knock at his door.

"*Sì?*"

"Don Vincenzo, it's Paolino's mother!" we

443

heard Signora Cavaldi call from the other side of the wood.

He rose once again and turned the metal handle. She blew in.

"Do accept my apologies, Don Vincenzo, I had so many things to attend to before coming here. Staff is not what one pays for, let me tell you that, but you, man of the cloth, know more about the human condition than I. Those tourists, bless them and their ways, but if you watch them long enough, you soon come to understand the world and how it's changing. One sauntered into our shop in her bikini this afternoon. I kid you not. Did you see her, Paolino? 'Course he did, couldn't miss that figure of a woman. Whole town is talking about it still." She patted her sweat but not long enough for anyone to offer a response. "The world is changing. That's why I told Paolino, if you're serious about the orphan girl, then there is no sense in waiting for the second coming. I mean another girl would expect all sorts of fanfare, but not Santina. She's a good girl, Don Vincenzo, simple life — I should know, I was the one who mothered her when hers died. I'm sure you've talked through all of this already, no?"

"Mamma. We just sat down. Let Don Vincenzo say what he needs to."

"Nothing needs saying. We're here to book in the earliest date."

We turned toward the priest, willing him to fill the silence before she whipped back up.

"Signora Cavaldi, may I get you some water? You look like the world has taken its toll."

She blushed at that. I admired his artful card, then found myself guessing which tack he'd operate on us? Condescension toward the young lovers perhaps? His expression told me that he guessed her insistence on speed was due to my being pregnant. It hadn't occurred to me till that moment. Did she think that too? This was the first I'd heard about a simple, hurried wedding. I felt my skin heat with indignation.

We watched Don Vincenzo pour her some water from a glass carafe. It silenced her for several gulps. He was a man who knew how to take charge of a room. With Signora Cavaldi present, it was no small feat.

"So, *fanciulli*. Jesus has shown you the art of loving one another. Over the next few weeks we will meet to teach you the ways to bring him into your marriage. For there is three in your marriage now, young lovers."

Three? I willed every fiber to stay rooted in the room, but my imagination raced the

445

steps, each of the four hundred and forty that led from the sea to the villa. I darted every nook, skipped two at a time, tireless climber, Cavaldi's mountain goat, till I reached our garden, slipped onto the chair beside the major. Till he and I gazed at the languid reflection of the dying sun, beckoned by the horizon, swallowed by the water beyond Capri.

"Do you agree, Santina?" Paolino's voice hooked me back to the surface.

"Do I agree?" I stalled.

"Don Vincenzo suggests the same time each week and an early winter wedding. Mid-December is the earliest he can do."

I watched the priest slit his eyes over to me, expecting some resistance no doubt, in view of my supposed pregnancy.

"That sounds beautiful," I said, a little too quickly.

"It's not a spring wedding," Cavaldi strode on, looking at Paolino, "but it will be festive, no? And less tourists squeezing the streets."

She was redder than before. Perhaps the stress of an impending celebration brought out the claustrophobia in her too.

"December is my favorite month," I said, reassuring the room.

Paolino looked over at me. His face was

dazzling against the pallid walls behind him, a sunbeam streaking the dark wooden shelves aching with Bibles and maudlin oil paintings of sneering priests peering down their noses at us.

"Simple and small is perfect," I added, feeling Paolino's hand squeeze mine and glad for it.

At last we were granted leave. Outside, the pealing bells announced the late Mass. I nodded to several of the older women I recognized from Paolino's shop as they waddled by me, clutching their rosaries like cherished memories.

Signora Cavaldi appeared behind us. "So that is that. Don't waste time with intricate details. What's the use of that? You've known us all your life, Santina. I feel blessed that I know my daughter-in-law as well as I do. I'm practically your mother already." I couldn't decide which was more disconcerting, her sudden tirade of possessive love or her vociferous disdain. "My children!" she cried, wrapping her arms around the both of us and squeezing us into her bosom. I smelled salt, oil, violet, and a wince of garlic.

She lifted my chin. "You've done alright for yourself, mountain kid. Thanks to you know who" — her eyebrows raised into a smile — "we've come to your rescue again."

"Mass has started, Mamma!" Paolino called, stretching an eager arm toward the door. He knew better than to tell her to stop. She gave her brassiere a stiff yank and waddled into the crowd within.

Paolino took my hand and kissed it. His eyes tipped up to me. They were laughing.

"Is this all a ridiculous game to you, Paolino?"

"You want me serious? I can be serious. You'll be bored after a month or two, but I can do serious!"

He began a pantomime, walking down the church steps and back up again like a gormless clown. People started to look at him.

"See! Look how serious I am, Santina!" He pulled an exaggerated mimic of sadness. The people passing started to giggle. He took a bow and watched them pass, then bounded back up to me, hooking my arm around his.

"Now, let's think about what other serious things we can do this evening. How's about a serious trip on my cousin's rowboat? Cool off after my mother?"

A laugh bubbled out before I could cork it.

"Santina — little saint — even she finds my mother almost tolerable. That's what catechism is all about, my love. If you can weather the mother long enough, the partnership has a future."

"You should wipe that grin off your face this moment, Paolino Cavaldi."

"Why? Only I know what I'm dreaming up this moment."

He stopped and took both my hands in his. "I want to give you the world, my love."

"I don't want the world. I want you."

"Same thing, no?" His face creased into a dancing grin I could no longer resist. He took my hand in his, and we strolled down toward the shore.

"I should get going, Paolino. I've already been longer than I said."

"Isn't the baby asleep?"

"She's not a baby. And yes, she is."

"So stay with your lover!" he replied, scooping both my feet off the shale, cradling me in his arms before I could stop him. Tourists lined the outside tables at Buca di Beppo, clinking another day of relaxation.

"What are you doing? People are looking!"

" 'Course they are. Most beautiful woman in town in my arms!"

His feet crunched toward the water. He stopped and sat me down in one of the smaller boats. Then, as I made to stand he gave it a shove and it slid into the water. I gave out a cry. He lifted himself in, took the oars in his hands, and began rowing us away from the shore.

"Paolino, what on earth do you think you are doing?"

"Taking my bride to my favorite place." He laughed.

My Positano sank into the near distance. His face glowed against the backdrop of my gray rock, houses clutching to the climb, the powder pinks, blues, bougainvillea reds, and primrose yellows dipping toward early evening. And with each lap of the wooden oar, more lights came on, till all that was left of our town was a cluster of color and twinkling lights, a terra-cotta model in the *presepe* at Christmas.

Paolino led us south of our bay and past the first pride of cliffs that rose out of the water. I looked up as we swayed on the sea, catching the final glimpse of our villa before he turned, following the craggy bend in the rock. We rowed a little way more but at the first opening beside us, Paolino twisted the rowboat to face the entrance and began rowing us under a concealed archway.

The oars eased through the water. We floated into a cave. The echo of slurping waves arched overhead. The sun's farewell streaked in like hope through the narrow entrance, reflecting through the blue be-

neath us, an electric cerulean, as if il-
luminated from below. The swells of light
danced across his face. He lifted the oars.
We rocked in choppy silence for a moment,
only the sound of the water sloshing up the
sides of the wooden edge percussed our
silence.

"Paolino, this is magnificent," I whispered,
hushed by the magical age of the place, an
imposter on antiquity, trespassing the hidden caverns of this mountain.

"I've wanted to bring you here since I met
you."

We swayed for a breath or two. Then he
ripped off his shirt, his trousers, and leaped
into the water. The boat rocked with a little
more momentum off the force of his leap. I
gripped the sides, searching for his silhouette gliding beneath the surface. He bobbed
up with a splutter.

"Come in with me, Santina!"

My face dropped.

"There's no one here! All the tourists are
on the shore now. Come on! The water is so
warm."

"Paolino, you have nothing on."

"Exactly!" he called, dipping under the
surface and spraying up to the top beside
me, treading water and holding on to the
side gentle enough not to rock it too much.

"You didn't say we were going swimming."

"See — you're thinking about it. Come on, *tesoro.* Before it gets too dark."

I looked at him. His eyes were so wide and inviting. The water lit up all around him. I rose to my knees and did the unimaginable. I let my skirt drop to the floor of the boat. I reached my blouse up and over my head. I unhooked my brassiere, then eased away my underwear. I looked over to him. He had swum to the far edge and found a small ledge to rest against. Now half his torso was above the level of the water. I knelt, across from him, swaying on the blue.

I felt alive.

"You are the most beautiful creature on this planet, Santina."

I felt the air blow over my bare breasts. Before I could think any further I stood up and let myself jump into the deep. Water rushed over me, an effervescence of bubbles. The blue quiet enveloped me. For a split second I was engulfed by the liquid silence of those muffled days after my mother died. Then, from the cool deep, I rose to the surface, propelled by sheer exhilaration.

I spied Paolino a little farther ahead and swam toward him. My breath grasped at the surface, giddy and frothing with laughter. I reached his rock edge. He leaned over and pulled me to him.

Our wet skin met, skittish, childlike. His fingers wrapped around my face.

"Yes, Santina. All of you. Just like this. Bare. No hiding. I want all of you inside me."

I think I was crying. My salt mixed with the ocean's.

His lips found mine. Soft, confident, bare. His hands traced my wet back.

Then, the slosh of another boat.

We froze.

Human stalagmites.

His eyes slid to the opening of the cave. The silhouette of two small boats stretched across the azure.

"Wait here!" he said just before leaping into the water. I watched his outline glide toward our rowboat. The sting of vulnerability replaced giddy liberation. He climbed into the boat and with fierce strokes rowed over to me. He clambered back onto our rock. I started to shiver.

"You lie inside. No one need see you. Cover yourself with your clothes."

I did as he asked. The sound of the echoing waves made me feel as if I were being pulled underwater, losing the strength to return to the surface.

That's when we heard the voices. At first, an indistinct garble of echoes. Then a familiar sound reached me. Every fiber of my body rose to attention, each minute sound reaching me like a dart. The sound of rowing slushed through into the cave. Paolino steered us behind an indent in the rock edge, clasping a crag to keep our boat unseen. My heart thudded against my ribs. I prayed I wouldn't become the ridicule of tourists. I imagined their sun-red faces gawking at my naked body. Shivers crawled over my body.

Three voices. Men. My breath snatched. The words were watered down. A few poked the surface. *Cavaldi. Drop-off.*

I noticed Paolino catch them too. His back stiffened, the top of his head rising like an antenna. I lifted my head so that my vision skimmed the rim of the boat. Around the edge of the rock, I could just make out the figures.

That's when the familiar silhouette pierced into focus.

My brother handed over a large packet to two men in another boat. I couldn't see his smile but could hear it on the sardonic twist of his voice. They shook hands. A further exchange. Their tone was clipped. Then Paolino and I watched them row away in opposite directions.

"It's alright, *tesoro*," he cooed after a while, "they've gone."

I sat up, clutching my clothes, cramped by my nudity.

"I recognized one of those men," he said, running a hand through his wet hair.

I stalled, not wanting to face the current of unanswerable questions: Why on earth was my brother rowing out here alone? Who did he meet? What did he hand over? How would I ever ask him? I shouldn't even be here, naked in Paolino's arms, swimming like a child. Or worse. Anyone could have seen me.

"Now," Paolino purred, moving over toward me, "where were we?"

My body was cold. I shook him away. "I should get back, Paolino. I shouldn't even be here. I don't know what we're doing!"

He could hear my panic simmering. I snatched at my clothes, pulling them over me with a jerk.

"*Tesoro* — there's still time before it's dark. Please, let's not rush away from this special place."

"It's not special anymore! Three strangers nearly saw me utterly naked like a common —"

"You think that's what I think of you?!"

455

"No! But strange men? Come on!"

"You care what strange men think, or me?"

I look at him square in the face.

"Take me home," I said plainly, our romantic escapade all at once childish, clumsy, pointless.

We rowed in silence.

Our town rose before us, dipped in violet dusk, a half-hearted invitation.

A distant yet familiar feeling swelled; who was that stranger acting like my brother?

CHAPTER 24

I closed the heavy door of the villa behind me, careful not to make too much noise. My hair was still a little damp despite the temperate air. A tease of breeze flew up from the sea. A solitary trickle of salt water traced the back of my neck.

"You had a gentleman caller this evening, Santina."

I turned in the direction of the major's voice. He was sat in his favorite spot, at the end of the lemon trees where the medlars replaced the citrus, alongside several peach and cherry trees. My feet crunched across the cooked earth. "I'm sorry I'm so late. I had no idea I would be gone so long."

"Please, no need to apologize. Though I would appreciate an explanation of why a very disheveled older man rang my bell after dinner?"

The description pointed to one man only. "What did he want?" I asked.

"To see you. When I told him you were out, he was quite insistent I give you this." He reached out his hand, holding a tired piece of paper.

"Did he tell you his name?" I asked, pretending I didn't know the answer.

"He said you would know."

His expression made me feel uneasy.

"Is everything alright, Santina? You look like you've seen a ghost."

"That's how I feel."

He shifted in the deck chair. "He didn't look like the sort of person I would have necessarily liked you to be meeting at night. If you need my help — in any way — you know to ask for it, don't you?"

He sighed a half laugh in the pause. "It feels almost ridiculous to reassure you now."

My eyebrows creased.

"You know, after everything."

I nodded, distracted, wondering what my father would have scrawled on that dirty-looking piece of paper.

"I'll stay out here a little while longer, I think," he said.

"May I bring you something?"

"Please don't worry, I'm quite happy to do that."

I took the note.

"I'm sure it's not important," I said, forcing myself to reassure him, but with little success.

"Good night, Santina."

I turned to return toward the villa steps.

"I'm glad I was able to be here tonight," he said.

I turned back.

"So you could begin your marriage preparations in earnest. I was flippant earlier. I'm sorry. You deserve every happiness. You will make a fine partner for that young chap. He's no fool. Knows a bright strong woman when he sees one."

I felt awkward, craving solitude. He intuited it without hesitation.

"My words are stifling. I'm sorry. Please, let me hold you up no longer." A wry smile now, but his eyes were full of warmth.

I sat on the edge of my bed and unfolded the note. My father's clumsy scrawl scratched across the surface.

> We need to talk. It's Marco. I know things.
> I wait for you at Fornillo beach.
> 10 o'clock tomorrow. Don't be late.
>
> Papà

His written Neapolitan was as slurred as

his spoken. The letters were big and round, not dissimilar to that of a child's. But the content I could not ignore. Why of all evenings did he turn up tonight? He wouldn't know that I had just discovered my brother floating with other shadows. That I'd narrowly escaped being discovered frolicking naked where neither of us were supposed to be.

Sleep evaded me. I twisted and turned in my darkened room. When I slipped into a light slumber, my dreams were fitful; I was back on the mountainside, my mother's elusive silhouette slipping out of sight.

It was no mean feat to reach Fornillo at that time of day with Elizabeth in tow. I made sure I took the longest route to avoid Paolino and his mother. Much as I liked to second-guess my father's ability to keep time I didn't want to run the risk of missing him. It sickened me to be at his beck and call, but I couldn't chance not knowing what he was compelled to tell me.

By nine o'clock the sun was already beating down, but Elizabeth insisted on halting at the weeds sprouting between the rocks along our descent, as we took the hidden back steps weaving parallel to the main road. It was a shortcut I had taken many times but never one I'd done at such a brisk pace. The only way to navigate our town was at a measured climb or descent. Galloping like the tourists tired a person quickly. This morning, however, I longed for Elizabeth to learn the nebulous art of cooperation, a talent that eluded her.

At the start of the ascent beyond the main drag of boutiques we took a sharp left and traced a very narrow alley that ran behind a curve of houses. To our left the deep gorge tumbled down toward the shingle and the *viccolo* curved inward. To our right a high wall rose to meet the main road. The flora beside our walkway was lush and green, for within the crags it remained in the shade for most of the day. Ferns spread their leaves up toward the light, bougainvillea trailed down from the rear terraces of the homes above. It was a small oasis hidden from most visitors and a passageway used by locals. At this hour, the only sounds were our footsteps and the steady crescendo of the cicadas, vibrating their impassioned announcement of incoming trespassers.

The church of Santa Maddalena just above us struck ten. Elizabeth flashed her bright blue eyes toward me, round, inquisitive, and alert, just like her mother's used to be.

461

My head was full of my father. Once again, his mere presence in my life, however sidelined, unsettled me to the core. I hauled her up onto my back and negotiated the steps down toward the beach, two at a time where I could, running the wider ones, deafened by the pounding in my ears and the ricocheting flip-flop of my soles against the stone walls.

At last we arrived at the beach. I let Eilzabeth slip down, but she was in no mood to leave my side just yet, grabbing my leg instead, urging me to lift her into my arms.

I caught my breath. Her clam-like attachment on me began to loosen.

That's when I saw him.

He was sat at the far end, his brown-gray pallor the perfect camouflage against the rocks. We walked toward him. As I drew closer, a familiar wet cold trickled through me. He glanced over and nodded, an awful knowing look in his glassy onyx eyes.

I sat Elizabeth down on the shingle. She seemed happy to stay close by for the time being. When I reached him, his grin broadened to a sickening smile.

"So you decided to show up at last," he croaked.

"What do you know?"

"Is that any way to greet a father?"

"I'm not here to discuss you or me."

"You're so full of fire for a young woman. Doesn't suit a girl like you. Besides, thanks to me you met your husband, no? This the thanks I get?"

I had even less patience for his slithering through facetious arguments than usual.

"What do you want to tell me about Marco?"

"I don't want to tell you anything. But I have a duty as a father."

I bit my lip so I wouldn't tell him that he wouldn't know how to behave as a father even if he tried.

"How much do you love your brother?"

"More than you ever will."

"You want to leave the angry young woman act at home and talk to me adult to adult, or we going to waste my time with recriminations again? You came here because you want to know what I do, but you're going the wrong way about it if you want me to spill."

I looked toward the emerald-green sparkle of the waves. Somewhere out there was the calm I needed to face this man. Trying to grapple it was like scooping sea water into my fist.

"Is Marco in trouble?"

"Could be," he said with a half-hearted

shake of his head. "You try to teach children how to be good people and this is how they repay you."

I didn't reply.

"You're not much better. Living like a princess up at the villa, marrying a jumped-up grocer. Quite the setup. Spare a moment for your father anytime? You wouldn't have had any of that if it wasn't for me!"

It was like being spat at. I stood motionless. All feeling cracking at the surface — a drying smear of caulk.

"That's it, silent treatment like your mother. You women are all the same. But you listen to me, Santina — that perfect brother of yours is in deep. Very deep. Police hunting for him as we speak. He's a dangerous man, Santina. I've warned him more than once that I can't live with what I know and keep quiet. But he threatens me too. What am I to do? And now the police are pressing down on me. Marco and I will be behind bars if I don't spill."

"What do you mean, dangerous?"

"Read between the lines, Santina. What do you think? Pretty handy in the line of work he does to be working at the cemetery, don't you think?"

"You're not suggesting —"

"No. I'm telling. And I can't live like this anymore."

It was impossible for me to tell if his bitter ramblings were that of a sorry drunk. My instinct urged otherwise.

"Why are you telling me this?" I asked.

"Because I don't want to send my son to jail. But I can't live like this either."

I let the pause hang.

"Here's the thing, Santina: you help me, or I talk."

"Talk?"

"The police expect me to talk tomorrow afternoon. Made a deal. I talk and they don't send me down. I don't, and they'll be after me before I can say *buon giorno.*"

The idea of my father locked away sparked a flicker of relief, but at the cost of losing my brother it was unthinkable, and he knew it. It made me hate him even more.

"Why would they send you down?"

"Nothing you need worry your pretty little head over."

"You said we'd talk adult to adult."

His eyes slid to the sea, then flicked back to me. "Small stuff. Didn't hurt anyone. Misplaced some things. Debts made and left unpaid. Let's just leave it at that."

I looked at his wan face, his skin tawny with drink, and felt the icy realization that he and I shared not only the same features but the same hostile privacy. The same steel stubbornness. I was looking into a warped mirror and the sensation was uglier than any I'd ever felt. Worse than knowing Paolino's love may not penetrate the surface of what the major and I had experienced, worse than the bitter taste of betrayal, or shame.

He took my pause as acceptance of my defeat. "So, Santina. You either pay me to skip town, support myself till I find my feet down south, Sicily maybe, Greece. Hell, I might even sail down to Africa while I'm at it."

"Or? Aren't threats normally an ultimatum?"

"Or, I go spewing to the awful pigs who are threatening to take me away from this paradise."

"You expect me to believe these lies?"

"Can you take that chance?"

I bolted him with my stare.

"Send daggers with your eyes, but the fact is, you help me, or I tell the police the truth about my son."

"What's he done?"

He gazed back out to sea. From a distance I'm sure we looked like a young woman speaking to a wizened fisherman, listening

466

to him knot his net of tales, of his life on the sea, of the perils and the triumphs. The conversation felt like quicksand.

"Terrible things, Santina. I wouldn't have imagined it possible. He was such a sweet child. Feeble maybe. But good."

"What have you done? Why do the police want you?"

"I've said all that needs to be said."

"You call me out here, scratch a note to my employer, get him worried about what's going on — you don't think he read that note before me? I run here to see this sorry state of a man only to be told I've heard all I need to know!"

I watched him tighten. It fueled my fury.

"You can let those filthy dreams about me bailing you out of your sorry state fly in the air, because that's all they are. Silly little pictures from a greedy man who never loved me, and now crawls back for his own good. You disgust me!"

"You ever think how I felt, Santina? Up in the hills with two starving children to look after? Not knowing whether we'd survive the next winter?! I chose to grieve for the rest of my life, giving up the two most precious things I had left in it, but you punish me again and again. What's wrong with you both? I gave what I could. Your escape!"

"No! Yours!"

"I did what I could do."

"You treated my mother like a rag! I cannot forgive you for that."

"And she me."

"Grow up!"

He shook his head.

Sudden tears shuddered through him.

I watched him wrinkle into his sorrow. I didn't know how to feel. I was so invested in my guarded numbness or fury at this man that there was no space for anything else. I watched him, like the replaying of a worn-out strip of film flickering onto a canvas screen before me, jerked motion pictures of a person I once knew.

"My children hate me" — he drooled — "all I need is a way out. You save your beloved brother. And have your father out of your hair. For good."

"You taught us that hate."

"Maybe!" he spat, wiping his nose with the back of his hand. "But it's all I knew. You've made no mistakes? You've done everything the perfect way?! Congratulations!" A second wave of tears struck him, with more force than the first. Again, the glassy reflection of my own shortcomings, my own warped choices. Only shadows between my father's decisions and mine, after all. I kept my lips pursed shut, I didn't want him to see me lose my temper any further.

"You have any idea what it's like?" he whined, clogging the argument. "Up in those godforsaken hills? You think my father was any better? You ever think to look at my scars? No. Young people? They are the victims always. You see to the end of your nose, no farther. You hate me that much, Santina?! Then give me the money I need, and I will be dead to you. Even more than I am now."

"How much are you expecting me to pluck from the air?"

"One thousand lire."

"Are you mad?"

"I'm desperate. I take away your brother or you get rid of me. What's it going to be?"

He stopped crying. There was a spindled strength to him, like a thin weed that will not be scraped away with a hoe. A final revelation that we grew from the same root after all. "How do I know you won't come crawling back as soon as you've drunk it all?"

He ran his fingers across his gaunt face. I could hear the *scritch* against his stubble even from where I stood.

"The police are in town today. If they

come to your house, you know they are on the scent. They are after Marco, Santina. They've already questioned you, no?"

I nodded, terse.

"They will be back. Harder this time. I wanted to tell you this last night."

I shook my head. His presence was as claustrophobic as ever.

"I'm sorry, Santina."

"Everything so urgent. Such panic." I tried to hold on to my resolve but it started to crumble, scuffed pebbles along the ridge of our cliffs, tumbling out of sight. Unwanted images blasted my mind, Marco's edge, the knife I'd spied in his hut, the robbery, the boat. It all added up to uncertain business but not necessarily dangerous. The picture my father painted was of a true criminal. He had no proof. Was I prepared to risk it? Could I live with the possibility that because of my stubbornness, my father might tell lies about Marco and send him to prison?

My rage knew no bounds. He could have skipped town long ago. He could have kept away. He needn't have swum into this watery mess. But that was my father all over. He delighted in this malignant play. He lived for this meddling. It was his fuel. And, should I even consider giving in to his demands, what was to say he wouldn't return week after week, demanding more? Threatening me again and again? Yet who was to say I could live with myself if I gambled my brother's freedom?

Around us, our Positano sparkled into primary-colored focus, the blue of the sea, the proud red of the bougainvillea, the yellow bursts of bikinis; a parallel paradisiacal fantasy. And here we stood, upon the shingle, our lives in the balance.

"I have no more to say, Santina. I turn to you because there is no one else who can save Marco. Or me. Our family never stuck together. Perhaps this once, we can make things good."

"You don't make things good with threats."

"Oh hell, call it what you like, Santina! You always had a way with words. That's why I knew you would be fine. You have a great life. Keep it that way! I'm reaching out! You just see punishment!"

We stared into the silence.

"You make your own mind up, Santina. I come to you tomorrow evening for the money. If the police have been, you know it's true. If not? What will be will be."

"Everything is so simple to you."

He let out a wheezy laugh then.

I did the only thing I could. I turned away

from that skeletal man, picked up Elizabeth, and began our hike back to the villa. This time I walked slower. This time I sent out thanks for holding her hand in mine. Marco's face blurred into mind. Motes of memory swirled inside me, catching at the back of my throat. I don't know who had hurt me more — my father whimpering for help with threats or my brother for being obtuse about his life? My rage turned inward; how did I let myself become so vulnerable to both of them? When did I become responsible for their lives?

It was time to uncover the truth.

Whatever the consequence.

CHAPTER 25

On our return, I butchered several handfuls of artichokes, taking out my needling frustration on anything other than the almost four-year-old prodding me at every turn. The heat usually left me unfazed, but today it bore down like a vise, walls inching closer, suffocating temperatures that made the simple act of breathing feel like a minor victory. Even the light had a dead weight, void of air, the act of moving through it a leaden exercise. I tore at the fluff at the middle of the leaves, scraped the hearts into a separate bowl, and quartered the florets. Elizabeth sat upon the terrace just beyond the door with a large enamel bowl of water she splashed in happily, making a delighted mess around her.

The slivers of garlic fizzed in the olive oil. I added the artichokes, threw in several wedges of potatoes, tipped in a fistful of parsley, a wiggle of water. A whoosh of steam rose up from the pan, pungent, promising, but providing little of the distraction I craved. My mind galloped on, pounding the same thoughts.

"Are you alright, Santina?"

The major's voice caught me off guard.

I spun toward him.

"Good heavens, you look frightfully pale. Perhaps you ought to take the afternoon to rest?"

I shook my head. My forced smile stayed locked in my mind, unable to break the surface. He stepped toward me, the sun beating down around him in painful dazzling stripes.

"I'm fine. Lunch may be a little late. I'm sorry."

"Not at all."

I would have liked him to leave then. Float back to his reading, or correspondence, anything other than hovering in my periphery. I could sense him standing there, waiting for a longer answer, eager to listen. I would have liked nothing better than to tell him everything right then and there. For a stark moment I knew he was the only person I could trust with the burden of all of this. I turned to face him again. He'd moved aside a little so that the rays traced the gentle sculpt of his jaw, his white skin luminescent in the copper air. It wasn't just the elegant outline that made him compelling, but the exquisite openness with which he held the space now, so attuned to my mood, eager for me to feel comfortable and explain. I'd seen that expression many times before. It was the one that drifted over him after a particular passage of a certain poem, a pert expectance, the ability to hover in unanswered questions for an indeterminate time. I'd seen him like that late at night sometimes, as I prepared the kitchen for the following morning. In the space between the open door and the dining area, he might linger by his favorite picture, or stop reading for a moment and let his gaze wander beyond our walls, to a space both private and vast.

"I have less patience than I normally do today. I'm sorry," I said.

"Awful condition, this human one," he answered with a bronze smile, which I mirrored, but mine felt like a paper cut.

The bell clanged.

I wiped my hands on my apron and walked toward the door, passing Elizabeth just as she lifted the bowl and tipped the entire contents over herself, squealing in watery delight, jumping up onto her feet and dancing wet footprints across the terra-cotta. On another day I would have enjoyed her delirium. Today I marked it as one more thing to attend to in the heat of the afternoon, scrubbing foot marks away.

The same two policemen greeted me. The taller snarled a diagonal smile.

"Signorina Santina. The pleasure once again."

I felt the major step in behind me.

"Gentlemen. What can we do for you this time?"

The sweaty one wiped his brow. Several mustache hairs curled toward his lips.

"Signore, *buon giorno*. We won't take too much of your time, of course. Just a few more questions for your employee here and we will be on our way."

The smell of scorched artichokes reached me.

"Excuse me one moment," I said and left without waiting for a reply, nor inviting them in. The kitchen was hot with a blackened smell. I turned down the gas ring to minimal, added a splash of water, watching it sweat over the scorched leaves. I placed the lid on top.

The men were already sat down, waiting. I picked up Elizabeth's overturned enamel bowl and gave a perfunctory glance around for the child.

476

"It's alright, Santina, Elizabeth has gone inside to play. No need to worry." The major wanted these two out of his house as quickly as I did.

"Please. Take a load off your feet, Signorina," the small man purred. He reminded me of a larded meat joint, rolled and ready for the oven.

I took a seat. My father's words echoed in my head.

"Last time we came you were quick to confirm your brother's whereabouts the night of the robbery, that is correct?"

"Yes."

"Since then, Signorina Santina — that's a quaint name for a housekeeper, isn't it, Giancarlo?" he perked, glancing over at his incumbent partner. "Little saint. Had an aunt called that, I think. My grandmother's cousin. She was anything but. What's in a name though?"

The tall one sniggered. He reminded me of an adolescent joining in with laughter a beat too late, desperate to demonstrate understanding. The major straightened his collar. It didn't go unnoticed by the small officer.

"But we tarry. Let us get to the meat of our visit."

"The juicy bit," interjected Tall.

Small slit him a look.

"So you see, Santina, we've had more witnesses wriggle out of the woodwork since we last paid you a visit. And we can now start to stitch together quite the colorful quilt. Your little brother is more than one sees with the naked eye."

I had expected a second snigger from Tall at the use of the word naked. I sat silent, trying not to let my converging thoughts trigger any expression. I wouldn't allow my eyes to wander over to the major for fear of reading any concern or, worse, kindness, that might have made my voice wobble of its own accord.

"I suppose I thought we'd be kind enough to stop by and see, if in the time we've been away, your memory might have jogged anything more to the surface? Because you see, when we gather all the evidence it's the people who are withholding information who are going to be punished alongside the criminals. You can understand that, can't you?"

Small's little black eyes flicked toward the major and then back to me.

"Family is a wonderful thing, is it not? I don't think anyone north or south of Napoli knows about family. Not what it truly means. We die for one another. And that is

478

as it should be."

He gave his mustache a perfunctory twiddle. It twisted straight back down to where it had been.

"I'm so sorry Santina isn't able to help you any more than last time, Signori."

Small and Tall turned toward the major. Though I knew he couldn't have understood the Neapolitan, he had read my body language and now translated for the men on my behalf.

That's when we heard the shrieks above our heads.

"Henry darling! Henry, my love! Look at our little painter!"

Our eyes followed the sound. Two faces gazed down at us. Both were paint-streaked. Adeline's patter sped up now, the words sputtered out at manic speed, her eyes dancing, part terrified rabbit, part victorious. Elizabeth's white skin was covered in red and yellow splats and smears. She giggled and waved a paintbrush down at us. That's when we noticed her tiny feet resting on the ledge that ran along the top of the stone balustrade the length of the upper terrace. Adeline's hands were around her waist, but the sight turned my marrow to ice.

I leapt to my feet and ran up the stairs. I reached Adeline's room and snuck inside without making a sound. I could hear the major talking up from the garden now. Cooing to his wife, keeping her talking, trying to make sure she stayed calm, prodding her with gentle encouragement to remove their child from the perilous perch.

Meanwhile, I watched Adeline's jerky movements, her spine rippling with hilarity, every small twitch a thorn, making the dispersal of my panic even harder. I watched her red-green-blue hands around her daughter moving as she spoke. I walked toward the balcony, registering the paint across the tiles, an overturned jar of water trickling brown-green sludge across the desk into a muddy puddle.

I was outside with them now, in the square of terrace beyond Adeline's double doors. Neither had registered me. Elizabeth started stamping her feet.

"Look at me, Papà!"

"Wonderful, Elizabeth! A real painter!" he called up, disguising every fray of concern in his voice. "Come downstairs now, my darling, and show me what you've painted, yes?"

"But isn't it marvelous, Henry darling? Isn't it just perfect, my love?! So long I've thought about this, Henry! She likes me, Henry! See this? After everything, Henry?

She likes her mamma, don't you, Lizzie?"

That's when she tickled her, and Elizabeth shrieked with laughter, rising on her toes, skimming the edge. Panic snaked around my throat.

"Addie darling, bring her down to the garden, let's paint down here, yes?" the major called.

"But do you see, Henry? The child understands! You should have seen the way she held the brush, Henry dear. An absolute natural! I feel immortal now!"

That's when her arms reached up toward heaven. In the split second she did so, Elizabeth lost her balance. I grabbed her just as her foot lifted up and over the edge. I clamped my arms around her, squeezing the life I'd saved back out of her.

Adeline whipped round. "Santina darling! Whatever is the matter with you, let the child go, look at her, she's screaming! Whatever's the matter?!"

"Sorry, Signora."

Adeline stepped inside to where I stood within the cool safety of the bedroom, disentangled my arms, and lifted the painted doll onto her hip, swaying this way and that, twisting them across the tiles in a maniacal celebratory waltz. Elizabeth's shrieks bounced off the tiles in wailing echoes. The light spidered over them through the shutters. I was watching a skeleton cradle the life it would never have.

The major stepped in.

"There's Daddy! Henry, look at her! Why did I never see how stunning this child was!" Her lips traced her chubby face, planting hurries of kisses all over it. I was unnerved by the whole scene, watching a conductor lead an orchestra through a frenetic passage, resisting their urge to keep time, swerving the tempo with players struggling to maintain rhythm. Around they twirled, sweeping over the tiles, leaving red paint smears as they did. The smudge of patterns was like the heaving evidence of a dragged bleeding body.

The major wrapped his arms around the both of them, lulling them toward stillness. I watched him retrace his daughter with gentleness, easing them all out of the narrowly escaped tragedy. Here was the life I was so woven into, yet invisible, gazing at it through smoky glass.

The major looked over at me, centered amidst the chaos, witnessing his own flurry of emotion without being consumed by it, a quality I could not relinquish my admiration of, this compelling ability to feel with such depth but remain at a safe, philosophical distance; a rowboat anchored, undulating on the sea without resistance.

"Do see to the men downstairs," he said, his voice soft. "I'll be down directly."

Small and Tall were wandering around the terrace, caged cats stalking their territory, hungry, restless.

"*Scusa,* didn't want to keep you waiting," I said.

"A child nearly falls to her death. We wait. Is no problem. You, on the other hand, look like a sheet in the wind," Small said.

"Anything more you need my help with?" I asked, surprising myself with the steel in my voice, despite the whirlwind of the past few minutes.

"Lunch maybe?" Tall cackled, sniffing the air like a pup.

"I am giving you one more chance to tell us what you know, really know, about your brother," Small interjected. "There are people, not such nice people as yourself, who are willing to tell us things. You understand that?"

"I will help any way I can," I replied, knowing that assisting them would be the last thing I could ever do.

Small searched me for clues. Tall stood motionless, a clay figure before the artist has etched in lifelike details.

"So, we go. And *buona fortuna* to you all. From the looks of things, you have your work cut out for you here. Part housekeeper, part nurse. There are places for women like her, you know. Someone should tell him this is no place for a child. Sad to see women ruined like that" — he shook his head with pantomimical sadness — "especially ones who must have been beautiful once upon a time."

His pomposity was nauseating. I knew if I let the words punctuating my thoughts fly out I would be doing nothing to divert suspicion. I opened the door.

They turned back, in unison, a well-rehearsed double act performing their encore.

"Be safe, Santina," Salvatore said, as they shuffled down the few steps to join the alley.

The major agreed to give me the early part of the afternoon off to recover.

I raced to the cemetery.

The gates were locked. I shook them until a sleepy Marco poked his head out of the hut.

"What on earth are you doing?" he slurred.

"Let me in this instant!"

"Shhh . . . you'll wake the dead!"

I rattled the cage a little more. His movements sped up at last.

"Everything alright, Santina?" he asked, his fingers unlocking the heavy padlock, pulling the chain out through the gap.

"No! Everything is not alright!"

"Easy, let me do the chain, you'll pinch your fingers."

"I don't care, Marco! After what you and Papà have done!"

Finally, the gate creaked open, I pounded through to his hut, while he shut the gate behind me. I noted his unhurried speed. It infuriated me even more.

Inside, my eye darted across his shambles. Half-spent candles, dusty votives, a large ceramic Madonna begged me for contrition. It made my stomach burn.

Marco closed the door behind me. Fear bristled up my spine.

"Now, you going to speak like a human or keep shouting like a witch?" he asked.

"I am no witch for feeling the way I do! And if you and Papà think you can squeeze the dignity out of me, you have another thing coming. I have every right to feel fire right now. First, he threatens me on the beach, next, I have the police sniffing around the villa after you. For the second time!"

He watched, impassive, no meager flicker across his eyes, no admission of guilt or passionate declaration of innocence.

The vacuum made me panic.

"What am I to think, Marco?"

His silence was a calm sea stretching beyond a horizon. I felt like I was spluttering in it, frantic jerks for air.

"Say something! My mind is full of bees! I can't carry on like this!"

He shook his head now. Smooth resignation. "There are a lot of people in this town, Santina, who can't bear the life we've made for ourselves. You in the big house, nice employers, a good life. You see how they live on the *viccoli*? You know the hunger down there on the alleys? The one the tourists ignore? The one we see year-round? Especially when the winter rolls in from the sea? And our sorry excuse for a father? He hates that we hate him. He's an alcoholic. An angry man."

"And?"

"And, what did he say to you?"

"He says he knows things about you. Says he will talk to the police unless I pay him to move away."

"And you believe him?"

The question hovered between us. I saw the skinny little boy chasing me downhill, desperate to keep up. I saw the quivering lower lip of the child being taken from me. And beyond, a metallic shiver of pride, a genuine plea for truth.

"I don't know what to believe," I said at last, the hot energy of anger wheezing through me like evaporating steam, leaving me empty.

That's when I saw his well-rehearsed veneer chip a little, imperceptible but to a person who had grown up registering his minuscule changes in humor.

"I can understand that, Santina. I haven't told you everything about my life, it's true. But it's to protect you. Have I been involved with the kind of people I wouldn't want you to know? Yes. Are you or I in danger now? Of course not. Does our father want to get what he can from you? I think we can both find the answer to that, don't you?"

I was tired, my fury fast fading to embers.

"I'm sorry, Santina."

I looked at him, hating myself for feeling forlorn.

"Here," he said. "Some relatives of Rosalia found this. Gave it to me for safekeeping, thinking I would see Rosalia before they would."

He reached for a knife inside a leather case, nestled between some water-stained vases and a jar of rusting screws.

"It belonged to Rosalia's brother they said, thought they would want it back."

"Why didn't they give it to them then?"

"I'm a gatekeeper, Santina. People do crazy things with me. They're in the whirl-wind of grief. Not so different from where you are right now. You feel totally let down by both of us. I'd be a clod not to under-stand that!"

I felt hot tears rise. I wouldn't let them fall till I left.

"And when people lose someone, they do funny things. I don't know why they trusted me with it. Perhaps they felt safe. I'm not a man of the church, but I'm the last human on the way to heaven. That's how they see it, I guess."

I looked down at the thing. It was the knife I already knew. A prickle of doubt shot through me. This weapon had been here since the burial. Why had he waited for this moment to give it to me? Every fiber in me urged me not to take it. But my hand reached out. And as I clasped its handle, I felt a great tear of guilt slice down my middle. The action was a pact of protection. I would deliver this to Rosalia, and then what? Assuage Marco's possible guilt? It wouldn't take long to trace it back to him, of course. It wouldn't take long for Small and Tall to work it out, that my brother had a murdered man's knife in his hut, and for this flimsy tale of having been given it by relatives to disintegrate.

"I'll take it to her," I said. My words fell flat, a thud of dough on floured marble. It was unthinkable that he was asking me to dispose of a weapon, surely? Perhaps I ought to receive the gesture at face value, proof of innocence.

Outside the garish white light was the unforgiving glare of brutal honesty. The beauty of the carved tombs, marble archangels, blanched so my eye saw only the sweat and toil of the sculptor, not the suspension of their wings mid-flight, the sea-salted dust roasting in the still air.

I turned to him, desperate to think of a parting sentence that would heal this rift. None surfaced.

We walked to the gate in silence.

I ought to have said goodbye. I ought to have looked into my brother's eyes and committed his expression to memory. I might have seen the truth there.

A lifetime would pass before I ever saw that face again.

My father never came for his money.

CHAPTER 26

The burnished summer faded, and with it, the termination of my duties to Elizabeth. As we edged toward autumn I watched a wan lady slip the child's hand into hers, a porter behind her with several cases. Elizabeth turned back toward me. Her expression was a painful echo. I was back at my family's hut, a small Marco pleading with me to turn the direction of events, feeling the brutal sting of being unable to do so. Her big blue eyes filled with tears.

I noticed my hand reach for the door, to steady myself and hold firm to the spot rather than dash after her for a third time. The tug knotted deep inside me, and, as the three of them turned the corner, out of sight, my mind floated behind them, recording every nook of the walls on either side, the long step she liked to jump down, the three cobbled steps toward the end of the steepest part where she would sometimes stop to count the ants. I hoped the lady would hold her hand tight as they reached the last curve, where sometimes the donkeys would cut in too close to the wall and, if Elizabeth ran that section, risked crashing into one. I hoped the car to the port wouldn't be too hot, but that they wouldn't open the window too far and let the draft spike a cold. I prayed for easy train rides through France and a smooth crossing to England. I tried to picture her school, her bed, her new friends, but the images lit up and faded, paper fast, burnt, whipping into ashes.

I heard the door close.

"It's the best thing, Santina. For Elizabeth. Not for us."

I looked over at the major. I watched grief streak across his face, tumbling clouds over a fast-moving sky. Then he straightened. I recognized the shift; he craved solitude.

"You'll excuse me now. Don't mistake it for brutal coldness. I just need to sit with my thoughts. We will talk later."

The abandoned terrace stretched out. The grapes overhead had begun to purple. Streaks of juicy promise patterned their green flesh. The large begonias in my prized terra-cotta pots were still lush, stretching higher each month. The wisteria rambled up the columns and over the high arches. But my garden was bereft. A noiseless place. No one would play under its canopy anymore.

I hadn't seen or heard from Marco since I'd confronted him. I'd visited the cemetery. He was conspicuous by his absence. A week later, I found his hut open with another custodian setting about clearing his disheveled collections within. He told me Marco had been placed elsewhere. He refused any more information, shrugging his shoulders to the heavens.

I tried to ignore the fact I was expecting a note to shunt beneath our door any day, an explanation, an apology. None came. Elizabeth was gone, now my brother. Mild disorientation filtered in at my periphery, the confusion of stepping into a room and at once forgetting what you had entered it for. I held on to the belief that at some point my brother would, of course, turn up, surprise me, clang the bell. I would open the door to his crooked smile, a sarcastic raise of his eyebrow, a relax-my-fretting-sister shrug, a sardonic shuffle across the terrace. And all would be, almost, as it was. But September sped onward, uninterrupted by unexpected guests in its glow.

October was marked by celebrations. I

longed for them to lift me up from the shifts in my life. I had my wedding to look forward to, and, with diminishing responsibilities at the villa, I had more time to spend with Paolino. But the month unraveled around me like a paper cutout. Rosalia's wedding marked the victorious end of the grape harvest. After Mass at the cathedral, the couple wandered down the streets, myself and her sisters holding out her train as the petals cascaded from overhead houses and terraces, and the car horns blew, and the people sang and shouted and cheered, and our town shook with noise and blasts of happiness. My best friend was luminous, and her light was enough for the both of us. It eclipsed the start of a retreat I felt inside.

Paolino filled the gaps left by the interminable silence of the villa, and the disappearance of my brother, with his usual effervescence. It rippled over me, water meeting oil. Signora Cavaldi reveled in my apparent virginal acquiescence to her endless tirade of plans and projected feasts, engagement festas and an endless list of people who would or would not be invited.

It was in the freezing mists of late November, when Positano boarded itself up against ebbing tourism and weather, that my fog rolled in. As I sat in that stark doctor's office in Sorrento, having made my excuses to both Paolino and the major, the walls of my tiny life began to crumble. Sea-weathered damage, a salty corrosion at the borders.

I was carrying a child I knew could not possibly be Paolino's.

That evening, I returned to the shop. Signora Cavaldi, event coordinator extraordinaire, was in full swing, lighting up the stone room with detailed pictures of our perfect wedding celebration. I listened in on the plans, sat around that kitchen table above the shop, and the conversation waved over me like radio signals from another room. And still I smiled, participated, at once the marionette and puppeteer, judging truthful tugs on the strings to affect the most convincing performance. I was deft at the job. And it terrified me. I held a scientific grasp of what I expected of myself. And I crafted Santina to perfection that evening; with humor, grace, a sprinkling of mischief even. Paolino was enrapt, his mother had a daughter, and all was well with their world.

December clawed down from the cliffs. Mist twisted down the alleys. We made our pilgrimage to the Christmas *presepe* during the early darkness of that month, surrounded by the town and its children, hymns warming the air above us, humming with hope and the delicate sanctity of new life. The abyss before me widened.

Paolino and I laid our own terra-cotta model house amongst the others, at the indent of the rock, a symbol of the homestead that one day would be ours, lit with candles. I felt only dread. The town gathered around the vast ramble of tiny houses surrounding the manger and a ceramic family of saints gazing at the holy child. The little children held their candles and warbled harmonies of holy silence and new beginnings. The darkness enveloped us.

The major insisted we deliver hampers to our neighbors. I'd dried the surplus fruits throughout late summer and autumn. The kitchen was burdened with halved peaches, apricots, plums, and figs, browned and sweetened with the autumnal sun, piled upon parchment across the countertops. And with each fruit I split, with each almond I spliced to the center, my mind chased an escape. I laid neat rows inside the baskets, alternating the fruits in pleasing patterns. Perfect lines of our gardening devotion surrounded me. I covered them in thin linen and tied wide ribbons around each.

I knew Paolino would be here to help me deliver them soon enough. I knew that each day my abdomen ripened a little more. The major and Adeline were at a regular doctor's appointment that afternoon. I decided that when Paolino arrived I would take him to my room. I wouldn't insist we waited till we were married any longer.

A knock. I creaked the door open. Paolino's face was ashen.

My first thought was that something dreadful had befallen Signora Cavaldi.

"*Tesoro,* what's wrong?" I asked, bristling with dread.

He removed his woolen cap, shook his head. I stepped back to let him in.

We walked into the kitchen in silence. I placed a coffeepot upon the stove and lit the ring, as I always did for him when he came to call.

He sat by the fire. I joined him.

"Santina, my love," he began. Then he stopped, stumbled over his thoughts, and fell silent.

I waited. The fire's orange shadows danced across his face.

"I don't know how to do this," he whispered.

I watched his fingers tighten around his hat.

"Paolino, just say whatever's troubling you."

496

He shook his head.

That's when his tears came.

I stood and wrapped my arms around him.

He looked up at me, reached around my face.

"What's the matter, my darling? Is your mother alright?"

"When I look at you, everything is well, Santina. Please, just kiss me."

Our lips met. Hungry.

I stepped back and lifted my sweater over my head. I let it drop to the floor. I unbuttoned my shirt. I loosened the catch on my skirt and felt it skim down my thighs. I eased my stockings down, then stepped out of my underwear. I unclasped my brassiere.

I stood before him. Vulnerable, free. A moment of sanctified clarity. And the light of the fire swirled over my body, and I felt warm for the first time in weeks. And the frigid fog I'd carried with me dissipated.

His eyes lit, then darted to the door. Fear slit through desire.

"No one is here," I said.

His breath quickened.

"Be with me, Paolino."

He stood and squeezed me to him. I felt him tear himself out of his coat, heard the *snap-slack* of his belt. His naked legs were against mine now. I think I creased his shirt

497

away. He sank back onto the chair and pulled me down onto him. The sting of guilt gave way to a deep softening. I felt him inside me.

Then his hands drew to a sudden halt.

"I can't do this," he murmured.

I tasted the vanilla-salt of his neck. I licked his tears.

He prized my face away.

"Santina, we have to stop!"

My body froze. His hands were around my waist. He lifted me off him.

I stood motionless. Like the thud of a stone dropping to a river bed, ripples of rejection shuddered up from my middle. My nudity at once brutal.

He picked up my underwear and handed it to me. A log spat.

We dressed.

I sat. "Please, tell me what is happening."

He snatched a breath. "I've never loved anyone like I do you."

I didn't reply. My hands were cold. I told myself my cheeks were hot with the fire, but I knew it was the scorch of embarrassment.

"What I'm about to do will feel like the cruelest act a man has ever done. And I want you to really hear me when I say it makes me ache more than I will ever be able to explain" — his head dipped into his hands, muffling the jagged sentences with sobs — "and I want you to understand that it is the best for you. You will hate me. For a long time you will wish me dead. But what I have to say means that you will be safe."

"You're not making any sense," I said, feeling the words slide out across ice.

He looked over at me. His dancing eyes sullen, as when gathering clouds dull our emerald sea to shale gray.

"I can't marry you, *tesoro.*"

A silence. It rippled over the strewn counters, that haze of red and blue ribbons, those baskets of good cheer. It snaked through me, leaving nothing but an acute awareness of my feet upon the stone, the spit of the fire, my wordlessness.

"Say something, Santina."

I couldn't.

"Please."

The ringing hush wouldn't let up.

"What are you begging me for?" I said, at last. "None of what is happening is making any sense. I don't know who is sat opposite me."

His tears escaped.

"Is there someone else?"

He raced over to my knees now, leaking onto my hands, begging for forgiveness. "No, Santina, of course not, I meant every word I said. You are the only person who would have made me the happiest man in town. But our marriage would bring you only grief. I have to leave town. I don't know when I can get back. But I'm doing all of this for you, Santina, I can't say why now, but you have to trust me. Please, just hear my promise."

"You're promising me nothing. I stood here naked. I wanted all of you. Now you run away like a scared boy."

His sobs shuddered deeper now.

"Maybe that is what I am, yes! But I am choosing this because I love you. And if you marry me, your life will be nothing but sorrow. I love you, Santina!"

His head dipped onto my lap. My skirt streaked with his tears.

"I want you to leave."

It was the biggest sacrifice of his life, he insisted, ignoring my request. His hands clasped around my thighs. I think he blubbered something about the greater good, about returning when he could, about situations beyond his control. But I had stopped listening. I could hear only the hum of stillness, the hiss of the coffeepot scorching the grounds, the distant call of a ship.

There were more words. I had the sensation of watching it all unfold from above, a snatched glance at a harried sketch; the outline of an ending.

At last, he left.

I watched the dance of flames, twisting licks of light fighting against the dark.

I sat there until white ashes dusted the grate.

I placed the major's morning coffee upon the ceramic pot holder. He dipped the edge of his paper down and thanked me over the top of it.

"I will deliver the baskets today," I said, shunting the sudden recall of last night out of mind, the slammed shut of an open drawer.

"I saw them on the counters last night when we returned, yes," he added, absent-minded. "Not to worry."

I wandered back to them. Each with their envelope pinned to the fabric covers: Rosalia and family, the American who had written Paolino's note for me, the German sisters up the street who'd held the party where Paolino had crooned to me across a packed room, an extra-large one for the widow who lived in the smallest house beyond them.

The major poked his head around the door. "Would you mind taking some of your wonderful broth to the lady next to the Germans? Her husband has come down with a terrible influenza, I've been told, I'm sure she'd appreciate it."

He'd caught me unawares. I didn't have a moment to draw the curtain over myself.

"Santina, whatever's the matter?"

I shook my head, brushing away his concern.

He didn't move. I felt myself curl in, the decaying edges of an autumnal leaf.

"You're gray," he said.

I didn't want to cry. I didn't want to crumble like that. I didn't want to feel his arms around me, filling me with the memory of our night, of the safety and freedom of his embrace. I pushed him away. He held my shoulders and met my gaze. I clasped at my vanishing courage, scrambling to hold on as it clawed at the edge of a cliff.

"There is nothing to say. Nothing you need to hear," I said flatly.

"Santina, please. You're hurting. A great deal. Let me in."

"Why?!" The words spat out too hot before I could stop them.

"Because I care for you!"

"Let go of me!" I shirked his hold and began unscrewing the coffeepot. A shake of grounds tumbled out in a damp brown heap.

His hand was on mine. "Santina, please."

I snatched my hand away. "Don't touch me! Don't jeer at me like that. Don't pretend concern. Not now. It's too late for that."

"Santina, you're not making any sense."

"Life doesn't make any sense!" I felt the red-hot steam of fury rise in my abdomen. "And it's your fault! All of this! Bringing me here! Taking away my dreams! Sending that beautiful child away! Imprisoning us with Adeline, our feelings, our hiding, our lying! And now I'm standing here like a cheap harlot, carrying your child, with a broken engagement! This isn't the life I wrote for myself. You did this! I allowed you to do this to me and I hate myself for it. And I hate you even more."

That's when my fingers clutched the side of the stove. When the full brunt of my grief burst out. My face was wet with indignation, embarrassment, anger, a fat sopping mess of the person I used to be.

He didn't touch me. He watched me disappear into the silent center of my tears.

He waited.

"Santina, I had no idea."

"You must have had some idea. That is

usually what happens when two people make love, no?"

My sarcasm crackled across the space between us.

"Come and sit by me." He pulled out a chair from the kitchen table and another for me.

"Do I look like I want to sit by you? I'm finished following your lead. I'm done with silencing what I came here to do. I loved your daughter like my own, I've cared for your wife, the woman you betrayed for a snatched night with me."

"A snatched night? Is that what that was to you?"

"Yes! A dream! A make-believe that sent me running into Paolino's arms!"

"That was your choice, Santina. No one forced anything on you."

"You lured me into a betrayal!"

"Of whom? Adeline? Where is she?"

"Upstairs."

"No. She left a long time ago. And I lost myself inside you."

"Don't speak like a guiltless party in this."

"Here is the painful truth. Are you ready to hear this, Santina? I orbited Adeline like a burning sun for years. She was my light, but did she ever let me in? I mean truly let me inside her very essence? Or was I simply captivated by her light? The moment I set eyes on you my whole existence was called into question. You tapped something so deep inside me. Something I'd never wanted to acknowledge before. And we've worked here, side by side, feeling the delicate intimacy of pure, complicit love. I felt you in the silences, Santina. I felt your every shift. And I felt you sensing mine too. Adeline is not my twinned soul. And you taught me that. And the lesson scorched. And I hated myself for it. And sometimes I hated you for it. For ripping me open."

His cold honesty was a wind surging through me.

"I was always Adeline's bystander. A loyal audience. She bewitched me because I would never understand her. Not fully. The distance was there before her illness. Perhaps it's the reason I fell in love with her. I knew I would never be able to reach her. Not fully. And so I knew she would never seek to pry into me. She wouldn't prize me open."

Our eyes were wet.

"Not like you have," he whispered.

We used what little resolve remained to not let those tears fall; he wanted me to believe what he said. I refused to let him know how impossible it was to stop loving him.

"I have to leave," I replied, dishonoring the burning truth inside me. "I will go to America as planned. You will help me complete the papers. I refuse to keep letting the men around me dictate what I need. Because in the end, they suit themselves! My brother, my father, my fiancé? They've all tossed me like seeds in the wind!"

"And you put me on that list too?"

"Yes!"

"Why, Santina? Because I followed my instincts? Because your fire of curiosity, determination, honesty, intelligence is utterly compelling to me? Is that reason to hate me?"

"I hate you for trapping my desires into your little world while making me believe you were preparing me to leave! It's insidious. At least Paolino just rejected me, straight down the line, you're worse. Marco was right, you just made me believe what you were doing was righteous, heartfelt. I should have listened to him."

"To him? Where is he now?"

"You have no right to talk about my family!"

"And you have no right to tell me that I am a hypocrite. My God, Santina, why do

506

you stand there so blind now? You chose your life with Paolino. He has hurt you. And I abhor him for that. But I will not stand here and let the woman I love rail against me with no recourse. Because I look at you now, raging, your face wet with pure venom for me, and I can't make those feelings go away, and I won't try because I will offer you only my truth: I am, and will always be, in love with you!"

He fought his tears now. I watched him force his breath to deepen. I watched him refuse to shirk the painful truth of what he needed to express. "Every aspect of you. I'm not in love with a picture, nor a promise, nor a future, because we know there can never be one. But for all my efforts to silence it, I am still utterly lost to my love for you. That is for me to bear. And you cannot insist I have no right to say it."

Our quickened breaths filled the little room.

"And we return to ownership!" I called back. "Again! Listen to yourself." I tried not to let his expression power through me, tried not to acknowledge the unbridled love I saw. I clutched my argument. "Paolino has abandoned our promise, and you step in! In the heat of my pain, you swing in with declarations! You should feel shame!"

"I don't, Santina."

His voice, all of a sudden calm; a summer storm tore through and left a glassy sea. He looked at me, still, strong. "I feel no shame for being lost in my love for you. I've clung onto the days this summer, knowing that you would walk out of here soon enough. I sent Elizabeth away sooner than I had planned in order to let you begin your own life away from here too. To spare myself the agony of waiting. To spare you the weight of my feelings. It is killing me." He looked into me. "Should I feel shame for loving you?"

"It's all words."

"You know that is far from the truth. I clung on to our studies, wading through those declarations of love because I couldn't do it myself. I didn't want to push in. I didn't want to spit it out like this, like I am now. It's clumsy. It's messy. I can see that. Any fool could. But it's true. Look me in the eye, Santina. Right now. See all of me. See every fiber of my being before you. And tell me that you don't believe that I love you."

The wintry light from outside slit in.

His eyes were bright with truth. "I'm laying myself bare."

I took him in.

"Can you do the same, Santina?"

508

I was translucent, weakened by my tears. "Look at me! I'm crumbling."

"Because you're allowing your terror and love and anger to shake through you? Is that crumbling? It's strength. You're standing here feeling what you feel, you're not holding back, you're not staying neat, you're not keeping up the perfected act of Santina. Is that weak?"

"Of course it is. You don't deserve to see it."

He took a breath. I watched his fingers trace the locks off his face.

That's when I let go, lying back onto the crisscrossing currents of my feelings, letting the watery emotions toss me downstream. I allowed the resounding truth to float to the surface: before me stood the man I had fallen into at first glance, in the gloomy London light of Mr. Benn's parlor. The person who loved me to the core. The person who fascinated me and lured me and grew me in every sense.

The only man I would ever love.

"There's nothing to keep me here now," I said, instead of the declaration burning in my chest, instead of falling into him with abandon.

He sat down.

"And our child? Where will you go?"

"To America. As planned."

"I won't stop you."

"You can't stop me."

"It will break me."

"You tell me to feel vulnerable! You tell me there is courage in that! So why don't you find your courage too?"

"I'm being brutally honest with you."

Another burning silence. Hanging. Unbroken.

I tried so hard to let the touch of his hand in mine feel real. But all I remember was the fast-vanishing sun, the night swallowing the light, the sound of my footsteps echoing up the stairs and across my room. The torturous darkness engulfed my twisting thoughts; I was staring at a blank page, yearning for an ending.

■ ■ ■ ■

1976

■ ■ ■ ■

Chapter 27

The summer sun was brutal: houses expanded and creaked, plaster blistering, waves of scorch lifting up from the pavement. The Positano tourists were undeterred, rather lured in deeper, charmed by the snaking heat. More homes mushroomed around us, etching further toward the mountains that loomed above. In town, the fishermen's modest homes were festooned with window boxes, fresh coats of paint in dainty shades of flora and sea hues, pale emerald, pistachio, watery teal, aquamarine, celeste, their windows adorned with theatrical displays of bay life, where once worn kitchen tables stood. Instead of a hearth surrounded by barely fed children, there were now glass buoys hooked to whitewashed walls, rooms perfumed with lemon; soaps, potpourri, wardrobe sachets of dried herbs. Decorative bottles of limoncello clustered the counters of the growing number of shops, never to be drunk, rather to stand like trophies for friends back home; proof of a visit, Positano corked for posterity.

Across low ceilings, displays of lace and linen danced, wafting in artful curves, stone boutiques filled with playful phantoms. Our bay was a celebration of all things beautiful, and the tourists worshipped their finds and told their friends. Boats arrived daily, heaving with hot bodies eager to take a little piece away with them, snap-shooting our cove in their little black boxes, sipping our *dolce vita* from large glasses ruby orange with aperitifs.

Over the past twenty years we'd witnessed my town's blossoming. The change whirring around us papered over the cracks left by my secret pregnancy. My hushed confinement that took me to Naples and the best hospital the major could find. My baby slipped out of me in the dead of night after a day and a half of laboring. I lost too much blood. A nurse later told me death and I skated seduction.

My girl was perfection and sorrow. I held her long enough to feed her once, an act the medical staff were loath to allow me, but I would not be stopped. I felt those tiny lips search my breast, and, as she swallowed, my tears raced down my wet face. They eased her out of my arms when she fell into her first sleep. My heart was ripped. I couldn't speak. I may not have ever left that sludge if it wasn't for the fact that my best friend had agreed to be her mother. Despite the nurse's insistence otherwise, Rosalia came to say goodbye with her, in the hours before their ship set sail the following day.

My friend handed me my baby and sat down on the bed beside me.

Tears broke through and my hands wove around her warm little body. Apologies tumbled out, breaking me in two.

Rosalia held me.

Her tears fell next to mine.

"I love you with all of me, Maddalena," I murmured, burning inside. "I always will. And your new mother is the best one I can give you."

Rosalia's body shook with mine. I felt her hands clasp around me.

Maddalena squirmed.

I looked down at my shirt. Milk had begun to wet the front of it.

Rosalia noticed. "You can feed her, Santina," she murmured.

"You don't mind? Just one last time?" I whispered, tears choking my voice.

She shook her head, her face streamed by tracks of joy and sadness.

I opened my gown. Maddalena jerked her head, flailed a little, then attached. I felt myself flow into her. I couldn't speak anymore. All my love and promise and apologies wove out of my body, wordless. There was no part of me that wished to rip this child from my best friend, I could think of no better life to give the babe I once thought would be an orphan cloistered with the nuns till childless parents took her in. When I had revealed my pregnancy to Rosalia, and she explained that Pasquale had decided that their lives would be in America, my decision to give my child to her took little thought. She always believed my child to be Paolino's. I never told her otherwise; that was my and the major's secret burden — not hers. Letting anyone else in now would seem like a betrayal more brutal than the first.

After Maddalena slipped into a milky slumber, Rosalia let me swaddle her one last time. I kissed the softness of her forehead, smooth with downy fuzz. I smelled her and committed that afternoon in May 1960 to every fiber of my memory, locked inside my body. The nurse eased her out of my arms and placed her in Rosalia's. She turned back to look at me from the doorway.

"I love you, Rosalia," I sobbed. "Allow

yourself happiness. That's how we'll all be free."

She couldn't reply. Her smile creased over a fresh fall of tears. We might have stayed that way, crying and laughing across the white room, if the nurse hadn't closed the door.

Twenty years later, on the afternoon of August 2nd, as the sun dipped toward the sea, Adeline's coffin sunk into the earth. Our neighborhood showed up to pay their respects. All the women and men the major had expressed care toward, never in person, but through the steady delivery of our garden harvests; jars of preserve in the autumn, dried beans and fruits in the winter, and a share of the first of the over-wintering cabbages, Romanescos, and kale. They arrived to put a face to the man who came to them in woven tales, pictures shared and morphed from house to house; the British hermit who was ever so kind and ever so invisible. A gentleman to be sure, a floating island offshore, shrouded in myth. I watched them look at him, reading the lines of grief, the stoic stance. I watched them waiting for the wailing, which, of course, would never come. I saw them study his daughter, Elizabeth, with her unpredictable energy, that left me feeling like I stood beside a horse desperate to be released from the stable, always liable to rear. Her red hair fell in heavy waves, a choppy sea, copper and brass catching the light. Her eyes were bright, like her parents', but there was a darting quality to them, as if she calculated the space and people around her at great speed. Gone was that tiny girl who would spend hours on the quietest of tasks, lost in the loose momentum of never-ending play. Now her tempo was cranked toward an insatiable restlessness, which she would always attribute to her great hurry to leave Positano.

She hated returning, of that we were all made clear.

I watched her look down at the wooden box. The grief I read made my heart ache. This was a young girl refusing to mourn the mother she never had. Her eyes raised as the priest said his final prayer. That's when the first cusp of tears glassed over. She didn't try to stop them. She didn't try to smile. She just looked at me. And for a moment we were back in the garden. She was beside me at the sink. Kneeling on a chair at the table peeling artichokes. Splashing in an enamel bowl of water.

I had never stopped missing her.

The crowd wove through the cemetery, filling the tiny walkways with a river of black, a peck of crows picking through the sorry mess of it all. Paolino insisted he host the wake and though the major resisted the idea of a public celebration of his wife, he relented, because not thanking the neighbors for showing their affection was rude, and despite having his home swarming with people he never wanted to entertain, any alternative was out of the question.

I received the flow of people, and the major hired several local girls to make sure everyone was handed drinks. It was a spectacular sight to see the villa so full of life, instigated by the sharp loss of it. I knew the major viewed it as some absurd celebration of Adeline's disappearance rather than a celebration of her life. But Paolino had been most insistent; he was thrilled to pay back the major for his many years of business, and refused the exchange of any money.

Along the terrace stood several tables, which Paolino used in his mountainside restaurant up the hill. They stretched underneath the vine canopy thickened with two decades of care. Upon the tablecloths lay vast trays of seafood antipasti, steamed squid with potatoes and parsley, risotto with wild asparagus zinging with fresh lemon, vases of raw vegetables, feathered tips of fennel, fresh endive. Paolino's signature cured meats took the center, ribbons of salty prosciutto, salami, and bresaola, cured in-house and sliced thin as rice paper. There were terrines of fresh anchovies drowning in green olive oil and local chili, enamel pots of shells; clams, mussels, and sea urchins, steaming with garlic-and-parsley-infused broth, deepened with his homemade white wine. I caught the major take in the feast. He looked over at me. The blue of his eyes turned cobalt.

He turned and headed up the stairwell toward the upper floors.

Once most of the guests appeared to be filling our terrace and filing out into the garden, I took a moment to follow him. I couldn't trust that the major's acceptance of the crowd invading his very private space would leave him any more equipped to deal with the challenge of this day.

A familiar rumble of voices reached me like a distant thunderstorm.

Adeline's bedroom door was ajar.

I heard Elizabeth's rasp. "What have you ever known about family?"

"I made sure you were both in the place that would help you the most. Your mother was too sick to understand, but you? Years of money and time poured into giving you the life and education you deserve, and you throw it back at me at every chance. Enough, Elizabeth. It's time to be a young woman, not this whining child!"

"My mother just threw herself from this balcony — I can whine like a child if I wish!"

His gaze slid away. He caught me in the shadows beyond the door.

"Can you talk sense into this?" he called to me.

"Don't talk about me like I'm not even inside the room. That's sociopathic."

"Keep your voice down."

"You hide away in here and outside everyone thinks you're a saint. Sending soup and food to a few neighbors does not make you a hero!"

I stepped inside. Our breaths filled the room.

I'd made the bed but left Adeline's paintings hung about the space. I'd cleared her collection of glasses, mopped up the paint dripping on the decorative tiles, the blue and yellow designs gleaming in the suffused light from the afternoon shafts streaming in through the shutters.

"It's time to join the others," he said, his voice soft.

"I won't go," she answered.

His eyes searched mine.

"Elizabeth," I began, "come down for a little while? Eat a little something?"

She turned in silence, walked away from us, across the room, and flung open the shuttered doors. She stepped out into the afternoon sun. When she leaned against the ledge of the terrace, she looked just like her mother. A shiver crawled down my spine.

"Why must it be like this, Elizabeth?" the major asked. "This is our chance to make things better."

"Don't tell me how to feel," she replied without turning back.

"If you had listened to me, we wouldn't be standing here like this now." His whisper was icy.

She flung round to him, her face crimson with fury. "You put that sick woman before me a long time ago! She needed a hospital, not sea views. Whose fantasy were you in? Rescuing all these women? My mother, Santina, me? It's like some kind of warped harem. You're a control freak."

"Keep your voice down, for heaven's sake!"

"You banished me from my own home, from Santina — my real mother. Tell that to the guests downstairs. Tell them how you imprisoned your wife, kept her from the doctors she needed. If you don't, I will!"

He turned away and began to walk out of the room.

It fanned her fire.

"Have you any idea how that felt?!" she yelled back to him, her voice chasing him as he left the room, as he descended the stone steps two at a time. She wouldn't let up. The faster he moved the louder she shouted.

"Have you any idea how it's felt all these years, people telling me how kind my father is, how he's done this and that for them, sent them soup when they were ill, for fuck's sake?"

We reached the drawing room beside the entrance to the terrace. Their sharp voices rippled out to the party, transmitting waves of hush.

"If you expect me to be around these people now and agree that you are in fact God, you have another thing coming!"

"If you'd just got in the cab from the airport, Elizabeth. If you'd just come straight home in the car I'd sent you, Santina would never have had to leave the house! If for once in your life, you'd done what I asked."

"Then what? Mummy wouldn't be suicidal?"

"That's no way to talk about your

mother!"

"My mother is standing right here!" She flung a manic arm out toward me. I clocked the German sisters take note of the erupting argument. Beyond them, several other neighbors drew to stillness, engaged in acute listening.

"See what you've put her through!"

"Don't speak for Santina — she has a brain too, you know!"

"Elizabeth, please," I interjected, "there's no need."

"To what? Say what you won't? I will. Because I don't play his games. I'm not a victim."

"When will you realize I'm your father, not a monster?"

"You stopped being my father when you sent me away!"

The metallic clang of the bell cut through the terrace.

The guests looked toward the door.

I felt an intense awareness of the sound of my shoes across the tiles and was glad when the voices rose once again — the swell of argument had been forced to ebb.

I opened the door.

Rosalia's smile cut through the years we'd been apart. I don't remember too much of those next few minutes, it was a sigh of tears and laughter and hands wrapped around friends who, since her move to America, hadn't embraced for two decades. Her hair had started to whiten a little, but her skin was lustrous as ever and her grin spread over her face like a sunbeam. She kissed my cheeks. She held my face. I cried again.

"I wanted to come here even before going to my sisters!" She squeezed me into her.

She pulled away from me to take a deep look. "Santina, my *tesoro*. We are old, are we not?" She giggled then, and in the sound was the dance of her youth.

Off my expression, her face fell.

"There was no way I could get the message to you, Rosalia," I began, my voice wavering, "it's Adeline."

"She's gone?"

I nodded.

"When?"

"Two days ago. We're having the wake now."

"Santina, I'm so sorry. I will come back tomorrow."

The major eased the door open behind me. "Everything alright, Santina?"

It was one of those snatched moments I wished I'd been able to grasp between my fingers and squeeze to stillness before it unraveled before me.

Maddalena stepped out from behind her mother.

My breath caught.

Her face was alight with fresh air, bronzed cheekbones. There was an alarming alertness about her. I noticed her one hand trace the rose brick around our door, not an absentminded gesture, rather stitching herself into our space with a sensuous luminosity.

"*Piacere, sono* Maddalena," she said, her voice woody, melodic, void of embarrassment even though you could hear she had studied the phrase well and that Italian was not her first language. Her hand slipped into mine.

"Mamma has told me all about you — that's where my Italian ends, I'm sorry — you don't mind, do you?" Her grin reminded me of Rosalia's. "You are more gorgeous than she said! This whole place is entirely magical. It's like I've stepped into a painting!"

Her blue eyes darted around our wooden doorway, alight with wonder.

"Maddalena darling," Rosalia began, "we've come at a bad time. Sorry, Signore." Rosalia's eyes flicked to the major. I thought I saw her blush a little.

"It's very nice to see you again, Rosalia"

— he stretched out his hand to her daughter — "and you, Maddalena. My name is Henry."

His voice didn't waver. Nor his hand. But I was certain that our glistening eyes were born from the electricity skating our skin, not from grief for Adeline.

"You're, like, from England?" Maddalena asked.

"Most definitely, yes. Please, won't you come on in? Half the town is here. You're most welcome."

Rosalia looked between us and Maddalena.

"I would love nothing more than for you to join us, my friend," I said.

They stepped inside.

I watched as waves of memory trickled over, as we waded through the town of people, familiar faces that had aged and slackened with time and stories. She held my hand as we walked through the terrace, tentative steps. On her other side, her daughter: I sensed her run her hand through the shaggy mop of thick black waves frolicking over her face.

Paolino walked over to us.

"*Dio mio* — I'm seeing things! *L'americana!* You back home for good? No one leaves Positano forever!"

He took her hand and gave her two kisses. She looked over at me.

"Paolino made all this for the major," I said.

"It's so wonderful to be home. It breaks my heart that this is all because of Adeline. I'm so, so sorry, Santina."

Her hand tightened around mine.

That's when Elizabeth scuffed out onto the terrace.

Her eyes were red. She looked poised for another fight.

I wondered how I might entice her away before it erupted again.

"This man, Signori! Take a look at this man right here!" She lifted an angry arm toward her father. "That's the man who kept my mother locked up in her own home!"

I watched as the neighbors checked each other for explanations. Elizabeth's feet seemed unsteady. She looked like she'd been drinking.

"Elizabeth, please, let's not do this. Not like this. Not here," the major said, walking across the garden toward her, taking her by the elbow and leading her inside.

"Don't touch me! Get your hands off me! This is all you! This is all your fault!"

She was kicking back against him now.

Flailing. I walked toward them. She didn't notice me right away. I took her head in my hands. I forced her to look at me. That's when she cracked into her tears. That's when she softened and I could lead her back inside and up to my room.

We eased onto the bed.

I watched her run through the memories of the past few days. The way she'd refused to get into the taxi her father had arranged for her at Naples, the way she'd arrived without advising us ahead of time. The way she hadn't reached the villa even when dinner had been and gone. The way I'd waited for her, wrung with worry while her father was in Amalfi on a business errand.

We sat in the silence and relived me choosing to leave the house to find her, or at least enquire what the abandoned taxi driver had gleaned from her, any possible details about her plans? I'd listened to him explain that she would be arriving later at some point, most likely by bus. I'd found her after dark, sipping drinks in the *piazza* by the Chiesa Nuova with some new friends. I'd hurried her home because I knew leaving Adeline was never advisable, even if she'd had a good month.

We returned to find her body.

A pool of blood drenched the dusty earth

beneath her head.

Forgiveness was a distant light in the sea's morning mist.

"I'm bloody exhausted." Elizabeth exhaled, dropping her head onto her hands.

She reached for my hand. Strong fingers wrapped around mine.

"You're my mother," she whispered as her tears fought their way out.

I wrapped my arm around her, welcoming her shudders into my shoulder. Her tears deepened. When she pulled away for breath, I took her face in my hands, wiped her cheeks. "I love you, Elizabeth."

A sad smile.

A voice at the door drew us out of our watery cocoon.

"Is the bathroom this way?"

We looked up. Maddalena stepped in.

"Oh gosh, I'm so sorry — only I'm, like, crazy desperate and downstairs there's already someone using one. I took a wander. Mamma's going to kill me when she finds out."

I watched the two women find one another, a faint blue snap of electricity between them, knotting across the space. I tried to believe it was just the language, a familiar sound in an unfamiliar time, an anchor for Elizabeth's torment. But this was not a connection based on language alone. Elizabeth jumped up and led Maddalena along the corridor. I listened to their voices echo across the marble.

CHAPTER 28

I left the bedroom, catching the two girls in the bathroom at the far end of the corridor, slim birches against the gray marble walls. Maddalena looked up and saw me. Her face lit up. For a disconcerting breath, time was a concertina, wheezing out the years, folding back into our snatched solitude, guilty feedings in the moonlight, the feel of her tiny lips against my breast. I inhaled another breath to hide my tears, which she mistook for those of a bereaved, which of course they were; for my brief glimpse of motherhood rather than for the English woman who had tumbled to her death. Elizabeth bubbled something to Maddalena, and she drew her eyes away from me, immune to the gravity of the situation around her and the heartache of the older woman at the end of the corridor. Maddalena was a tonic for Elizabeth.

I wished she might have been the same for me.

In the lower terrace, Paolino made sure everyone was overfed and glasses topped up. I watched his wife, Martha, cross the terrace and reach him, wrapping her thin white arm around his widening waist. She was willowy, flowing blond locks lifting on what little breeze wafted up from the sea. Not long after he had terminated our engagement she had sailed into our bay, met the grocer who would become the wealthiest impresario this side of the mountains, and fallen in love. He was dazzled by her elegant otherworldliness, her Canadian fascination with Italy, and, I suspect, his ability to have triumphed over the advances of the other Positanese, or North Americans for that matter. They married three months later. She loved to retell the story at every chance, and the tourists melted between the lines, hoping they too might join the host of travelers who come to visit and never leave. The sea washes them in like shells, precious jewels from beyond our horizon, revered by locals.

I watched her regale one of the neighbors with choice anecdotes. I'd heard them all before, and maybe they had too, but she had the innate ability to spin a yarn as if afresh, the subtle twist of a sentence here, a flick of punctuation, an embellishment when the listener least expected it. I had wondered over the years how they communicated with her dexterous use of English compared to her jagged Italian, and vice versa. I had a memory of Paolino boasting that when in love language pales into insignificance. Of course their bond was born upon little more than carnal attraction, which, for Paolino at least, perhaps was indeed enough. And she seemed delighted with her Italian lover, however portly he had grown, however much he seemed to enjoy the attention of other young admirers.

I joined the girls filling the guests' glasses, for a moment enjoying my ability to melt into the background, under a protective layer of invisibility. From here, I was afforded the freedom to observe everyone else, and by now, they knew better than to pry. I watched them offer the major sage advice, condolences. I saw them uncomfortable with the lack of emotional displays until the major asked for everyone's attention.

A surprised hush descended.

He cleared his throat and straightened. The hair at his temples had begun to whiten but otherwise remained a fiery red, and his eyes had not lost the vigor of his youth. His skin was lighter perhaps, his freckles unchanged. There was no resignation to age but rather a softening toward it, a lengthening. Adeline's death was a violent loss, but I know, for him at least, it was also a release. She was free from the torment of her decaying health at last. She found her escape as she always wished it.

"Before you all leave our villa, I want to take this moment to thank each and every one of you for being here today," he began, the faint whisper of a crack in his voice floating away as quickly as it surfaced, a tuft of cloud in a taintless sky. "Adeline was a very troubled soul. We came here and found the respite we so desperately needed. Her years here were happy ones. And that is what I will remember."

There were murmurs from the English speakers in the crowd. He then began an angular translation in Italian, which elicited a hearty applause from the Positanese. Rosalia caught my eye from the far side of the garden, where she stood beside the German sisters. A lifetime apart eclipsed the space.

The guests took their cue to leave, which was not common, but the major's farewell speech seemed to elicit the desired intent. In town it was more customary for the bereaved houses to stay full till the moon began its acquiescence to dawn. The major stood by the door and shook everyone's hands. Martha whisked over to me. "Thank you so much for letting Paolino do all this for you! I can't tell you how happy he was!"

"Our pleasure, of course," I replied.

She squeezed my hand. The gesture caught me somewhat off guard. "I really am so very sorry," she cooed, the gentle lilt of her voice the perfect accompaniment to the wisps of hair licking her face below her languid blue-green eyes. She still had the grace of youth, a childlike wonder about her, as if she too still couldn't quite believe the way her life had unraveled.

"You go, *tesoro,*" Paolino called out, "I'll stay and clear this all away for Santina and Signore."

The major's name and mine coupled in a sentence. Perhaps he'd said it a thousand times, but I'd never heard it. It unsettled me.

"I'll collect my offspring — once I find him!" She laughed, pulling off her wide straw hat and fanning it over her face. I watched her scan the garden. After a search, she found a group huddled around Elizabeth and Maddalena, holding court in the shade of a lemon tree. Maddalena had hooked their attentions. Her gestures were hapless, free, and her eyes were bright at the center of whatever story she was describing. The small herd of youths burst into laughter. I noticed Paolino's son throw her a sideways grin. He was the picture of his father with his swagger and feckless energy. I don't think there were many young girls on our hill who hadn't been attracted to his back-footed charm. His mother reached the group and I watched them stiffen a little. I saw her turn back toward me. Maddalena left the crowd and spoke with her mother. Rosalia reached me upon the terrace, where I was managing to keep up the work of clearing the table.

"Here, Santina, let me help you now," she said, slipping in beside me.

"I can't take my eyes off her."

"Not many can, Santina," she said, turning toward me. "I haven't done half as good a job as you would have."

I looked at her, still not quite believing my favorite woman in the world was beside me again at last. "She's luminous," I said, determined not to cry, "like her mother."

"You took the words out of my mouth."

We smiled then, years creasing into little lines around our eyes, glistened with tears.

"We'll cry later, yes, my friend?" she

laughed through a sniff, lifting a heavy ceramic terrine from the table, the remnants of olive oil and parsley smudging the base. She followed me into the kitchen and began wiping out the bowls before filling the sink with hot soapy water.

"Listen, Maddalena wants to go out with Elizabeth and the others, is that alright with you?" she asked.

"With me?"

"Well, I don't know if her father is in any state to make these decisions, do you?"

"Where are they going?"

"Down to the bay, I guess — I can't keep Maddalena in one place for long at the best of times!"

Her face widened into a broad smile. I put down the dish in my hand and wound my arms around my friend. We laugh-cried.

"It is so wonderful to stand next to you, Rosali'!"

I could feel her shudder into me. "Tell me why I keep wanting to hear that you forgive me, Santina?"

"Because you forget what we did was out of love."

"I stole the most precious thing from you. It's a knife inside." Her cries deepened.

"No, my Rosalia," I whispered into her ear, my voice thin and watery now, "we gave each other what we needed most. Because we love one another. My heart could burst with what I feel. And now you are here. There is no better gift. She is a special girl. And that is because of you."

Then the words trickled away into more sobs, because no clever sentences could express the elation and pain we had carried all these years; for the child she thought she'd never have, for the child I thought I may never see again, for the long-lost newborn who floated in the periphery of my dreams like a nebulous shadow, trailing my waking hours each time I met a child at the market, next to me at church, wailing on the street. The memory triggered at the slightest prompt, catching me at inopportune moments, so that I'd be forced to hide in a doorway in the middle of town while the tears fell and dried. Even years later, the scar toughened by time, it took the briefest glance from a tiny soul to make my heart split in two, and for that moment I was back in my room, cradling the mewling infant, her charcoal eyes glinting in the shuttered moonlight, minuscule fingers wrapping around mine.

Rosalia and I pulled away from each other, and we wiped our tears, the young help clattering around us, mistaking us for mourners.

"I'll tell them the girls can go, yes?" Rosalia asked, wiping her cheeks with her fat fingers, smeared with watery makeup, which she never used to wear.

"I'm sure that will be fine."

I left the kitchen to bring more plates inside. The major was face-to-face with Elizabeth. I watched the pack of youth wind out of the door to mischief.

He closed the door and looked at me.

I walked over to him.

His eyes were glazed. "Maddalena is astonishing."

I nodded, sighing a faint laugh. The sound of her name from his lips was molten. A moonlit kiss.

"There is some sort of bizarre beauty in the absurd timing of it all, Santina."

He looked into me then. For the third time that afternoon, the order of events seemed to flow through unexpected conversations. "Everything has a way of returning until it is well and truly dealt with," he added.

His expression was calm, his eyes lit with unquestionable warmth. "That child was born out of something very beautiful."

The memory careened through me like lightning.

"Sorry," he stuttered, off my silence that he mistook for disdain, "that was clumsy. I didn't mean to —"

"I know what you intended."

"Of course you did," he said, his voice a warm whisper.

"And I know how I feel at this moment."

"Tell me?"

I stumbled then, censoring my thoughts. Too many years had passed. Too many growing seasons where we had worked at a pleasurable, respectful distance, nurtured our trust and friendship like well-fed soil, vital with volcanic minerals, endless possibilities for growth. I wasn't about to ruin it now, at Adeline's wake, with a confession that from the moment the girl we made together stepped onto the terrace this afternoon, I saw everything around me through the filter of our night together. Reality slipped into the moonlit shadows of my memory. Every touch, brush of his lips, fingertip trace upon my body rushed to the surface, like a hot spring, tingling my skin with a ferocity I had long buried.

"Full and hollow," I replied, finding my voice because the words were desperate to escape. "Lost to a yearning I thought I'd fed and satisfied. But I haven't. Not really. Perhaps *that's* the truth of what we have to face right now?"

His face lit with an echo of a smile, at once sad and hopeful, unnerving in its openness. There was nowhere he'd rather be standing at that very moment. Twenty years of cultivated friendship, platonic peace, was forgotten for a heartbeat. I crushed the thoughts because I suspected only I was thinking them. We stood wordless, hovering in our unspokens, in the mechanical sounds of the dismantling wake around us. We were back in our shuttered secret. A familiar fear crawled over me, like a spider weaving a deft web in haste. I watched him relive it too. This wasn't the place for this conversation, and we both knew it. Or maybe, in the safety of the crowd, it was the perfect place; it's why we dared inch toward the watery edge of this shared memory now, stepping back from the lapping cold at the first lick of our toes. We daren't wade in. Not just yet.

I left him upon the terrace, reaching Paolino at the far end of the garden, where he was folding the several dozen deck chairs he'd lent for the occasion.

I lifted one.

"No, Santina — I've got this," he said.

"A chair isn't going to break me, Paolino."

He stood and leaned on the folding chair

in his hand.

"You're amazing."

"You're drunk on praise."

His leathery skin cracked into that familiar smile.

The pause lasted a little too long.

"Someone dies, it makes you think about what's important, don't you think?" he asked. His eyes were shrouded with a philosophical gloom.

"I'm exhausted," I replied, "that's the only thing I'm thinking just now."

He nodded and broke his train of thought. I watched him choose to increase his pace and start folding and piling up the chairs with renewed energy.

After a few clanks of the wooden frames I offered an apology.

"I didn't mean to sound cold, Paolino — I'm just empty and full. My best friend is here, and I feel more alive than ever. But the picture of Adeline across the earth is not going to leave me. Not for a long time."

He stood still and looked at me, unhurried. For once, silent.

It was unnerving. "Say something. You're making me feel . . ."

My words trailed off, all of a sudden useless, like they often are after a funeral. I slipped into the cooling silence, the gentle respite of early evening creasing across the garden, impervious to the storms that had coursed through the villa over the past few days.

"I know what I want to say and that you may not want to hear it," he said, at last.

I recognized that look, and I knew he was right.

"But I think I'm going to say it anyway." His tone slipped into a soft whisper. "I need you to know something, Santina."

My eyes lifted to his.

"I want you to know why I did what I did."

"Please, Paolino. We've made our peace. You've got a wonderful family. There is no need."

"For you maybe. Not me."

"Why have all the men I've known been so anxious to get me to hear their side of the story? Perhaps it's fine that they don't? Have you ever thought about that?" My hair slipped out of the pins I'd used to pull it off my face, and several strands fell in front of my eyes. I whipped it away with irritation. "Perhaps silencing the thoughts is fine. Because thoughts and explanations are part of a past — and a past doesn't exist any longer. Our strength is looking ahead. Or even, just looking at the precise moment we're in, no further."

"For you maybe."

"For all people. Men or women. It doesn't matter. But what does matter to me is this continuous need for people making me stop to listen. I've listened a lifetime. What I've witnessed over the past few days makes me wonder whether it's not time to stop listening for a moment? To really enjoy the silence."

We hovered in it. A beautiful pause. His face framed with the passiflora trailing along the end wall of the garden, a purple flash of floral halo.

"Isn't that what death teaches us, really?" I asked. My speed ebbing now because I was sure he wouldn't, at last, interrupt me. "Silence is a beginning and ending. A little silence while we live is a wonderful thing."

"I have been silent! For a lifetime."

Why I thought he wouldn't find a fight I couldn't know.

"And I'm tired of it killing me," he concluded.

"Killing you? You own half the town! Everyone loves you. You have a beautiful life. The only thing that's killing you is that I won't give you an audience." My hands tripped now, forceful twists and turns like a dancer deep inside the music. "I'm the one person who won't hang off every word. Your

545

ego is killing you, not your silence."

I turned to leave. He grabbed my wrist.

"That's no way to get me to listen!" I spat, under my breath.

He loosened his grip.

"Marco threatened me."

His words halted my stomp toward the villa. I turned around.

"He told me that I was on their hit list. That if I married you, you would be a widow within the year. He was protecting you, he said. He told me no one else would be kind enough to give me the heads-up. I was a broken man, Santina. I couldn't do that to you."

I stood, frozen.

"He made me disappear, till it was safe. He made me promise I'd never say anything to you. He told me he was in grave danger, and so was I if I didn't listen to him. He looked like a madman when he told me. Eyes bulging with panic. He was a sweaty mess. No more cool, cocky Marco. It was awful to see him like that. And terrifying. I didn't know what to do."

"You waited twenty years to tell me this?" I choked, through a whisper.

"What was I supposed to do, Santina? I came back knowing it was too late to fix anything. I loved you too much to put you through all that. To tell you who your brother really was. To tell you that my family was wrapped up in the sorry mess of Rosalia's brother's murder."

I let the white noise of the admission penetrate me. Familiar memories brandished my mind with flickering images, snatched pain, buried pleasure, like glass smashing to a ceramic floor, piercing shards splintering across it.

"What are you doing, Paolino?"

"Telling you the truth at last."

"Why now? Why today, with everything happening around us? What's the plan — see how far you can push me till I break?"

"No! Because I can. That danger that's hung over my head for years is finally gone. Marco has seen to that. You have no idea how I've lived all this time!"

"What do you mean, Marco has seen to that?"

He shifted then. Regretting his outburst. "I promised I wouldn't say any more than that. Your brother, he saw to things. Made good. I did as he asked all this time, so he pays me back with my freedom. My safety."

"You're cruel. Spouting lies about my brother. About what *you* chose to do all those years ago. You stand there trying to get me to believe that criminals were waiting to kill you for marrying *me*? An orphan from the mountains?"

"Don't you see, Santina? Watching all this today makes me see how little time there is for all of us. You deserve the truth."

"No. I deserve space."

"You deserve a wonderful life." He scooped my hand in his then, cradling it. His voice eased into the familiar song I recognized from our youth. "You live here but none of this is yours. You're still the wallpaper. You deserve more. And I want to give that to you. I can do that. Now more than ever."

"Paolino, you sound more mad than usual," I replied, trying to diffuse the situation and failing.

"Death makes us drop our shields. Even your soldier man was able to talk to the whole party and seem like he was enjoying it."

The nerve was hit like a bull's-eye, and he knew it. I whipped that stubborn strand of hair from my face. "I'm tired of you talking about the major like that. Enough."

"I hate the hold he has over you."

"I work here!"

"Call it what you like. I see what you don't want to. And it breaks my heart, Santina."

"Why? Because from the moment you cut

off our engagement I threw myself into my work, my life, rather than collapsing? I chose to survive, yes. I chose not to live in your shadow, yes. That's called strength. Did you want me to jump off a cliff for the memory of you?"

"No. Because I never stopped loving you. Your temper. Your strength. Your ability to pick yourself up and do whatever you set your mind to. I can think of nothing more exciting in a woman than those things. And you made me realize how weak I'd been. And I know you probably hate me just as much as I hate myself."

I pinned him with my glare.

"Stare me down all you like."

I had to laugh then because I didn't want to cry. "Now you want my pity? Or you just going to stand there and tell me I'm irresistible when I'm angry and then I'll run into your arms?"

"Be serious, Santina. You haven't watched this charade today? All these wasted years."

I took a breath to slow down my racing thoughts. "You have a beautiful family, Paolino. You disrespect them talking like this."

"No. I mean them no harm. I have a right to tell you how I feel."

"Do you?"

He adjusted his linen collar. The pale pink set off his sun-kissed neck.

"Maybe not," he replied, "but look at me now and tell me you're happy not to have a lover light up your body?" He cocked his head a little to one side; Paolino the puppy. I hated myself for admitting his age hadn't diminished his charm, nor his ability to shine a light where there appeared to be none. My anger evaporated like steam. His far-fetched story about my brother seemed all of a sudden like a frantic fiction to get my attention, which it did, and I berated myself for it. Childish games for a faded childish romance, that was all.

I shook my head with a sighed laugh. "You will always make me smile, Paolino."

I turned away from him then, listening to my feet crunch across the cooked earth. He stepped in before me. I was sure someone would start to notice.

"I want to give you what I meant to years ago, Santina. Let me do that."

I stood motionless. My mouth was dry.

"You will step aside and let me return to my work," I replied, after a beat. "We will forget this crazy conversation of an older man who's been in the sun too long. You're *sciroccato,* that's what this is! That *scirocco* wind from Africa that wailed through here

550

last week has left you with your brain inside out." I laughed.

"I will win you, Santina," he said, as I brushed past him, reaching the reassuring clink of cutlery within the kitchen. I fitted in between the team of girls restoring the villa to our usual order. One by one they left. Paolino may have called out to me from the garden during that time or he may have slipped into a sturdy silence once again, piling up the chairs beyond the door. The rest of the afternoon faded in echoes of clunking furniture, stacking of crockery, the rhythmic swish of the mop or cloth, aimless chatter; the percussive eradication of death.

The last girl left.

Rosalia and I sat on the terrace, a small teapot steaming upon the table, offering a light reassurance; I had become more British than I would like to admit.

Paolino reached us. "So, that's it, all packed up."

He pulled his shirt down over his round abdomen and hovered for a moment in the awkward pause; we were all young again, unskilled navigators; his words from earlier still prickled, tiny thorns along my skin.

"You've done so well, Paolino," Rosalia said, coming to our rescue.

"Says the *americana*!"

Her smile was warm, if a little guarded.

"It's not so easy as people say, you know. Pasquale worked like a horse. Perhaps if he hadn't had to struggle so much for us all he would still be here today. His time was used up too soon. But Maddalena has what she needs. That's the important thing. It's good to be home. Grass is always greener. But you knew that already."

I watched emotion ripple over his face, which he let crease through him. I admired him that. He wasn't scared of feeling. He welcomed it, lived by it, even. Perhaps I envied him a little.

"Well, ladies, I'll let you alone with your twenty years to catch up on. It's good to see you, Rosalia. Santina — I'm sorry if I upset you before. It was a little selfish, yes. I hope you'll accept this apology? Don't answer now."

He turned to leave, then spun back toward us, his eyes alight with a mischief it was hard to admit I'd missed. "I spoke to the major's daughter before. She and Martha have their hearts set on a trip out to sea over the next few days. Salvatore's idea. He knows his Papà will never say no to taking our yacht out for a ride."

He shifted his weight from foot to foot, his age slipping away with each gesture.

"That's enough from me — never did learn when to stop."

I didn't reply. Rosalia didn't fill the gap either.

He left.

We watched the shadows lengthen, moon rise, stars etch little glimmers of hope in the sky. In the darkness, we traced our years apart, linking the dots with darting lines, constellations of anecdotes that sparked off in welcome tangents. Then we slipped into comfortable silence till a clatter of voices caught our attention.

I reached the front door and opened it. Maddalena was beside Paolino's son Salvatore, his eyes slit, gazing across at her with mischief. Elizabeth stood before me, trying to block my view. Her eyes were glassy with alcohol, the fumes of which puffed toward me on her breath. She flicked a lock from her face, the waves more erratic than usual, then brushed past me.

CHAPTER 29

In the hush of the villa I sat upon my section of the terrace beyond my bedroom. The milky moon struck the water with languid ripples. Adeline's room lay abandoned above me. My eye flitted back to the corner where Elizabeth's bed once stood, where I had sensed her every shift, murmur, anticipating her needs.

I cried then.

A recurring ache. A child is time, before your eyes it charges through space, conscious and unconscious, refracting your own life toward you, while to them you remain unmoveable, unchanged, the elder, the fixed point from which they can spin away, an axis that will anchor them against their will. Adeline scored this emptiness I'd kept locked away. The loneliness and despair that led to her death forced me to reflect on my own. Now I faced a string of missed connections throughout my life; a recipe cooked out of order, misread, half remembered, improvised without skill. The ingredients demanded attention; my lost daughter, my lost lover, my lost brother. I couldn't sense what would remedy this unavoidable sense of displacement. I was floating offshore with the current lapping me farther away.

What sort of life could Positano possibly offer me now?

I did everything I thought possible to avoid joining the proposed party at sea. I knew Rosalia wanted to stay in town with her mother, and I was happy to join her — but Elizabeth would hear none of it. When she stood beside Maddalena that morning and the two of them begged me to join, I couldn't refuse. To spend a day beside them, on the water, was too beautiful a chance to walk away from. Besides, they were a force, each on their own, and together they were like that *scirocco* which left Paolino's frame of mind askew and most likely several others in town if my years in Positano had taught me anything. These young women powered through the house, unstoppable, shifting everything within it, including the major and me.

I stepped out onto the terrace with a basket of fruit. Elizabeth had her arms woven around the major's neck.

"You're finally listening to sense, Daddy!" she exclaimed, kissing him with a skittish pout. His face softened. He caught my eye. Seeing his daughter in such a light, loving mood, it was as if a great weight had been lifted from him. His shirt buttons were undone a few more than usual and his white linen shirt reflected the light onto his face with a youthful bounce.

"Daddy is coming with us too! Can you believe it, Santina? He's actually leaving the prison for once. Would you like us to cover you in a sheet while we walk down so no one sees you?" Her laughter frothed out. He was delighted she was happy; her sarcasm was left ignored.

We met Paolino, Martha, and Salvatore by the main bay, Spiaggia Grande. Martha charged across the shale to us and planted polite kisses upon our cheeks. I watched the major relinquish to her lead, though I knew he felt uncomfortable with the enforced physical contact expected in our corner of the world and which foreign visitors usually took to with great aplomb. Paolino was dressed like a skipper, a beam of white against the azure. Salvatore jumped onto the jetty and made an unsurprising beeline for Maddalena, all too willing for his attention, and the three youngsters followed, stepping on board.

The yacht was pristine, with a glossy deck and a generous amount of space for passengers to lounge both at the bow and the stern. Paolino stepped down onto the jetty and shook the major's hand. "Signore, I'm so glad you finally come onto my pride and joy, *si*? Come, please!" He stretched out his other hand and helped him aboard. By the padded canvas seats at the stern, there was a huge bucket of ice and inside two glass bottles of fresh lemonade beside a plate of pastries; Paolino's palace upon the water. I quashed the sensation that these thoughtful touches were more for my benefit than the major's, especially when Paolino tossed me a provocative smile from the helm, which I brushed off with a roll of my eyes. It made him chuckle. A few minutes later we left the bay, sailing in the direction of Capri.

The water grew darker, sapphire blue replacing the shimmering turquoise. The white spray lapped up the edges of the yacht as Paolino and his son moved with well-rehearsed ease, shifting beneath the sails, steering farther away from Positano. It was a beautiful dance, father and son swaying in turn at the helm. They doted on one another. Fatherhood suited Paolino well. He would have liked more children. I knew he longed for a house full of noise. We'd dreamed up our gaggle sometimes, on our Sunday afternoons, colorful pictures of a band of children, fearless girls, sensitive boys, brave souls who would stand by their mamma and papà, shaping their slice of Positano into an idyll where they lacked for nothing, not food nor love. The memory slumped like a heap of stringless marionettes. I tore my gaze away, and looked back toward the shore. The people on Fornillo beach were minute-colored specks of tourism now.

"Please! *Mangia!* Today we celebrate life, Signore!" Paolino called out.

Martha's face spread into a freckled grin. She pulled the rim of her wide straw hat a little lower over her eyes and reached the plate out to the major. He took a small lemon puff and she poured him a glass of lemonade. Upon the bow, Maddalena and Elizabeth had already stripped to their bikinis, their white skin set off by the dark blue around them. With each bump of the waves below, they squealed like children. Elizabeth turned back toward us at the far end of the yacht. "Isn't this heaven, Daddy?!"

He smiled, lifting his hat and giving it a

slow fan over his face.

Martha nodded toward the two beauties lying in the sun with a compelling lack of self-consciousness. "I'm so glad you came, Henry, Paolino was most insistent we do this. As was my son. I think we can imagine why, can't you?"

"This is perfection. Adeline adored the water too," he replied, looking out toward the jutting rocks, prehistoric nubs of volcanic eruptions, and took a deeper breath. "Quite fitting to be here today. It is as glorious a day as you could wish. I could burst into song!" He laughed at himself, as Martha's face widened into a dazzling grin. "I had hoped that living surrounded by such musical people I would have inherited some measure of their talent," the major continued, looking more relaxed in new company than I'd ever seen him, "but alack, no, I shall leave it to Paolino, yes?" He waved up to the captain. "To burst into song at the breathtaking beauty around us, yes? But I'm sure you're used to that sort of thing, Martha."

"When we were young, perhaps!" she cooed, with her gentle Canadian lilt, a slit of sadness, which disappeared as quickly as it surfaced. "We lost my mother when I was about Elizabeth's age. I wish my father had

559

been so eloquent about her as you are about Adeline. I'm sure it would have helped him — and me — a great deal. I didn't think you necessarily needed a day out at sea, but my husband does love to force feed. It's really a wonder I'm not the size of a house!" She laughed a little too loudly.

The major caught my eye. I felt at once trapped. Unsure whether I was partaking in the conversation or whether Martha assumed, as the help, I ought to remain mute. It was hard to express our relationship beyond the villa walls. Within, we had a delicate understanding of our quotidian rhythms, a pleasure in an unspoken, effortless compatibility. But beyond, we were an awkward pair. I felt a keen sense of outsiders projecting their versions of what we ought to be upon us, even if today they were unaware our grown child on board had spun us off axis.

"Who wants to swim?" Salvatore called out.

"*Sì, grazie!*" Elizabeth yelled back.

"Just up here I'll set anchor!" Paolino called out.

"He loves to come here, Henry," Martha explained, as if the beauty of our surroundings needed qualifying. "It's where he proposed." She smoothed her linen sundress. "Now we've both shared a little, yes? You can feel quite at ease, Henry." She chuckled. The major mirrored her. I wondered how much she enjoyed receiving the undivided attention of a distinguished, handsome English gentleman.

A little farther on, where several rocks jutted toward the sky and Capri floated in the near distance, Paolino dropped anchor. Emerald waters lapped up to the edge of the boat. The two girls walked along the edge and plunged into the deep, shooting up for air, their faces lit with delight. Salvatore dove in after them, then his mother, her delicate alabaster frame slicing into the water with grace. The major stood up and let his linen shirt drop to the floor and followed, cutting into the sea without a splash. The laughing heads bobbed in the water, cleansing away the sorrow of the week. I watched Maddalena lie back and allow the water to lull her to the surface. Her eyes closed with bliss. Then she pivoted back to vertical, peddling the water. "Santina! Will you come in with us?"

I laughed. "I wasn't planning to!"

"Yes, Santina!" the major called, flicking his hair away from his face, sending rivulets splattering behind him. "It would be sinful not to, it's glorious!"

Just then Paolino swept past me and took a flying jump into the water to shrieks from the others. White spray lifted up into the sun. Before I allowed myself to stall, I too stepped out of my sundress and dove in. The cold bubbled up my sides, shooting me to the surface. There we floated, breathless with laughter, the dancing water reflected in our eyes. The major looked like the man I'd met in that parlor in Hampstead all those years ago. Till now, he had always insisted on private swims. No one had ever accompanied him. It was strange to see him half naked, dappled with sunlight alongside the youngsters. His body was sinewy, taut with an energy that belied his years.

"Not so long ago, Santina and I snuck around these caves, no?" Paolino cackled.

I joined his laughter, upended by this unusual collection of people, stripped of normality by the leveling water, undulating in the shadow of those monumental cliffs. I pretended not to note the major's expression. Nor Martha's.

"When we were children, yes! And the only yacht you got your mucky hands on was a rowboat that belonged to an uncle!" I replied, feeling the pressure of the cold upon my chest, sweeping away the stinging pictures of Marco in the caves and Paolino's feeble accusations from yesterday. That morning I wanted to allow myself unadulterated happiness, I wanted to mimic the girls' abandon.

"We will be hungry after our swim, no?" Paolino asked, gliding back toward the yacht. "Come, Santina, you help me with the pasta, yes?"

It wasn't a question. He had already hauled himself up the ladder. By the time I'd reached him in the galley, he had a deep skillet of tomatoes melting with crushed garlic, a pile of fresh fish and shrimp beside it, already cleaned and ready to be tipped in for a *zuppa di pesce.*

"This smells amazing, Paolino."

"You won't let me make love to you with words, so . . ."

For a moment the light slit in through the round window. It caught the rich chestnut of his eyes. We could have been youngsters again, give or take the odd line. His grin was unchanged. The events of the past few days were a free fall through memories, like marine knots tied in haste, unraveling, slipping out of their ill-practiced grip.

"Some people don't change, no?" I asked, matching his grin. I wanted him to know that his clumsy flirtation neither intimidated nor affected me.

I wrapped my towel tighter around my middle and threw two packets of linguine into the simmering salted water upon the two-ring gas stove and gave them a twirl. He tipped the seafood into the skillet and coated it with the deepening red sauce. We slipped into silence, percussed only by the rhythmic clangs of the pan and the gentle clatter of the shells brushing against one another. Beneath us, the boat rocked upon the gentle waves, our kitchen a shifting space, lulled by the water. I watched his deft hands chop the parsley at great speed, cup a fistful in his hand, and sprinkle it over the *zuppa.* He zigzagged a spray of white wine and the steam rose up in a fragrant *whoosh.* He turned to me. "It's wonderful to cook with you."

"You're not as clumsy as I thought," I replied, acquiescing to the simple pleasure of the moment. There was nothing wrong in what we were doing. A moment's complicit intimacy in the tiny galley, surrounded by our sea, and the distant chatter of the swimmers, our real lives just beyond the round glass. Then a pang of sorrow; this was the life we forfeited. From the moment he left after breaking our engagement, I shifted all my feelings into a tiny compartment of my mind. He joked about my cloister, but it had been my choice alone, and I had made peace with it. My celibate life had a delicious purity and simplicity to it. Not void of pleasure but uncluttered, meditative, healthy. Now Maddalena had stepped back into my view, a part of me long forgotten was awoken with a brutality that excited and terrified me.

"You saw the way Martha looked at the soldier?" he asked without taking his eyes off the pan. "You think that's a woman in love with me? She's always known my heart has belonged to someone else." He gave the pan several flicks with his wrist. The fish were sent up into the air and back down into the salty broth.

The sides of the narrow galley inched closer.

"I'm not a words man like him. I've cooked this today so you will feel my love. It's the only way I know."

I could have pushed him for answers that day he left the villa. I clammed up instead. Now all these shunted relationships pounded at my heart, and I wondered if I had the courage or passion left to revisit them or give them the love and attention they had deserved all along. Was I old enough now to let someone in at last? Had I been alone enough to feel whole?

He gave the pan another shake. The shells opened a little more.

Perhaps I was.

Martha poked her dripping head below deck. "Oh dear Lord, that smells divine, darling! *Grazie mille!*" She swung back up to the group.

I lifted a stem of linguine out of the water and tasted it. It was perfect. I reached past Paolino for a cloth to wrap around the metal handle of the heavy pot. I turned off the heat, gave the pot a heave. He swung in behind me and wrapped his hands around mine. I could have elbowed him back, snorted a witty retort to make him laugh, or move a little farther forward so I couldn't feel his breath on my neck. But I didn't. I let the ribbon of heat unfurl a ripple down my spine. We tipped the pan toward the colander placed inside a large rectangular plastic bowl. We stood there letting the steam swirl up and over our faces. His chest moving against my back with the light rise and fall of his breath. I had forgotten the weight of him, it was a sip of velvety cacao before sugar has been added, bittersweet, indulgent, almost irresistible.

Salvatore's steps split us apart, just in time for him to appear, dripping and buoyant. Paolino took the colander and tipped the linguine into the saucepan. With every turn, time wound forward to the present, clock hands twisting me out of our past with reluctant revolutions. His boy left with the pan in hand. I lifted the ceramic bowls from the counter where Paolino had stacked them. He stepped before me.

"I know you feel it too, Santina," he said, his voice a murmur, his expression softening. I wasn't being pursued. We met in that narrow gap between guilt and innocent pleasure, an underwater space; deep enough to be surrounded but close enough to the surface so that shafts of sunshine could cut through the blue.

I forced myself to leave the galley for the table by the stern. The major rose at the top rung of the ladder. The sun cut shadows across the definition of his muscles, rippling beneath his fair skin. The water trickled down the length of his torso. He brushed his hair off his face and lit with a smile. I had never seen him so alive, his eyes the exact same shade as the cerulean sea.

"Santina, something smells beyond wonderful!" He laughed then, surprised by this great wave of happiness. Like his daughters he was at once a beam of energy. The boundaries I'd been used to seeing at the villa had sunk away into the water. Gone were his angular movements. Something about this day at sea had loosened everything about him, as if an artist had scuffed the sharp outlines of his portrait with fast charcoal-dusted fingers.

We sat around the table at the stern, twisting Paolino's declaration of love around hungry forks. Maddalena's nose was dotted with freckles from the sun. Elizabeth looked pink. Salvatore inched close to Maddalena, jet-black hair scraped off his face, his bronzed skin a deeper shade of olive.

"Do you like Papà's pasta, sir?" Salvatore asked, his English dancing with a tinge of Canadian lilt and Italian vowels.

"It is the best pasta I have tasted at sea. But I have to be careful, you understand, the best cook in town is sat opposite me." He looked directly at me, fixing me with a youthful grin. I thought back to Adeline on the terrace describing her subjects' colors. At that moment she would have seen the rich bronze reds and oranges of her husband. She might have splayed him with slashed yellow, or violet even.

The realization flowed through me like a splintered shot of electricity.

"I fear if I praise your father too much," he continued, "Santina will serve me porridge for the rest of the week in protest."

Everyone laughed at that. Paolino looked over at me.

"Paolino darling," Martha interjected, "he says you're a match for Santina!"

I pretended not to read more into his diagonal smirk. Martha filled in the lulls in conversation with sublime ease, which I could see did not go unnoticed by the major. Paolino then paraded his deck, pointing out his joinery, his varnish, the way he had restored the old masts with years of care. The major did a fine impersonation of interest, looking over to me between regaled details of such and such workmanship, his eyes dancing.

Why was he here? At first I thought it had been Elizabeth's insistence, but as I watched him enjoying the youngsters dance around one another in the water, I realized he was here for the very same reason I was: Maddalena.

We took in her every move. Every flirtatious smile to Salvatore, every time she elicited hearty laughter from Elizabeth. We observed her long limbs, the ease with which she swam, her natural habitat it seemed, as if life on land was something learned, adjusted to. But most captivating was her élan, unfettered, unself-conscious; we had gifted her the freedom we lacked.

She ducked in and out of the water oblivious to the two adults reliving their ill-timed flicker of love, their meander through their shadow selves. And there, before us, the miraculous reminder of what we shared and sacrificed.

We did a fine job of disguising our stares.

When the sun eased past the most ferocious part of the day, and Paolino set a pot of coffee to simmer upon the stove, everyone settled into their own thoughts. The major looked up from his book for a moment. His eyes found mine; we were still at sea.

The sunset streaked across the deck, stretching out, lengthening mast shadows across the water before us. Paolino raised the anchor and the boat cut through the deep, to our left, the jagged gray cliffs. The salty breeze caressed my face, but despite the charge of the yacht, I felt as if the sea carried me without direction. From out there the pink plaster of the house was visible amongst the villas perched higher on the hill. It looked at once like a stranger's home, somewhere I visited in a memory. Every element of my life was tossed in the air, droplets of seawater mid-flight, and I was unsure as to where they would land.

Martha sunbathed at the bow, a sleeping

Elizabeth beside her. Maddalena stood beside Salvatore, his wandering arm slinking around her waist when he thought no one was looking. The major was sat in front of them, reading. Paolino sat beside me.

"All this can be yours, Santina," he murmured.

He was hapless, relentless, adorable.

"How easy it could be for you to just be happy, Paolino? You're always chasing. Or running away. Is middle age really so terrifying? I feel like I've just woken up. I think middle age is my great escape from the traps of youth. The unanswered questions. The doubts. The desperate search for roots. I think we're old enough to not care. Aren't we?"

"Talk poetry if you want, Santina. I want to follow my heart, not just talk about it."

I looked at him then, his fuller cheeks no longer the golden perfection of the young lover. In his eyes the sparkle of our youth was replaced with a quiet desperation. Maddalena let out a hearty laugh, Salvatore wrapped around her, assisting her command of the helm. She wore Paolino's skipper's hat.

"I know she's yours, Santina."

I snapped round to face him. At first I thought I'd misunderstood.

"And I know she's not mine."

I felt my blood drizzle down toward my ankles.

"I'm not so stupid after all, am I?" he continued, with a half smile that told me he thought the bait was hooked. "You disappeared for those months. Stories flew around. I haven't told a soul. I wouldn't do that to you. I'm telling you now not as a threat. But so you know my love isn't blind. That's how you know it's real."

I didn't want to defend myself. It would only provoke him further.

"You think the major feels this way? All these years in the house and did he ever make you happy in the way you deserve? You were never his lover. Always the help. But you stay because you think what you feel is love. Loyalty. Duty. Friendship. But it's not. It's guilt. We all have it. You and I have lived in two shadows cast by the same unforgiving sun."

I couldn't ignore the thorn of truth stabbed between his words. It smarted.

"Guilt is your cross to bear, Paolino, not mine."

"Not anymore."

I stared at him.

"The tides have turned, Santina. Your runaway brother owns Positano now. I heeded his advice all those years ago, a debt he's more than happy to reciprocate."

"What are you talking about?"

A grin creased over his lips. "Your baby brother made good, Santina. Quite the man now. There's no dagger over my head anymore. Your Marco ran away from those forcing him to prepare to murder me. He cowered in the shadows long enough till he was ready to ruin them. Who do you think runs things now? And that makes me a free man; time to let the truth shine at last."

My heart galloped in my chest.

"You think that Englishman loves you like you do him? I hope he does."

He left me then, and took over the helm, steering us back to our bay — a different place to the one we left that morning. I felt naked. We stepped onto the jetty, paid our thanks, exchanged polite kisses. Paolino beamed — after twenty years we'd finally had the most frank conversation of our lives; a warped victory was his at last.

The girls walked ahead of us. The major fell into step with me. Tourists wove around us. I knew the cacophony of early evening would not be pleasurable to him. As we climbed the curving, stepped alleys, I realized that I was, as always, focused on his state of mind before my own. Paolino's words echoed in my mind.

"Are you alright, Santina?" the major asked. "Would you like to pause a while? I think we've had too much sun for one day."

"No. I'm fine."

"You're a dreadful liar. And I love you for it."

He grinned.

An American tourist walked between us, arms loaded with paper bags from the boutiques; the sharp corner of one scuffed my elbow.

"I want to be home," I said.

And in that moment I knew home had never been and would never be the villa. Home had been anywhere the major was. Home had been anywhere he took me, through the history books, the poetry, the garden.

It was time I found home for myself.

I pretended not to register his expression, nor the way I could intuit he had sensed my thoughts. We walked on in silence, restaurants tinkling with holiday makers sipping their aperitifs, diving into plates of antipasti like maniacal last suppers, an endless hedonistic chase for pleasure and escape. I filed the pictures like snapshots, a memorized album of one of my final nights in Positano, squares of photographic paper curling in on themselves in the dying light.

Maddalena was in no hurry to leave. She and Elizabeth took a bottle of chilled wine and put the world to rights out in the garden beneath the lemon groves as the sun streaked the sky purple pinks and fire orange.

I laid the table with a light dinner, charred zucchini from the garden, a salad of fennel and orange, a large wedge of fresh ricotta, and a basket of small rolls I had baked that morning. The major called to the girls, who wound their way up to us, sandals in hand, feet browned with the dusty earth, and not a care in their worlds. It was hard to believe Elizabeth had lost her mother only a few days ago.

They took their seats. I turned toward the kitchen.

"Please eat with us, Santina," I heard Elizabeth call out.

I turned back.

"I think that's in order, don't you?" the major added.

I walked back to the table. He pulled out a chair beside him. I sat down.

"To Mummy," Elizabeth said, lifting her glass. We clinked and remembered Adeline. Maddalena caught my eye. Her father's death must have felt recent to her still too.

"To absent friends," Maddalena added, "isn't that what we're supposed to say?"

"Always do what you're supposed to, Maddie, yes?" Elizabeth asked.

I noticed the start of a frown on the major's face, which melted into a sun-kissed smile. The deep pink of his wind-kissed cheeks was edging toward brown.

The doorbell cut through the silence.

I answered it. A tall young man with long hair stood before me. He wore a backpack stretching the length of his back, sandals out of which I spied filthy toenails, a worn rusty-colored shirt, and baggy linen trousers that begged a wash. Before I could ask who he was, Elizabeth dashed across the terrace, stepped before me and wrapped herself around the young man.

The major stood up.

"Daddy!" she gushed, leading the worn-out boy into the terrace by the hand, his eyes wide with surprise, as if he'd never seen so many lemon trees in one place. "This is Eddie. My fiancé."

CHAPTER 30

"Are you completely out of your mind, Elizabeth?"

The major's voice cut through the silence of the downstairs rooms. I was sure Elizabeth's fiancé could hear him, though he was showering in Adeline's bathroom at the top of the house.

"Did you expect him to ask for permission? What year are you living in?" Elizabeth replied. The thunder began to rumble in her voice.

"I guess I'd better get going," Maddalena said, following me into the kitchen with the bread basket.

"I'm sure Elizabeth would prefer you to stay, but maybe yes, it's probably best."

She set the basket down. I felt her looking at me.

"My mom has told me so much about you."

"First person I met when I came back

from London."

"I like her face when she talks about you. Kinda sparkly maybe? That sound crazy to you?"

I smiled. She mirrored me. Our lips were the same shape, though hers were fuller, and had the knack of creasing into an oblique smile like the major's.

"It's nice to hear that," I said.

"You're pretty quiet, like she said. She calls herself the foghorn. I remember at parent-teacher conferences I was always so embarrassed, you know? She'd yell across the room. Half in Neapolitan, half in English. Not so cool."

"That doesn't surprise me."

I watched her fold the dishcloth around the rolls to keep them fresh for the next day.

"It's like I already know you. Weird, right?"

I took her hand in mine. Her fingers were committed to memory and uncharted maps. "That makes me happier than you'll ever know."

Then she stepped forward and kissed me on the cheek, following her impulse without a moment's doubt. "Thank you for the heavenly dinner, Santina. This entire day may have been the best of my life. Does that make me sound like a kid?"

"It makes you sound like a happy woman."

She danced out of the kitchen. Then her head popped back through the doorway. "I'll be back. Think up some embarrassing stories about Mamma — I know there's a lot she won't tell me, right?"

I smiled. I could hear her light footsteps across the tiles, then the heavy creak of the door and its weighted close. The quiet was no longer comforting. It seemed like the calm before the storm already whirring in the next room. I opened the kitchen door that led to the lobby. It wasn't difficult to hear the major and Elizabeth.

"I just don't understand the rush. You've got your whole life ahead of you. Why are you promising yourself to someone you barely know? It's insane."

"Insanity is sending a child away at four, Daddy. Falling in love is what people do. You keep telling me how much you loved Mummy. Why can't I love Eddie that way?"

"Of course you can. But why promise your life to someone who you can't have been in love with for longer than a year at most?"

That's when she swung the door open, almost banging it against the wall inside. She brushed past me and out onto the terrace. He followed.

"Why do we have to argue, Elizabeth?"

"Can't you just be happy for me? For once in your life just say, well done, Elizabeth, you're marvelous, just as you are. You are enough. But I'll never be enough, will I? And you command me back here every summer and I have to suffer the same old shit. I'm so bloody tired of it."

The major ran a hand through his hair. "Why didn't you even mention he was coming? Don't you think Santina would have appreciated that? What are we? A hotel? She doesn't have to run after someone else just because you decide. Why didn't you tell *me* at least?"

"Because we would have had this argument already, that's why. Just be happy for me!"

He let out a terse sigh. "I will not stand here and be lectured to by someone who doesn't know what it means to be in love! To really love someone so that you know what their thoughts are even before they say them, or think them. What do you know of that? Of meeting a person who makes you the very best version of yourself, forces you to grow, to be better, to listen better, to them, to yourself? What do you know of that?"

"Is it so hard for you to think that Eddie has fallen in love with me? Am I really so

580

ghastly?"

He softened. I willed him to use his Adeline voice, the one that would always ease her back into the room when her mind had taken flight to frightening places. Yet in that moment I felt the painful realization that he was as terrified of Elizabeth falling in love as he was himself.

"So just enjoy each other," he soothed. "Get to know one another. Why do you have to plan on marriage? It's too fast. It's unnecessary."

"I want it! He wants it! That's the end of it."

The major stiffened. He took a long breath.

"That is *not* the end of it. You are inviting someone into our family. Someone I don't know. Someone who shuffles in with sandals and his house on his back, gawking. I don't like it. Not one bit."

"So?"

"You marry that man, Elizabeth, and you forfeit your own plans. Put yourself first. You've worked hard all these years. You're a bright, inquisitive, argumentative woman. You could put your mind to anything."

"And being in love means I sacrifice myself?"

"Yes!"

"No — *you* did that. You gave everything away because of Mummy. I'm not going to make those same awful mistakes. You put your whole life on hold. You locked yourself away, and me for that matter, and now you think that's what it means to be in love. It's pathetic!"

I watched them from the other kitchen doors, swung open onto the terrace. Elizabeth brushed by him and stomped upstairs.

The evening slid into night. Elizabeth and Eddie shuffled downstairs to raid the fridge. I was sat on the terrace reading. I heard them dismantling my careful order. When I went inside, there was lettuce torn in strips upon one of my chopping boards and several jars opened at the same time; sun-dried tomatoes, pickled zucchini, olives. Eddie's face lit up.

"This is phenomenal. Thank you so much!"

"Santina is like my real mother. She's the lady I've told you all about," Elizabeth purred, her face flushed.

He reached out a hand. I shook it, feeling some olive oil clinging to his fingers, from where he'd scooped them into one of the jars no doubt.

"Daddy's being ghastly. Our bags are

packed. We'll head out tomorrow."

"Elizabeth, give him a little time. Give yourself a little time. A lot has happened the last few days."

"I'm so sorry," Eddie interjected, wrapping some bread around a heap of cheese and zucchini. "I wanted to be here. My friends and I got held back in Naples. Crazy place. Missed our connection."

He kissed Elizabeth on her cheek.

"I'll write to you, Santina," she said, at once hollow.

"Things will be different in the morning," I urged.

Eddie looked at her. I could tell what he preferred to do, but she shook her head.

"We'll head to the beach, *tesoro.* That's where I need to be," she concluded.

And she stood, planted two kisses on my cheeks, and left, her puppy close behind. I looked down at the debris upon the table and counters.

The major had long since retired upstairs when they left. He didn't come down to say good night.

I returned the kitchen to its original state, then headed upstairs. I looked toward my room, then along the corridor to the bathroom, noting the wet towels Eddie had left strewn along the floor. I headed upstairs to Adeline's instead. I hadn't said my own goodbye yet, and with the major most likely asleep, I could steal a private moment of reflection before we stripped her room. I owed myself that.

I stepped into the dark and opened the windows and doors onto the terrace. It was a beautiful night, the sea a sheet of glass reflecting the stars, the horizon wrapping around the far distance beyond Capri. Overhead, her paintings fluttered on the careless whisper of breeze, ferocious scrawls of color now black and white silhouettes in the dark, as if they had lost their light along with her. They crinkled above me, exhaling her spectrum and all the fury that accompanied it. I allowed my own breath to release. I followed the moonlight onto the terrace, steeped in a chrome glow, shafts of onyx shadows of the surrounding trees and trailing bougainvillea cast across the blanched plaster.

"She won't be told. Just like her mother."

I turned toward the major's voice. He was leaning on the balustrade at the opposite end of the terrace that ran the length of the villa. His silhouette's outline was a nimble sketch of silver, his face a shadow but for the glint of his blue eyes in the metallic light.

"Or her father," I replied, deciding not to shy away from the truth.

"It's such an awful feeling, Santina. To know you've failed someone so deeply. She despises me."

"She thinks you despise her."

I would have left him to his solitude then. I would have hidden in mine elsewhere in the house. But his words pinned me to the spot.

"I'm taking my anger out on her. Adeline hurt her and me in the cruelest way she could, and I'm not ready to forgive her. Not by a long shot. Elizabeth's right — I put everything on hold for Adeline."

His expression darkened. "I made the biggest sacrifice for her and it's been a shocking waste. I'm supposed to feel pity. I'm supposed to understand her suffering. But do you know what, Santina? I feel utterly rejected. And I scream at my daughter because I envy her new love. I envy her freedom. What kind of father does that make me? What kind of man?"

"The most honest man I've ever known." The words slipped out before I thought them, a fish sliding back into the water from a fisherman's net. But no fear followed. I stood upon the liberating precipice of truth and decided to jump. I had nothing to lose now. Paolino was right, when someone dies a person does become heightened to their fleeting existence.

"The man I have loved in silence for twenty years."

I was quivering. The powerful admission shook through me.

I might have fled then. I didn't.

He walked over to me.

In the lunar glow he looked like marble, sculpted at the hand of a master, his face chiseled with a passion I knew he had never let me see, not like this, not till now.

Our words twisted up into air like the flurried ribbons of smoke from flickering flames. Now there was only the feel of his lips on my neck. They pressed onto my skin like a forgotten song. The powerful sensory return to our silenced past rushed over every fiber of my body. In a breath we were beyond the walls of the villa, beyond the boundaries of memories and thoughts. I let the current of energy score through me, the fierce realization that our bodies were but fiction, the illusion of a shell. And we peeled away the layers, within and without, our clothes at our feet, moon-kissed bare bodies, the door frame pushing against my back.

The long-ago feel of the major inside me made my breath catch.

He stopped.

So did I.

My legs were around his waist.

He looked into me.

His eyes were wet.

"Let them fall," I whispered, my hands around his face. And his cries shuddered through him. And so did mine. Then the laughter broke out through the wet and our lips celebrated. Our breath deepened. He pushed farther into me.

The main door downstairs creaked open. We froze.

He slipped out of me and leaned over the balustrade.

"They're back," he whispered.

I grabbed my clothes and dashed down, closing myself in the dark quiet of my room.

Rest evaded me because my body was on fire. I had awoken from a twenty-year sleep. I watched my clock tick toward twilight, pretending I couldn't hear the engaged couple make love in the room next to mine.

Breakfast was silent but not sullen. Elizabeth seemed more relaxed than the night before and Eddie surprised the major by proving to be more articulate than he had judged by his appearance. The major even appeared to take some interest in Eddie's

587

plans to work in the Far East, a place Eddie explained he had been fascinated by since he could remember. Then Elizabeth sliced through the pleasantries.

"We're leaving today, Daddy. Eddie and I want to travel south to Sicily. We might cross to Greece or Africa, follow the wind."

"Elizabeth, that's not necessary. Please, stay here as long as you wish."

"I hate this house, Daddy. I always will. It's Mummy's sanatorium. Only worse. Because it reminds me how you both wanted me gone."

I watch him take a deep breath, fighting the bristle rising in his throat and the embarrassment at her blunt delivery in front of the young man he barely knew.

"Don't look embarrassed, Eddie darling," Elizabeth threw his way, "you need to hear this. It's best out in the open."

"For heaven's sake, Elizabeth," the major replied, "the poor man is caught in the middle, he has every right to feel uncomfortable."

Eddie stood up. "Elizabeth, I'll head on up. You two hash it out in private, yeah?"

"Eddie, my love, it's totally fine," Elizabeth replied.

"I'm going to pack," he replied, and left. His forthright attitude surprised both the major and I. His direct reply reassured the major. Elizabeth may have met her match after all. Perhaps this was a true partnership?

"Elizabeth, I've always wanted what's best. But if you marry someone none of us know, I can't tell where it will find you."

"So let it be, Daddy. You stopped protecting me the moment you watched me leave for school. That's the hard truth. You gave control over to others that day."

He wiped his mouth with a napkin. It enforced his silence a little longer, which I presumed was the intent. Then he straightened.

"Look after yourself. I will cease to bail you out of predicaments, sending you money, like I have till now, anytime you take it upon yourself to go somewhere with someone or other with no mind whatsoever to the consequences. You are impetuous and careless."

"I don't want your money. Never have. And I don't want to be summoned back here either."

The major didn't rise to the bait. "I'm not going to tell you what to do, Elizabeth. But I'm going to remind you that you are an intelligent, brave, powerful young woman. It breaks me to see you throw all that away."

Elizabeth turned toward the sea. His reaction caught her off guard.

This wasn't the father of a few days ago.

"But don't come running back here expecting me to rescue you. You walk out and start your life with Eddie, then it is on your shoulders. You hate this place so very much? Then let's not call it your home any longer."

"Again the ultimatums," she sneered.

He stood. "Call it what you will. One day you might accept that I've only ever wanted you to be happy."

She rose to meet his stare. "Peculiar way of showing it."

She left her final word hanging like a hovering arrow.

The major saw me. His eyes bowed a little.

The couple said their goodbyes. The major shook Eddie's hand. Elizabeth held her hand out for her father to shake. It broke my heart. She came over to me and squeezed me tight. "None of this is your fault, Santina, nor mine," she whispered in my ear. "Mother could have taken her life at any time, tell me you know that?" She pulled away and looked at me. "I will write to you, yes? I will tell you every juicy detail." Her face widened into a beaming smile. Her eyes blinked away hidden tears. Eddie followed her out.

The major pressed the door till it clicked shut. He turned to face me.

"I didn't sleep a wink," he said.

"Me neither."

His words wrapped around me like tentacles. In that moment Paolino was right. If his feelings for me were as profound as mine, he wouldn't be at sea. He would be running into my arms. He would be unfolding his heart to me. There was nothing to hold us back any longer. Yet he stood, motionless.

"These walls have absorbed so much sorrow," he began. "Elizabeth is right. It is a prison. You and I have been trapped inside it too."

"Can't we be free now? I decided to be honest with you last night before I could think. And I'm glad. I love you, Henry. And you have broken my heart for too long. I let you do that. Because I preferred to stay close to you than live a life without you." I knew my honesty would challenge him, but at last my own feelings surmounted his.

His expression withered. "I seem to have hurt the people I feel the most for."

"This is the time to look me in the eye and tell me you don't feel the same way."

He looked at me square. His eyes filled with tears he refused to let fall.

"I'm not prepared to ruin what we have, Santina."

"What do we have?"

I watched him snatch a breath to speak but the words caught. I stepped forward.

"Look at me, Santina," he blurted out. "I have never been so terrified in my life: I may never see my daughter again. The woman I thought I once loved threw herself away from everything I provided for her. Maddalena is here and I feel the twist of the knife of how much we gave up."

His breaths became tighter, lighter, inhaling away the tears rattling the ends of his words. "Fact: I have ruined the lives of the three women I cared most for. And I'm not going to hurt any of them anymore."

I longed to hold him.

He shook his head as I moved toward him.

"No, Santina. I won't do this. I won't hurt you anymore. I'm so sorry. I'm so dreadfully sorry."

We held each other. Our chests beating against one another's tear-streaked shoulders.

Someone rang the bell. I wiped my tears with the back of my hand.

The major darted inside. He abhorred how this period of mourning had made our home an invitation like never before.

I pushed back the catch and opened the door.

A bronzed man stood before me, hair slicked back, a crisp white shirt with long lapels taut across his chest, tapered in at the waist where it met pale blue tailored trousers. A heavy gold chain was reflected in the gleaming toes of his loafers. Two men stood either side of him, a foot or so away from the door, a questionable triptych.

"I know it's been a while, Santina, but I hoped for a warmer welcome than this."

Only then did the voice of my little brother slam me into reality. My mouth was dry. I may have been trembling, but I couldn't feel much below the stone dropping to the pit of my stomach.

He leaned in and kissed me on either cheek. Then he stepped inside and signaled to his cronies to wait where they were. He walked to the center of the terrace like he owned it.

"Well, still the same, no? You keep this place like an oasis." He turned to me where I stood, still gawping at him by the door. "I heard what happened. Came to pay my respects."

I fought for words, but they prickled the side of my mouth like thorns. "Where on God's earth have you been? Have you any idea what you put me through?"

"Some. A lot actually. I kept a close eye. From a safe distance. I knew you'd be furious."

"I am speechless with fury. Have you any idea, any at all, what you've put me through?"

My tears weren't dry from my conversation with the major and this disorientating nakedness made me fear I would not control my emotions with my brother as much as I would have liked. He nodded with a polite smile. He reminded me of a priest who listens with an impartial ear, inviting confession and absolving with grace. Quite a skill, considering he was the blatant wrongdoer.

"You have every right to be, I suppose," he replied, his voice so smooth and distracted it made my fury sink even deeper. "Even if I was the one who made sure that sorry sack of shit of a father never bothered you again. Even if I was the one who made sure you weren't a widow at age twenty-three. You have any idea the danger I put myself in to save you that? I didn't want to kill Paolino any more than you wanted to live as a widow. I had to hide myself for a long time, Santina, because I protected you and your lover boy. Because I didn't want to do what I was told."

His words boxed my ears.

He gave a raspy sighed laugh. "Times have changed. I got my revenge on those pigs in the end. And enough years have passed — I ought to take credit where credit's due, no? In the end, we all like a pat on the back."

I stormed across to the far end of the terrace, where he'd reached the table and taken himself a seat.

"The gall you have, coming in here like this!" I panted.

"I thought I'd do business the proper way."

"Why are you here?"

"Englishman is planning on selling. And I'm planning on buying."

My feet rooted to the tiles, but I felt like shaking him.

"I'd like to speak with the Signore. Tell him I'm here."

"I'll do nothing of the sort."

He looked up at me. His eyes were flint. "Oh I think you will."

My head was spinning.

"Good afternoon, Signore," I heard the major call out behind me. "What a surprise to see you here."

Marco stood up and shook the major's hand.

"I came to pay my respects."

"Thank you."

The major didn't offer Marco a seat.

"I won't take your time, Signor Major, but I wanted to leave my card. Anything you need, anything at all, you just call. I have a lot of" — his hand fiddled with the air for the right word — "business in this area now, and I'm always happy to help. It's been a long time I know. I hope you don't mind me just turning up like this."

The major shot me a look.

Paolino's words thudded in my mind. His story seemed less of a fabrication than I'd assumed. The man before me was not my brother. The transformation was so complete that if it weren't for the voice I would never have believed it to be the same man. His dancing eyes were hard. There was a flinty edge to his movements and speech, a sense that his body was poised for attack at a breath's notice; we were in a tiny cage with a hungry lion.

"Santina — I will call for you again in the next few days," he said, prowling toward the door. "We have a lifetime to rediscover. I'm happy I'm finally able to come back home." His smile was crooked. It sent a shiver down my spine. He turned toward the door. When we reached it, he spun back to me.

"I've behaved like an ass. I know that. But

I'm a different man now, Santina."

"I can be sure of that," I replied, my voice a shiver.

"I can make this up to you more than you will believe. You're in shock. I am too. I'm just hiding it well. Comes with years of practice."

I shook my head. "I don't know whether to hug you or punch you."

"I can count on you for the truth, that's for sure. It's why I'm back. To own up to some sorry business you needn't have been hooked up in. I screwed up. This is my penance. I don't waste time with church." His eyes widened into a wounded expression, as if it was up to me to absolve him of his unforgivable behavior, disappearance, blatant lack of respect by turning up like this. It was such an excruciating tendency of all the men I'd been closest to: to irritate the life out of me, push me to my edge, watch me explode, then do their best to make me feel like I'm the one committing cruel victimization for which I must offer an unquestionable apology.

He lifted my hands and kissed them with unhurried lips. Then he raised them to his forehead, bowing toward me like I was a queen.

"Please let me make this up to you. At

least explain."

I pulled my hands away.

"I'll call again soon, alright? I can't say when, but soon."

His men straightened to attention. They walked away.

I clicked the door shut. That metallic shunt signaled I was done waiting; for Marco's explanation, for Paolino's next maneuver, for the major's declaration of love that might never come. The thoughts smudged like the powder-pink and purple strata of the sunset, and beyond, a sublime clarity, pure like the glassy equilibrium of the water beneath it.

It was my time now to set sail.

CHAPTER 31

In 1977, Rome's Trastevere quarter was a political furnace. At first it made me feel alive, filled with a youthful verve I don't think I'd ever allowed myself to experience before. The students huddled around tables sipping wine and spouting manifesto against the fascist pull of the city at that time. I took a job that the major offered to arrange for me through a friend who owned a tiny bookstore on Via Moro, which sold a number of English texts much to the delight of eager American and British customers living and studying in the city for their slice of *dolce vita*. In the first few months there I reveled in the quiet order of my days around books, with simple meals in between cooked in the room in which I lived above the store. I hadn't said my goodbyes to either Paolino or Marco. My memory of leaving the villa was a watercolor wash. Each day I added more liquid in my mind so that the images bled into an anonymous brown; the expression that struck through the major's eyes, the way we both fought to keep our tears at bay, the way our hands managed to not grasp for one another's. I arrived in Rome a woman in her forties. Alone.

One evening as I strolled home to this medieval quarter, across Ponte Sisto, the bridge that arched over the Tiber, my eyes caught a familiar shadow outside my building. I shook off the dread beating through my limbs. There was no way my brother could be in the area stalking my every move. But the feeling trailed me through the next month. When the memory filtered my dreams, and I gasped awake in the dead of night, I realized that my fleeing Positano to a city only several hours north was a meager grasp at freedom. I needed to leave the life carved out by the men who surrounded me once and for all. So, as August slipped toward September, I boarded a boat for England.

The world I'd left as a nineteen-year-old had disappeared. London was emerging from its psychedelic verve, and I couldn't be sure I longed to be a part of it. It was no surprise then when a day out to the southern coast turned into a permanent stay. I visited Broadstairs in the southeastern county of Kent as an antidote to the city. I needed a little fresh air to think through my plans, how I would best use the severance pay I'd first refused from the major but which he insisted I accept.

When I arrived in the town, there was something familiar about the cobbled street warrens winding around the squat cottages that echoed Positano. The curve of the sandy bay at the bottom of the hill enclosed pale blue water, resplendent in the summer sun that greeted me. A wooden pier stretched out into the sea where visitors inhaled fried fish and fat chips, seagulls cawed, children shrieked, and the small town hummed with a modest celebration that appealed to my need for space from city life and what I'd left behind. I found affordable lodging in a room within a house, which faced the promenade. It was on the top floor of the Georgian terrace, its narrow front garden slanting downhill toward a view of the beach, lined with a squat hedge and dotted with rosebushes, colorful blooms fragrant in the salty seaweed breeze. Inside was a bed, a small table with two chairs, a two-ring gas stove, and shared use of the bathroom with the other, mostly holiday, visitors who came to stay and took breakfast downstairs in the landlady's dining room.

The walls were lined with a pale pink wallpaper, net curtains hung in the windows that opened up toward the coast. For the first time in years, I felt at home.

My landlady kept to herself and didn't express affront in me doing the same. Anonymity was mine at last. After a few weeks, the family at Morelli's, the prized Italian gelateria along the promenade, learned of the new Napoletana in town and were quick to offer me work should I need it. I stepped into the foreign cliché, joining the large team of ice cream scoopers, letting the stereotype flit over me like a veil. I cared little for what the locals thought of me and soon was accepted as the older server who longed to be alone. I knew their little minds might be darting around my possible history, why I was unmarried, why I had no children, why I had started this solo life in a seaside town where I knew no one. Their fictions skimmed my surface and left no trace. I found the simplicity I craved.

In the evenings, I revisited the Dickens books the major and I had pored over. I lingered over those words, knowing that this was the very town in which the writer had been inspired to craft several of them. That this sea was the one he too had gazed at while composing, bringing his family to reside here for their summers.

After a year, my tiny room heaved with books, stacked by author. My literary cloister and the sea air was what I needed, and a fresh new life blew through me, the stony memories of the villa crumbling with each day, in its place the silence of my solicitude and the great passion of someone else's stories and characters I'd lost myself to.

I scooped ice cream through a second summer season. I watched the sea darken through the autumn. I found great pleasure in those barren trees of the narrow streets, their spindling silhouettes mourning summer, reaching up to the graying skies of late November. The sea roiled, ashen.

The rain pounded the glass panes of the tiny tea shop where I liked to sit after an early morning stroll along the seashore, or on the days when my feet urged me north to Botany Bay, the chalky cliffs breaking up the cove, several rocks rising from the water, their deep green tips damp with years of rain. I adored the shades of this English coast, which sometimes leaned toward my childhood in the mountains but reassured me I was far from the Positanese world I'd fled.

I cupped the warmth of the tea in my palm and watched the water slide down the panes. Beyond, the gray sea blackened with winter.

That's when his silhouette approached, his hair plastered to his head with the pounding rain. A raincoat's collar flicked up over his neck. At first I resisted my instinct to step out. I knew my memory was playing bitter tricks. Then my cup dropped to my saucer. I was outside, the rain streaking my face as it did his.

"I couldn't keep away from you any longer," Henry murmured, his voice floating above the beating drips around us, bouncing up from the glistening cobbles.

"How on earth did you find me?"

I could hear my voice crack. I could feel the ground melt beneath me, shifting sands as the tide pulls out.

"Can we go somewhere? I'd like to talk," he replied.

I looked back at the steamy windows of the café, then turned and led him toward my lodgings instead. All the while my heart pounded in my chest, refusing to believe that any of this was happening. We left drip marks up the stairs. I heard the landlady unlock her dining room door that led onto the hallway just as we reached my room. I'd never had a visitor before.

I took off my sodden coat and shook it,

hanging it behind my door, and reached out my hands to him to do the same. He did. Our movements were sharp lines in the space, stilted, awkward, trying to puzzle our way through it without colliding. I gestured for him to sit at the small table by my window. I set a kettle to boil upon my stove. I took a seat whilst it heated.

We both took a breath and spoke at the same time.

"Please, Santina, do go ahead. I didn't come all this way to speak over you."

"What are you doing here?"

His eyes were more penetrating than I'd let myself remember. He looked toward the sea through my net curtains, wiped his hair off his face, and turned back to me.

"The past year has been a living hell, Santina." He paused. "I did everything I could to forget you. I traveled the length of Italy. I'm embarrassed to say I followed you at one point to Rome and when I saw how settled you were, I knew it would be unforgivable to barge in."

That haunting shadow rose into view. It hadn't been my brother after all.

"I returned to Positano, determined to sell the villa, determined to set up an anonymous trust for Elizabeth, Maddalena, and you. But when I sat in the lawyer's office,

605

my pen hovering over that page, your brother rubbing his hands with excitement, I couldn't do it. I couldn't do it because it was the very last thing I had in my possession to remind me of you. If I sold that place, I would relinquish my final tie to you."

His words flickered like flames. His handsome face, creasing with emotion while he tried to make sure every syllable was formed and delivered with grace, broke me.

"I've spent all these months growing my own life," I began through the ripple in my voice, "out of your shadow. Training myself to not want to hear these words. I don't know if what you're saying is beautiful or cruel."

"I promised myself I wouldn't cry. I promised myself I just needed to tell you how I feel, without it being a vise around you." His words trailed off then. A tear skimmed his cheek.

He reached his hand across the table. I slipped mine into it, feeling that familiar warmth send a flight of birds soaring from my chest. He kissed my fingers. He turned my wrist and kissed the softness of my creases there. Our lips met, tender and searching. Everything I'd cocooned myself inside slipped away. We were light in the gray. I could no longer sense where I ended and he began. My bed rose up to meet me and we tipped onto the eiderdown. We tumbled inside one another.

The kettle's whistle cut across the sound of our love.

We awoke several hours later, knotted together in my small bed, a scrunch of sheets and crumpled clothes. I felt his breath on my neck.

"I have dreamed of this, Santina."

"You have a filthy mind."

"Small mercy."

I could hear the grin in his voice. I reached my arm underneath his and stroked his fingers with mine.

"What on earth is happening, Henry?"

"We've waited long enough, Santina."

He lifted his hand and pushed up onto his elbow, resting his cheek on his palm. I turned to let his gaze glow over me. The time for fleeing was over. I let him see me.

"I love you, Santina. I'm not terrified of you seeing through to the very heart of me any longer."

"I think you're the most beautiful person I know."

"So come and be with me, Santina. Let's make the villa our home. Together. As equals. As lovers."

"If I let my life here slip away after one afternoon of lovemaking I'm not sure that makes me an equal."

"I'm not here to abduct you. I want to love you. I want to grow with you."

He tipped his head down and kissed me. His tongue etched my lips, wound inside, and danced around mine, unhurried. I rose up to meet him. He fell onto his back and lifted me on top of him. I arched, straddling him, feeling the softness of the stretched skin of my belly fall in creases, my breasts hanging a little lower than the first time we played this game. This was the body I honored for all its crags, the beginnings of age plotting a course like an unfinished map. I looked down at him, bare. I felt the white cold sensation of vulnerability score through me, brutal and fortifying.

"Santina, you will always be the most beautiful person I know. I didn't fall for a young woman who would kowtow to her employer. I fell into the woman I saw refract like a thousand shafts of light."

I eased him inside me then. I abandoned everything I thought I ought to be. Until I caught sight of the clock, which struck panic, spiked pinpricks, over my entire body. I lifted myself up from him, threw on my work uniform, begged him to be discreet and stay there till the end of my shift. Then I ran down the stairs, fussing my hair back into some version of order, braved more rain, and took up my position behind the counter for the afternoon. There was a surprising amount of customers, for which I was glad, though as I served each one of them, my mind was somewhere beneath my sheets, beside my lover.

I returned home to find the room strewn with candles and the delectable scent of a feast. How Henry had whittled it out with only two gas rings and a couple of pans was a marvel. He'd even borrowed two wine glasses from my landlady. I daren't ask what he had explained to her. Now two plates stood with a steak upon each, drizzled with a tempting peppercorn jus surrounded by wilted spinach and chard.

"This is beautiful, Henry."

"I'm glad you like it. It's not bribery. It's not seduction either. It's a celebration."

He gestured for me to sit down. He reached for an opened bottle of wine and poured me a glass.

"You've been planning this evening for some time." I smiled. "Or were you trying to get me to believe you just spontaneously threw it all together?"

His laughter lifted through a sigh. "If after tonight, you tell me your life is better without me in it I promise I will never haunt you again. But if you tell me you will consider my offer and live with me in our villa, I will make that happen. Right away."

I looked into his eyes, the flickering candlelight dancing across the irresistible dapples of darker blue. There was no place I would rather be.

CHAPTER 32

The following six months at the villa were luminous. Winter offered us a privacy we longed for. We retreated into both a new and familiar rhythm. Time was our ally. We made love during the day. Fed one another without hurry. Retraced our steps through the books we had shared. As spring budded through the gray, we took long, unhurried walks most mornings. Henry enjoyed the challenge of the bracing cold of the spring sea, something I only permitted myself once we had eked toward the warmth of May. That's when we took a steady descent to the shore without the crowds. We swam as far as our hearts could take us, and as I began to tire, we'd float back toward the shore, gazing up at the cloudless blue. One warm morning, after sipping a coffee and pastry on the shore, our hair still dripping, we embarked on our daily climb back to the house. We passed the first warren of boutiques and the start of the morning's shopping flow. Our route led us a sharp turn back toward the rock along the alley where the artists had set up a row of stalls selling their paintings and jewelry beneath a thick canopy of wisteria that the tourists gawked at, romanced into purchasing the beauty around them. We crossed Via Cristoforo Colombo and took the staircase up toward the road above. That day, for some reason, the final steps of the four hundred and forty that led us from the water's edge to our home loomed as a daring vertical before us. I turned back toward Henry. He had one hand upon the rock that flanked our ascent, just below the lit votive upon a stone shelf where a statue of the Madonna looked down at him with pity.

I called down to him. "Are you alright, *tesoro*?"

I didn't like his expression as he caught my eye. I ran down the steps.

"Good heavens, don't worry, Santina. Look" — he pointed up above his head to the statue — "she only wanted me to pause awhile, has some important message apparently. Can't understand the woman though, my Aramaic isn't as good as I thought it was after all."

I joined his laughter, wishing the pallor of

612

his skin was a little more pink than gray. Onward we climbed. When we were under the final covered archway near the villa, he slipped his hand in mine and turned me into him.

"We're pretending to be teenagers now?" I smiled, as he wound his arm around the back of me.

"Absolutely."

His salty lips met mine. A droplet of sea water fell off his hair and traced my face. We heard footsteps and pulled away. I let the giddy sensations trickle through me. We reached the villa, and he stormed into the kitchen.

"I shan't be inside today, my Santina — my legs need to walk some more! Take me to your hills! That's an order!"

"Perhaps I'll take a shower first, pack some food?"

"No need. I like it when your lips taste of the sea, and I've already prepared some treats." He ducked into the kitchen, hooked a basket in his arm, slipped his hand around my face, and planted his lips on mine. I let my hands trace his back. I heard the basket reach the floor. I let him lift me up. I cackled like a schoolgirl as he descended the steps. We didn't lose ourselves into silence until we reclined beneath our trees.

Until I felt the sun on my bare legs and the entire weight of him rise up and inside me. We lay there after our lovemaking, feeling the sweat smudge between us, the wetness crease down our legs. He rose up onto his elbows.

"It is quite wonderful to be children, don't you agree?"

"The most delicious state I can think of, my love."

"I try not to think about how much time we denied ourselves. All I want to enjoy is the beauty of this soul lying with me now, parched grass staining her skirt, earth powdering her arms."

"Henry. I'm happy."

He leaned down and kissed me with soft, warm lips. I held his face in my hands, feeling the width of his jaw, the smoothness of his skin between my fingers.

We spent that afternoon high above the Path of the Gods, watching tourists in our periphery way below us, tracing the beaten path from our hidden perch amongst the carob trees. No one could see us making love up there. No one could hear our laughter, watch us feed one another, watch him trace his lips on my bare breasts. We lay upon a large blanket, gazing up at the carob leaves dappling shadows over our naked bodies, trodden with age, warmed with love.

Our fingers interlocked. Our breath rose and fell in unison.

"So much simpler to be the carob, Henry."

"Quite."

"I mean to say each bud is both male and female. There's no need for pollination. It is self-sufficient."

"From now on I shall call you Carob."

I flicked my elbow into his rib cage.

"I'm completely serious," I said. "And as usual, you're finding any reason to resist listening to my wisdom."

"Therein lies ruin, don't you know, listening to wisdom."

I turned my head to his laughing eyes.

"That's why they used it as currency," I continued. "The carob. Without this marvelous tree, life would have been quite different for a lot of people."

"You're incredibly attractive when you talk trees."

His lips pressed against mine, his tongue gave them a little flick.

I pulled away and looked above us again. "Then demonstrate a little more respect for my knowledge, sir. We're literally under the tree that saved the Amalfitani, and their cattle, from hunger and invaders. They

615

traded it, ate it, used it as currency."

He rose up onto his elbow. "Once you've finished your sermon, I would be much obliged if we experimented in further activity of the partner orientation."

"Must the Brits be so wordy when asking to make love, Henry? I think it undercuts the intent."

"You adore my wordy foreplay more than you'd like to admit."

"I think twenty years of it is quite enough, no?"

He smiled down at me. I felt the earth rise up beneath me, smelled the shaded parched ground. A solitary carob leaf fell onto my forehead. He picked it away.

"I love you, Santina."

We eased inside each other, our lips dancing, our limbs knotted.

Several weeks later, as the spring blossoms burst open, our bell clanged to life. I opened it. Our daughter stared back at me. A miniature version of herself stood beside her, clasping her hand, a mane of dark hair fallen down in waves over both arms.

The telegram Maddalena told me she sent never reached me. My dearest friend Rosalia had died, and her daughter longed to return to the town she'd fallen in love with.

"Come on in, *tesoro,* please." I showed

them through to the far end of the terrace, aware that I was still shuffling around in my dressing gown even though it was edging toward midmorning. Maddalena retraced the last days of her mother's life. We cried together. She clasped my hands. I noticed the strength of them.

"This is Bianca, my daughter. I took a lot more away from here than I had bargained for." Her face wrinkled into a watery smile. "She's my Positano. Salvatore doesn't know, of course." Her hand traced her daughter's face and she planted a soft kiss on her cheek. The little girl looked up at me, expectant. I realized she and I had the same shape face, and her eyes were deep brown, with a glint of mischief, inherited from her grandfather Paolino, no doubt. It didn't take but a moment for me to fall in love with her.

Henry stepped out onto the terrace to see who had come to call. His face registered the same shock as mine. Two weeks later, when Maddalena was due to return to America, she broke down in tears. "Santina, I don't want to go home. There's nothing for me there. I feel alive right here. I'm a different person here. This is where I want to become the artist I long to be." She wiped her face with angry hands. "Sorry

I'm such a blob. Look at me! It's ridiculous, I know. Mamma's sisters are all I have left now. I don't feel I can ask them if we can stay. They're not really interested in a single mother, even if I'm their niece."

"Stay here," I blurted, without thinking to ask Henry first.

Her face lit up. "Are you sure? I will pay you. I don't want charity. I just need a little time to find our feet. Are you serious? You're about to make me dance with joy and that's not a sight you might like, I warn you!" Her voice fizzed into laughter, and our arms were wound around one another, and her daughter clasped my legs, and I wondered if time had at last agreed to knit us all together.

Our living arrangements grew to be the talk of the town's gossips. We were impervious to it all and settled into a beautiful rhythm, which revolved around the education of Bianca and the creation of an artist's studio for Maddalena on the top floor. Maddalena, a little surprised at my relationship with Henry at first, was then her usual breezy self. We watched Bianca lengthen into a child bristling with intelligence and affection, while Maddalena set up a stall alongside other street artists selling their work beneath the wisteria-canopied walkway to the sea.

That September was luminous. Bianca gardened beside us every evening. Maddalena transformed her rooms on the top floor into a magnificent celebration of her art. The chaos of Adeline was replaced by a transcendent atmosphere, delicate organization, watercolors in various stages of completion. When she was by the bay, selling, I would linger inside her sanctuary, letting the playful sketches of light and color uplift me. One afternoon Henry stepped in behind me.

"It is beyond glorious," he murmured, planting his lips on the back of my neck.

I turned around to him. "Do we owe her the truth?"

"I don't know," he replied, in that beautiful way he now had of expressing his uncertainties without pride or fear. "For whose benefit would that be?"

"Mostly ours, I suppose."

"We love her. She knows that. She feels that in the way her life is plaited with ours. With the unhurried hours we spend with Bianca. She is a light."

"She adores you."

"And good poetry."

I laughed. He traced his fingers over my hair, lifted my chin and kissed me. For a fleeting moment, his skin looked ashen.

"Are you alright?" I asked, noticing his pallor and wondering if he was coming down with a fever from the subtle shift of seasons, though outside it was still very much late summer.

"No need to fuss," he replied, kissing me again, then pressing me into him. His heartbeat was a steady thud against my ear. "Nothing good ever came from fussing," he added, his voice a murmur through my hair.

That night we made love with the doors open and the moonlit breeze dancing across the linen curtain. His soul eased into me, his fingers ran over my limbs. I'd never felt more beautiful in my life. The next morning when I first opened my eyes I noticed I'd left the doors ajar, the sun cast a corridor of light across the foot of our bed. Henry lay beside me. It was unusual. He had a knack of waking with the dawn most days and enjoying a little solitude before we gardened or prepared breakfast. I sat up, holding the sheet over my bare body, reliving the night. Then I turned back to look at my lover. I shifted down into my nook at the top of his chest. That's when I felt how cold his skin was next to mine. Choked with panic I shifted my ear to his chest.

I never heard his heart beat again.

■ ■ ■ ■

Signor Antonino, the lawyer, looked at me, expectant, from his side of the desk. I'm not sure if he'd prepared for an emotional outburst, to comfort a Neapolitan lady at the mercy of grief. Of course I offered him none of the above. He looked a little disappointed.

"Santina, do you understand everything?"

"Yes. Perfectly well," I replied.

"You asked me about his daughter, Elizabeth. She is not mentioned in the will, no."

"I see."

"You'll need time to adjust to your new situation. As executor I will, of course, oversee the financial and legal arrangements."

I nodded, silent, his words a wave of punctuation and singsong vowels. I left his office, sun batting down with an unforgiving glare.

Three days later Henry was buried, beside Adeline.

We returned to find Elizabeth at our door.

She looked up at me, in her eyes neither questions nor grief. "I found out he's gone," she said, her voice a thin line.

I walked up the last few steps and hugged

621

her. Maddalena eased in and wound her arms around her friend. I slipped my hand into Bianca's, the only person who kept me grounded, forcing me to stay present, looking at his death with courage and honesty. There's nothing like incessant questions of a young child to make one realize the absurdity of life and death, the incorrigible surrealism of our existence. And I was thankful for her, even more than I had been before.

The women and I entered the villa. Elizabeth sat at the table, taut.

"Can I get you something?" I asked.

She shook her head. "I'm here to pay my respects to you, Santina. You're the person who held this family together for me. I suppose I should feel like I'm free now."

I sat down opposite her. "He loved you very much, Elizabeth. He was a sick man. None of us knew that. The doctors told him his heart condition meant he would not likely live past fifty. He sent you away so that you might be spared your mother's illness. And his."

"You always defended him."

I could feel the prickle of my pride rise up my spine. I'd kept my emotions intact for Bianca and Maddie, but listening to Elizabeth now forced me too close to the edge. I wanted to blurt out that the depth of our feelings could not be couched in words, recriminations.

"I wanted to be here to help you pack up the house. Sort things out." Her callous tone nailed me to my chair.

I paused. "There is nothing to sort out, Elizabeth."

Her expression iced. "What do you mean?"

"Your father left the house to me."

I watched the statement land. With a breath, her anger fired. "I came all this way when they told me. I came to help, for God's sake, and all I get is a kick in the teeth. Fucking typical."

I stood now. "If you want to tarnish your father's name, do it! But not here! Not now! There are other people grieving here!"

"I'm sorry, Santina, I didn't mean —"

"You're not sorry! Your hate for him consumes you, and in the end who does it harm the most? You!"

She sat looking at me, red faced in my hot wind of honesty.

"You have every right to feel hurt, Elizabeth," I continued, before she could respond, "no one can take that away from you. But do you honestly want to live in that shadow forever? Don't you want to

623

really be free?"

"So now it's my job to free myself? Never mind that the sorry excuse for a man never apologized."

"And he never will!"

We stared at each other across the table.

"Elizabeth, I loved you as best I could. I held you when your dreams ripped through you. I reveled as you took your first steps. I watched you see things for the very first time. When you left, you took a piece of me with you. Do you think there was ever a time when I wasn't wondering how you were?"

"I never doubted that."

"So don't doubt my love now. Take it for what it is. Everyone has always wanted what was best, why don't you choose to see that?"

"Because the man who should have loved me the most — didn't."

"You want to keep that hurt like a thorn inside?"

I heard Maddalena come out of the kitchen behind me. "Everything okay?" she called to us. "I can bring you something maybe?"

"We're fine, Maddie. Perhaps take Elizabeth and show her your rooms upstairs?"

"Rooms?" Elizabeth asked, piqued.

"Sure, I'll be right back."

Elizabeth turned to me for explanation.

"We let her rent the upper floor. It was empty and she needed a place to stay. Maddie and Bianca have breathed life into this place. It's become the home it should always have been."

Elizabeth's eyebrow raised.

"How's Eddie?" I asked.

"I don't know."

I held the silence.

"Turns out he wasn't the best choice for me after all."

"I'm sorry, Elizabeth."

"You don't have to be. Just glad Daddy isn't here to hear that."

I reached for her hand. She withdrew.

"Your father didn't give you what you needed, no. We can agree on that. But he gave you what he thought would make your life free. Why don't you let me love you now?"

Elizabeth's eyes filled up. I watched the tears tip over the edge of her lashes.

"I don't think I could come back here, Santina, without dragging up all this pain. I don't want to put myself there again. When I'm here, it just all flies in my face."

That's when her tears shuddered through her. I wrapped my arms around her. I let myself cry with her.

Our breaths quieted. I again heard the tide come in from below.

"I understand how you feel, Elizabeth. And I want you to be free of this shadow you've cast yourself under. I'm able to take care of your father's finances and you will be looked after."

"I don't want his money."

"It's *mine* to give you. And I do so because you're the first infant who stole my heart. I don't give out of guilt or to patch up a past that wasn't mine to heal. No one can do that. I want to do this because I love you."

A tired smile then. "The first?"

Maddalena stepped out to join us. "Elizabeth, I'm really so sorry. Santina has been so wonderful to me and Bianca. I know you don't want to hear this, but your father too."

"You're right, Maddie," Elizabeth replied with a sighed laugh. "I don't want to hear how nice Daddy was to you. But I like you a great deal. And I do so want to stop crying, so be a darling and say something to change the subject? It's what us Brits are usually so very gifted at."

The sisters looked at each other. I watched them slip their hands into one another's and head inside. I left the terrace for our room upstairs. I sank into the quiet of the terrace save for the rattle of the cicadas and a soft rumble of waves.

Two days later, Elizabeth left.

It wasn't long before Paolino surfaced. I'd learned about his divorce through twisted tales from neighbors and that his life had taken him to Naples. One lazy Sunday morning he stood before me at our door. His skin looked like he was no stranger to wine and partying; I couldn't shake that sense of an older man clinging on to a lost youth. He paid his respects, his features hard.

"So, he made you queen at last, Santina."

"I'm not surprised you see it that way, Paolino. People usually say they're sorry for someone's loss."

He smiled then. Somewhere inside, I caught a glimpse of the young man, but it disappeared as soon as it surfaced.

"How can you be sure Bianca is my granddaughter?"

"Have you looked at the child, Paolino?"

He cracked a grin and nodded. "I'll do the right thing," he began, all business. "For once. They stay with you? I'll make sure you get something toward their keep, *si*? And maybe a little extra too, you know, when the *fanciulla* is grown."

"That's kind, thank you," I replied, resisting the instinct to throw him a callous

627

observation that his way of solving most things was through money. I was tired of fighting, and it struck me that he yearned in his way to do the right thing for the first time in his life.

He left that afternoon, and the final whispers of our past evaporated, inconsequential mist in the shadows of my mountains rising, immortal, around us.

■ ■ ■ ■

POSITANO
2005

■ ■ ■ ■

"Do you want me to write what the doctors said?" Svetlana asks me, shock creasing her brow.

"Well, of course. It won't make any sense if I don't."

"It's a bit morbid, no?"

"Oh give it to me, I'm fine. Or, I will be fine with some tea." I shoo her away. I know my bad temper is something the dying become accustomed to. I saw it in our neighbor when I nursed her after Henry passed away twenty-five years ago. Now I have become the crotchety old woman.

I don't write any more from where I tapered off. Svetlana is right, I'm not up to very much this morning. I ease myself off the bed and shuffle to my dressing table. I comb my hair off my face, admiring the silver strands. I reach for my notebook and rub my thumb across the rose printed on the cover. I flick open to a page I'd been lingering on during the night when the morphine had begun to ease its grasp: "The day of my birth my death began its walk. It is walking toward me, without hurrying." Jean Cocteau's words. Words Henry had me think about early on in our lessons. My finger traces the sentence. I breathe in the still warm air of the villa, the palace I will gift the girls, the home where my daughter has lived beside her mother, without knowing it, for the past thirty years.

Bianca creaks open the door. She pokes her head around the corner, asking for permission to enter.

I smile. Her smile is like the reflection I used to see in the glass. She sits on the bed beside my dressing table.

"You want me to help you, Zia Santina?"

"That would be nice, yes."

She takes the comb from my hand and weaves the teeth through my strands with gentle, unhurried strokes.

"I love you, my Bianca. So very much."

"I love you too."

She stops for a moment, and we catch our faces in the mirror side by side. The resemblance, even in my weary state, is startling. People used to comment on it. The point of her chin, her high cheekbones, her unruly hair. And beyond all these physical markers, the mountain air about her, a fearless gait which draws people to her and which allows her to dive deep inside herself for reserves of determination and strength few can hope for.

"I wrote you a story, my Bianca."

"Yes. You told me yesterday."

I raise my hand to my shoulder. She places hers upon it. The touch ignites a stream of memories; how she became my shadow in the kitchen, the garden, anywhere I needed to be. How it ached to watch her move like her grandmother, love me as her grandmother without anyone knowing the truth, her laugh, which escaped like bird song, staccato, bright, cutting through the trees.

I take in my paper skin, behind me the glory of those painted ceilings, golds, ochres, reds, azures; beautiful and meaningless now. My gaze shifts toward the terrace to the never seen beyond, the horizon that once beckoned me so, urging escape only to lure me back on its inescapable current. I catch the metallic shimmer on that afternoon water, hopeful glints dancing in the suffused sun. I smell pine and hibiscus and thyme on the toasted air. My house creaks in the heat, like its owner. I feel Henry's invisible hand upon me now, the warm murmur of his voice. I see his oblique grin that made me feel at once teased and loved and understood. I see that sparkle of intelligence in his eyes, full of unanswered questions, a passion and respect for life in all its expression. The man I loved with every part of myself, who embraced his frailties and helped me value my own so that I could share my heart and soul with abandon. A moment in time. That is all we ever have.

I turn away from my reflection.

ACKNOWLEDGMENTS

It truly takes a small army to produce a tale, and I'm so very grateful for the brilliant team supporting me. Thank you so much to John Scognamiglio and his wonderful team at Kensington for their continued encouragement and support. Deep gratitude to my agent, Jeff Ourvan, at Jennifer Lyons Literary Agency, for always asking the trickiest, juiciest creative questions without pressure for immediate answers. Warmest thanks to the lovely Anna Baggaley and her brilliant team at HQ Stories and HarperCollins. Thank you to Stefan for his insistence we visit him at his magical home. His feasts — mental and edible — fed my imagination. *Grazie mille* to Signora Rispoli and her family for filling this writer with pasta and stories, sharing her love and photos of Angelina whilst offering me a comfortable bed with breathtaking views of her coast. Thank you to Zia Lilli for connecting me with her sister Teresa, who cooked me spectacular linguine and offered an insight into her Positano life. Thank you, Adele and Carl, for the gelato by the Kentish coast and time at your country idyll for editing. As our firstborn approaches tweendom I'm obliged to conjure an embarrassing motherly gush, both for him and his younger indefatigable brother. Mum and Dad, please know you make this all possible. Thank you, Ma & Pa English, for always being happy for me to hide away in your blue room to write. And lastly, but not without fanfare, to my funnier, song-and-dance other half, whose buoyancy keeps all of the above family afloat, even on the choppiest waters.

ABOUT THE AUTHOR

Sara Alexander graduated from Hampstead School, London, UK and went on to attend the University of Bristol, UK, graduating with a BA hons. in Theatre, Film & TV. She followed on to complete her post-graduate diploma in acting from Drama Studio London. She has worked extensively in the theatre, film and television industries, including roles in much loved productions such as *Harry Potter & the Deathly Hallows, Doctor Who,* and *Franco Zeffirelli's Sparrow.*

LP

Four hundred and forty steps to the sea